SHAKESPEARE MINUS 'THEORY'

Shakespeare Minus 'Theory'

TOM McALINDON

ASHGATE

Published by
Ashgate Publishing Limited
Gower House
Croft Road
Aldershot
Hants GU11 3HR
England

Ashgate Publishing Company
Suite 420
101 Cherry Street
Burlington, VT 05401-4405
USA

Ashgate website: http://www.ashgate.com

British Library Cataloguing in Publication Data

McAlindon, T. (Thomas), 1932–
    Shakespeare minus 'theory'
    1. Shakespeare, William, 1564–1616 – Criticism and
    interpretation 2. English drama – Early modern and
    Elizabethan, 1500–1600 – History and criticism
    I. Title
    822.3'3

Library of Congress Cataloging-in-Publication Data

McAlindon, T. (Thomas)
    Shakespeare minus 'theory' / Tom McAlindon.
        p. cm.
    Includes bibliographical references.
    ISBN 0-7546-3981-9 (alk. paper)
    1. Shakespeare, William, 1564–1616 – Criticism and interpretation. I. Title.

PR2976.M286 2004
822.3'3–dc22   200365068

Printed on acid-free paper

ISBN 0 7546 3981 9

Typeset in Sabon by J.L. & G.A. Wheatley Design, Aldershot
Printed and bound in Great Britain by MPG Books Ltd, Bodmin, Cornwall.

Contents

Preface

This collection of essays seeks to defend and demonstrate a method of close reading and historical contextualisation of Shakespeare and his contemporaries that it has been customary of late to describe (most often derisively) as traditional and liberal humanist, and which, although still widely practised, seldom advertises itself as such. There is, however, a strongly oppositional thrust in the collection. Three of the nine essays are critiques of the claims and methods of radical, postmodernist criticism (new historicism and cultural materialism especially); they illustrate my conviction that some leading scholars in the field of Renaissance literature and drama, who deserve credit for shifting attention to new areas of interest, must also be charged with responsibility for a marked decline in standards of analysis, interpretation, and argument. I am not the first to protest against this development, but our numbers are few. Liberal tolerance in relation to oppositional views, respect for innovation, misplaced regard for the political idealism of radical theory and practice, and professional prudence have too often combined to allow parodies of rigorous scholarship to pass as the real thing.

The remaining six essays are interpretive studies, all but one of which involve challenges to radical readings of the plays involved. The chapter on *Henry V* is much the longest, its length being due to the fact that I am here challenging a traditional as well as radical views of the play. The concluding chapter, on Marlowe's *Doctor Faustus*, is included because it gives some idea of the thoroughness with which major non-Shakespearean texts have been forced to fit the radical template; because it focuses on theatricality, a subject of almost obsessive concern with many new historicists; and because it highlights Marlowe's (serendipitously) ironic perspective on a famous scholar's fatally selective reading of a key text.

Acknowledgements

For permission to reprint, I am grateful to the editors of the following journals, in which Chapters 2, 4, 5, 7, and 8 have already appeared: *Studies in Philology*, *Shakespeare Survey*, *The Modern Language Review*, *The Review of English Studies*, *Studies in English Literature*. I am similarly indebted to Cambridge University Press and The Gale Group for permission to reprint Chapters 6 and 9.

I would especially like to thank Rowland Wymer, Robin Headlam-Wells, James Booth, Angela Leighton, and John Roe, whose comments on one or more of these chapters have proved most helpful.

List of Abbreviations

Shakespeare's Plays and Poems

AWW	*All's Well that Ends Well*
Ant.	*Antony and Cleopatra*
Cor.	*Coriolanus*
Cymb.	*Cymbeline*
Err.	*The Comedy of Errors*
Ham.	*Hamlet*
1H4	*Henry IV, Part 1*
2H4	*Henry IV, Part 2*
H5	*Henry V*
1H6	*Henry VI, Part 1*
2H6	*Henry VI, Part 2*
3H6	*Henry VI, Part 3*
JC	*Julius Caesar*
Lr.	*King Lear*
Luc.	*The Rape of Lucrece*
Mac.	*Macbeth*
MM	*Measure for Measure*
MND	*A Midsummer Night's Dream*
MWW	*The Merry Wives of Windsor*
Oth.	*Othello*
Per.	*Pericles*
Q	Quarto edition
R2	*Richard II*
R3	*Richard III*
Rom.	*Romeo and Juliet*
Son.	*Sonnets*
Tim.	*Timon of Athens*
Tit.	*Titus Andronicus*
Tmp.	*The Tempest*
WT	*The Winter's Tale*

Periodicals and Series

CQ	*Critical Quarterly*
EETS	Early English Texts Society

EHR	*English Historical Review*
EIC	*Essays in Criticism*
ELH	*English Literary History*
ELR	*English Literary Renaissance*
ES	*English Studies*
MLR	*Modern Language Review*
OED	*Oxford English Dictionary*
PMLA	*Publications of the Modern Language Association of America*
RES	*Review of English Studies*
SEL	*Studies in English Literature*
SQ	*Shakespeare Quarterly*
ShS	*Shakespeare Survey*
ShakS	*Shakespeare Studies*
SP	*Studies in Philology*
STC	*Short Title Catalogue*

Chapter 1

Taking Stock: Radical Criticism of Shakespeare

It is now time to take stock of these advances . . . these major steps forward
. . . [beyond] traditional modes of Shakespeare criticism and scholarship.[1]

1

Fundamental to the essays in this book are the following intentions: to concentrate on what I judge to be the play's intended meanings; to take due account of the entire text in the process of interpretation; to attend where profitable to aspects of historical context other than the political; to enhance appreciation of the dramatist's conscious art; and to encourage readers to empathise with his perspectives on character, action, and life. Clearly, then, these essays will not have contributed to the great march forward celebrated by John Drakakis as he surveys the years between *Alternative Shakespeares* (1985) and *Alternative Shakespeares*, Volume 2 (1997), landmark collections of critical essays which typify the radical or postmodernist criticism (deconstructionist, Marxist, new historicist, cultural materialist) that has dominated Shakespeare studies since about 1980.[2]

As my stated intentions indicate, I have a number of objections to radical criticism of Shakespeare. First of these is the fact that it disallows in the student the sense of wonder, excitement, and admiration which his plays inspired in me from my own undergraduate days to 'the pupil age of this present twelve o'clock'. The radical attitude to Shakespeare (characteristically and slightly dubbed 'the Bard') varies from suspicion to condescension and even outright hostility, reflecting a determination not to be daunted by his great reputation or seduced by 'the aesthetic dimension'. It sees him primarily as a social thinker submerged in his own historical moment and not as a great artist whose imagination and craft gave enduring life to his characters and their experiences. His art, both tragic and comic, is effectively ignored, and if passing reference is made to it, it is usually to characterise it as a dangerous distraction. Thus one of the beliefs to which radical criticism is opposed, says Terence Hawkes, is that Shakespeare 'is entertaining. He makes us laugh and cry like billy-oh, and can command our rapt attention like no other writer.' In fact, adds Hawkes, his plays should not be thought of in terms of 'anything as forbidding as Art'; we should reflect rather on the 'collective role' of the audience responding to the plays 'as in a modern football stadium', viewing them not as art but 'as part of an ensemble of spectacular entertainment . . . one which included bear-baiting, brothels, the stocks, the pillory, the exhibition of the mentally disturbed, public beheading and evisceration, and royal processions. These competed – on equal terms – with the theatre for an audience.'[3] The origins of this line of argument are political and go back to the turbulent 1960s and 1970s, when Louis Kampf, President of the Modern Language Association of America, endorsed the newly fashionable view that art is elitist, claiming that 'the very category of art has become one more instrument for making class distinctions'.[4] 'The fountains [at the Lincoln Center]', he said, 'should be dried with calcium chloride, the statuary pissed on, the walls smeared with shit.'[5]

Critics who write about Shakespeare in the Hawkesian manner reveal an impressively iconoclastic self-confidence; and indeed there is an obvious correlation between the current demotion of Shakespeare and the promotion and self-promotion of the critic, the latter apparently competing at times on equal terms with the former. In the new dispensation, the critic does not listen to the dead author but seeks to 'engage in a dialogue' or a quarrel with him; the critic is no longer an interpreter of the text but a 'producer' of its meanings or, as Terry Eagleton puts it, a 'co-partner'. 'Shakespeare was not great literature lying conveniently to hand', explains Eagleton, 'he is great literature because the [literary] institution constitutes him as such.'[6] As a prominent member of the institution and one of Shakespeare's most restive partners, he announces on the first page of his bestselling *William Shakespeare* that '[t]o any unprejudiced reader – which would seem to exclude Shakespeare himself, his contemporary audiences and almost all literary critics – it is surely clear that positive value in *Macbeth* lies with the three witches. The witches are the heroines of the piece, however little the play itself recognizes the fact.'[7]

This reverse valuation of creative writer and critic is not confined of course to Shakespeare studies (although when Shakespeare is the demoted writer in question it does have a singular audacity); the attitude is typical of postmodern theory and criticism as a whole. Barthes's alleged Death of the Author, and Derrida's assurance that every text 'since Plato' lies waiting for its unintended contradictions to be unpacked in the academy ('Derrida has shown us . . .'), inaugurated what W.J.T. Mitchell has hailed as 'The Golden Age of Criticism', a period when 'the dominant mode of literary expression . . . is not poetry, fiction, drama, film, but criticism and theory'.[8] Until the sales of radical theory and criticism begin to challenge those of fiction and poetry, and audiences desert theatres and cinemas for public readings from avant-garde critics, we can dismiss this claim as absurd. But in the academic study of Shakespeare the success of radical criticism is such that its iconoclastic assertions and daring 'productions' have to be taken very seriously.

2

A major symptom of radical criticism's hostility to Shakespeare's art is its persistent sneering at the attribution to his plays of an essential unity, an attitude whose primary sanction is to be found in the work of Marxist theorists such as Pierre Macherey[9] and Frederick Jameson.[10] The offending attribute is 'an imaginary coherence' allegedly imposed on the plays by liberal humanist (or 'traditional' or 'conventional') critics driven by 'certain pressing ideological imperatives'.[11] 'In the old days', explains Alan Sinfield, 'the thing you were meant to do with a literary text was to point out how whole and complete it was. The trick now is to do the opposite, to look for the gaps and silences and stress and pressure points.'[12] And elsewhere he adds that 'coherence is a chimera . . . No story can contain all the possibilities it brings into play; coherence is always selection.'[13]

There is a degree of error and confusion in these observations. In the first place, no critic writing in 'the old days' would have denied that coherence always entails selection; in fact since the time of Aristotle, who introduced the metaphorical concept of organic unity to dramatic criticism, it has been taken as axiomatic that artistic unity is entirely dependent on selection, and that the drama, being subject to a strict time limit, is of necessity the most economical and compressed of all literary forms. Moreover, the maxim of Ferdinand Brunetière (1849–1906) that 'conflict is the essence of drama' was generally accepted, and A.C. Bradley subsequently established a long tradition when he analysed Shakespeare's tragedies in terms of behavioural and emotional conflict and found at their heart an unresolved metaphysical contradiction (the radical critic substitutes ideological and political contradiction). The effect of the New-Critical tradition too was to stress in Shakespeare's plays a combination of both formal unity and inner contradiction (or ambivalence, or paradox). A clear instance of this combination is *Richard II*, where structural symmetry and ironic circularity reinforce a profoundly complex if not ambiguous attitude to the rights and wrongs of the Richard–Bolingbroke conflict, leaving us with a final sense of pattern and closure and yet with an awareness that for Bolingbroke and England 'the really difficult part was only just beginning' (to quote a Chekhov ending).

As Richard Levin has observed, the radical critic's denial of artistic unity to Shakespeare's plays involves a confusion of formal unity and ideological uniformity.[14] A play would not succeed if it did not dramatise a conflict of ideas, attitudes, feelings, values; but when it is conflictual in that sense it is not in consequence artistically disorganised. It would seem that the root cause of this denial of artistic unity is a determination to equate all Shakespeare's meanings with ideology, and with ideology defined not simply as the prevailing social norms but as the ruling class's endeavour to smooth over the conflicts and contradictions of the social order.[15]

There is abundant evidence in Shakespeare's plays of an entirely conscious concern with ideas of unity and disunity. As we shall see in Chapters 3 and 6, they are grounded for the most part on a well-established notion of unity – in nature, society, and the self – understood as an intrinsically unstable system of opposites. Thus the *raison d'être* of Shakespeare's focus on unity is not, as Jonathan Dollimore and Alan Sinfield maintain, to 'occlude' conflict and contradiction,[16] since it acknowledges them as always inherent and potentially dominant in every stable structure or state of affairs. And the implication that signs of deep disunity or contradiction in the plays invalidate an intended impression of unity, and have been detected only by vigilant radical critics, is very wide of the mark. Such beliefs, however, serve to legitimise the claim that the critic's role is to 'construct meaning out of the contradictory discourses which the text provides',[17] which in turn promotes the practice of strategically selective quotation, bits and pieces from Shakespeare's carefully wrought designs being reassembled to fit a prefabricated interpretive paradigm.

3

Intimately related to radical criticism's negative attitude to Shakespeare's art is its hostility to his humanity, more often referred to as his universality. Ben Jonson had the latter in mind when he declared that Shakespeare was not of an age but for all time; but it was Samuel Johnson who gave most forceful expression to the idea, and he has in consequence been pilloried by critics such as Terence Hawkes[18] and Christopher Norris.[19] High on Hawkes's list of beliefs to which radical criticism is opposed is 'the belief that the Bard's . . . work is universally valid and speaks to human beings across the ages as clearly now, had we the wit to see it, as then . . . that, construed aright . . . Shakespeare's plays are able to address all people at all times, and everywhere'.[20] On the contrary, Shakespeare's plays have historically specific significance and no more; his supposed universality is founded on the false and dangerous notion of a permanent human nature (dangerous because it serves to obstruct social change); moreover local, contemporary relevance (which most traditional critics acknowledge in Shakespeare) and universal significance are mutually exclusive, cannot coexist.[21]

The idea that it is impossible to effect social change if one believes (rightly or wrongly) in an essential human nature is disproved by the biographies of countless men and women who have been responsible for major advances in social thought and practice, and by the fact that even radical critics would never abandon the appeal to 'human rights' when challenging the activities of brutal regimes. And the suggestion that a play which is manifestly rooted in its own time and place cannot have universal significance is baffling. The case of a play which antedates Shakespeare by two thousand years is sufficient to establish its obtuseness. Sophocles' *Antigone* is undoubtedly embedded in the religious, ethical, and political culture of fifth-century Athens (BC); but its dramatisation of a conflict between the state and the individual, between the inhumanity of rigid law and the strength of human love and moral conviction, is such that it found its place as a play-within-the-play – a mirror image of the contemporary context – in Athol Fugard's *The Island*, a veiled attack on the injustices of South Africa's apartheid system and its most notorious prison. Moreover, the actor who first played Haemon, and was arrested on his way to the theatre and sentenced to seven years hard labour on Robben Island, gave one-man performances of *Antigone* in the prison quarry for the benefit of his fellow prisoners. Could anything better demonstrate the timeless significance of great art?

Shakespeare, wrote Johnson in 1765, is

> above all writers . . . the poet of nature; the poet who holds up to his readers a faithful mirrour of manners and of life. His characters . . . are the genuine progeny of

common humanity, such as the world will always supply, and observation will always find. His persons act and speak by the influence of those general passions and principles by which all minds are agitated, and the whole system of life is continued in motion.[22]

As Nicholas Rowe pointed out in 1709, 'the severer Critiques' of the time complained that Shakespeare broke all the (neoclassic) rules; and he was rebuked and patronised accordingly. And yet 'the generality of our Audiences' loved and admired his plays (remarked Rowe), they grew in esteem with the passing of time, and his greatness had to be both acknowledged and explained.[23] Johnson was doubtless wrong (or at least overstating his case) when he said that Shakespeare's characters are not modified by contemporary and transient peculiarities; but his universalist argument is essentially a response to a question which the severer critics of today invariably ignore, and which every academic should consider an elementary part of the teaching process: wherein lies the special virtue of this particular play or body of plays? Why is is that four hundred years of cultural change have not diminished its appeal to audiences and readers alike? The question has to lead us back to humanity and art.

Against the anti-universalist argument one must also set the perpetual tendency of Shakespeare's characters themselves to utter generalisations on human nature and experience, or simply to express feelings and ideas that time never antiquates:

Silence is the perfectest herald of joy. I were but little happy if I could now say much.

How bitter a thing it is to look at happiness through another man's eyes.

Such men as he be never at heart's ease
Whiles they behold a greater than themselves.

Tomorrow, and tomorrow, and tomorrow . . .

    Thou'lt come no more.
Never, never, never, never, never.

     There sir stop.
Let us not burden our remembrance with
A heaviness that's gone.

We are such stuff
As dreams are made on, and our little life
Is rounded with a sleep.

And so on. The more distant Shakespeare becomes from us, the more important is the work of historical contextualisation if we are to understand and enjoy all that he has to offer; but the task is worthwhile in the first place because utterances like these, heard or read in context, capture with arresting authority what is not historically contingent and absorb us into the life of the plays.

4

Since the 1970s, individual theorists such as Derrida, Althusser, Foucault, and Lacan have been granted iconic status and submissive intellectual regard by radical critics in the United States and Britain ('heroic' is Catherine Belsey's word for Althusser);[24] and although their theories have been subjected to rigorous and extensive demolition work, the reverence in which they have been held west of Calais still persists. In some cases, too, radical critics of Shakespeare indulge in repetitive self-reference and autobiographical excursus, blending for the supposed benefit of the reader their own intellectual and spiritual lives with the concerns of the world's greatest playwright. Yet the cult of the individual is sternly condemned by such critics in relation to Shakespeare himself ('bardolatry'), his characters, and character in general.[25] According to Graham Holderness, we should not be 'thinking of Shakespeare as an individual genius', since in doing so we are reinforcing 'the individualism of bourgeois culture' and ignoring 'the collective achievements of Renaissance popular culture'.[26] Stephen Greenblatt pursues the same point more engagingly. Although elsewhere he accords Shakespeare a dangerous and sinister individuality, in his essay on 'The Circulation of Social Energy' he conducts a subtle attempt to dissolve his identity and deny his manifest superiority to all his contemporaries. Echoing Derrida's theory of difference or trace (that which avoids presence or identity), he re-defines Shakespeare's plays as 'textual traces in which we take interest and pleasure . . . signs of contingent social practices'. Adapting an idea from Foucault, he suggests that 'the life' that textual traces like *King Lear* 'seem to possess long after the death of the author and the death of the culture for which the author wrote is the historical consequence . . . of the social energy initially encoded in those works'. The questions we ask of them 'cannot profitably center on a search for their untranslatable essence. Instead we can ask how collective beliefs were shaped, moved from one medium to another, concentrated in manageable aesthetic form, offered for consumption.'[27] From this perspective, Shakespeare begins to resemble a nameless functionary pressing keys in the Central Cultural Supply Station. His 'traces' are no longer identifiably his. Testimony to Greenblatt's magisterial authority as a radical critic can be found in the way this perspective re-states itself a decade later at the beginning of Lisa Jardine's *Reading Shakespeare Historically* (1996), where Shakespeare's plays become 'the textual residue of "a great author"'. Scare quotes signal that it has become an embarrassment for sophisticated critics to acknowledge the greatness of the author who continues to obsess them; outside such quotes he is at best 'the quintessentially canonical dramatist of the early modern period in Britain';[28] and as we have been told often enough, 'canons' are no guarantee of intrinsic superiority.

Shakespeare's characters too are demoted and de-individualised. According to Kiernan Ryan, the causes of tragedy in *King Lear* are 'housed beyond the conscious culpability of individuals in the iniquitous structures' of society, a Marxist analysis which functions deductively in accordance with a universal law of causation which renders the intentions of both author and character irrelevant.[29] Terence Hawkes rejects the belief that the tragedies exalt the individual and is mystified that the developing relations between characters conceived as 'single, unitary individuals' are still seen by many as 'the core of each play's interest'. This, he at first surmises, is due to an individual critic, A.C. Bradley, whose popularity and influence throughout the entire twentieth century he finds 'astonishing' (Bradley's arguments being for the most part 'dogged', 'flat-footed', and 'manifestly preposterous'). On the other hand, identities are ideologically constituted, Bradley cannot be held responsible for his own popularity and influence, and the correct explanation for the generality's belief in the importance of character in Shakespeare's dramatic art must be the fact that a 'concern with individual personality' lies deeply embedded in 'Western ideology'.[30] Catherine Belsey takes a similar position in her theoretical work and in her book on the tragedies of Shakespeare and his contemporaries. Citing Althusser as her authority, she writes that the conception of people as 'unique, distinguishable, irreplaceable identities' is an ideologically determined illusion.[31]

Any critic who holds these views on Shakespeare, his characters, and character itself has to contend with more than a few generations of benighted forerunners. It must have been hard for the ambitious and egotistical Ben Jonson '[t]o draw no enuy' and admit it, but in 1623 he did: it 'was all mens suffrage', he confessed, that Shakespeare was not to be compared or confused with any one of his contemporaries. Forty years later Dryden more than agreed: 'the age wherein he liv'd, which had contemporaries with him Fletcher and Jonson, never equalled him in their esteem: And in the last Kings court, when Ben's reputation was at its highest, Sir John Suckling, and with him the greater part of Courtiers, set our Shakespeare far above him.'[32] Many critics writing in the New-Critical tradition undoubtedly ignored Shakespeare's indebtedness to his predecessors and contemporaries and wrote about one or more of his plays as if they were autonomous artifacts divorced from their informing cultural context; but the opposite extreme of relegating him to the level of participant in a cultural collective is ludicrous. Unless one refers to the whims of 'the canon', it leaves us with no answer as to why, for example, George Wilkins's *The Miseries of Enforced Marriage* (1607) is known to none but the scholar when *Romeo and Juliet* has been read and played to the delight of the generality ever since it was written. Worse still, it implies that the question is uninteresting or even unanswerable.

Discussing the relationship between *King Lear* and Harsnett's *Declaration of Egregious Popish Impostures*, Stephen Greenblatt intimates that the work of earlier critics who studied *Lear* in relation to its sources is wholly inadequate: all they do is 'provide a glimpse of the "raw material" that the artist fashioned'.[33] The subordinate clause on the artist's 'fashioning' momentarily and unintentionally allows us to forget the anonymous circulator of cultural energy and reflect on the fact that source study as performed by Kenneth Muir and Geoffrey Bullough in the 1960s and 1970s has thrown into relief the figure of Shakespeare as a dramatic artist with definable, individual intentions and extraordinary shaping powers.[34]

Unique as an artist himself, Shakespeare was credited with a rare capacity for creating unforgettably distinct characters. As a practising dramatist, Dryden fully appreciated this gift, ascribing it to Shakespeare's extraordinary understanding of human psychology – the feelings and dispositions whose particular combination in each of us makes us who we are: 'If Shakespeare be allow'd, as I think he must, to have made his characters distinct, it will easily be infer'd that he understood the nature of the Passions: because it has been prov'd already, that confus'd passions make undistinguishable Characters.' Even before Dryden, Margaret Cavendish (in 1664) had rhapsodised at length on the chameleonic imagination which created so many distinct and uncannily lifelike characters:

> [S]o Well he hath express'd in his Playes all Sorts of Persons, as one would think he hath Transformed into every one of those Persons he hath Described . . . Who would not think he had been such a man as his Sir John Falstaff? And who would not think he had been Harry the Fifth? . . . nay, one would think he had been Metamorphosed from a Man to a Woman, for who could Describe a Cleopatra Better to the People, than he hath done, and many other Females of his own Creating, as Nan Page, Mrs Page, Mrs Ford, the Doctors maid, Bettrice, Mrs Quickly, Doll Tearsheet, and others, too many to Relate?[35]

And before Cavendish there was the young Oxford scholar Leonard Digges, who in 1635 or earlier praised Shakespeare's 'plot, [and] language exquisite' but reserved all his enthusiasm for the characters who outshone those of Jonson and packed the playhouse to bursting point: Brutus and Cassius, 'honest Iago' and 'the jealous Moor', Falstaff and Hal, Beatrice and Benedict and 'Malvolio, that cross-gartered gull'.[36]

There is also the testimony of the actors down the centuries. All the great plays are named after individuals, and sometimes the subtitles draw attention to a particularly impressive secondary character. Every ambitious actor has aspired to play one or more of these characters (Paul Schofield worried in middle age that Richard Burton, his exact contemporary, would get to play Lear before him). Moreover, the creator of these unforgettable characters clearly believed (*pace* Althusser) that there are 'unique, distinguishable, irreplaceable identities'; he expressed that conception with compelling eloquence in three words: 'You alone are you.'[37]

What the radical critic seems most to dislike in the 'bourgeois individualist' tendencies of traditional criticism is the notion of character as 'unified'. In his *Introduction to Literary Theory*, Terry Eagleton rejoices repeatedly at the way in which one continental theorist after another leaves the self or subject (as well as the text) 'contradictory', 'shattered', 'decentred', 'pulverised', 'subverted', 'exploded', 'split'; and in his Derridean version of *Macbeth* he claims that the witches 'shatter' and 'engulf' the protagonist's illusion of a unified self, turning him into 'a floating signifier' doomed to pursue 'an anchoring signified'.[38] Catherine Belsey follows a similar path, stating moreover that 'the unified subject of liberal humanism is a product of the second half of the seventeenth century, an effect of the revolution . . . when the bourgeoisie is installed as the ruling class'. She concedes that some might find it 'tempting' to see in the self-assertion of some Elizabethan-Jacobean protagonists ('I am myself alone', 'I am / Antony yet', 'I am Duchess of Malfi still', 'Alone I did it') evidence of belief in an essential, unified self; steeled by her theoretical commitments, however, she herself is not so tempted, dismissing these seemingly humanist claims on the grounds that they are shown (presumably by authorial intention) as monstrous, ironic, or pathetic. The disintegration of the hero in the tragedies of the period, she maintains, proves that these plays do not reveal the existence of a unified selfhood, the latter being simply liberal-humanist criticism's projection on to the plays of its own imaginary fullness.[39]

We may suppose that 'unitary' or 'unified' means lacking in multiple elements and propensities, consistent and non-contradictory; in which case Shakespeare's most famous characters, from Richard II and Falstaff to Cleopatra and Coriolanus, are certainly not unified; and indeed it would be difficult to find any traditional critic who would suggest otherwise. However, the complexity and changeability of these characters – even Cleopatra's 'infinite variety' – is always within its own unique, kaleidoscopic pattern ('What is your substance, whereof are you made, / That millions of strange shadows on you tend?');[40] and even a radical critic would never be guilty of confusing any one of them with another. To each it can assuredly be said, 'You alone are you.'

Belsey's assertion that the notion of a unique, distinguishable identity is a specifically bourgeois phenomenon and a product of the later seventeenth century is historically incorrect: it was a thoroughly familiar notion in Shakespeare's time and can be traced back to classical antiquity. When Webster's heroine declares 'I am Duchess of Malfi still', every educated spectator or reader in 1614 would have heard the words of another victimised and rebellious (though morally very different) heroine. Warned by her nurse against seeking revenge on her faithless husband, since the Colchians are no longer on her side and nothing is left of her wealth, the protagonist of Seneca's *Medea* replies: 'Medea is left ['*Medea superest*'] . . . Fortune can take away my wealth, but not my spirit.'[41] Medea may be a villainous heroine, but her assertion of selfhood in the face of disaster is meant to command respect, and it echoes a central theme in Stoic and Neo-Stoic tradition. In fact, however, we can trace the conception of an innate identity, and the possibility of swerving from it, as far back as Sophocles, four centuries before Seneca: 'All is offence when a man hath forsaken his true nature . . . return even now to thy true self', says Philoctetes to the noble young Neoptolemus.[42] It is incorrect also to assert that innate identity is disproved because the Shakespearean tragic hero, and Macbeth in particular, collapses into a state of disunity or doubleness, loses his 'single state of man'. That collapse is shown as a tragic fall from an anterior integrity or wholeness, which in Shakespeare's thinking, I contend, is a state of unified duality (or multeity), something to which the transformed hero is at least partially restored at the end of the play. Attention to intellectual history or the history of ideas (rather than the political history exclusively preferred by radical criticism) would have taken these critics much further in an investigation of the contradictions and dualities which affect *Macbeth* and the other tragedies so profoundly (see Chapters 3 and 6).

5

Autonomy is another attribute of character which traditional criticism allegedly emphasises and the radical critic scorns: 'the Individual of . . . bourgeois humanism', says Louis Montrose, is 'freely self-creating and world-creating', but now, thanks to the work of postmodernist critics, he is 'defunct'.[43] Involved here is a caricature of liberalism's emphasis on the liberty of the individual as the primary social good, and of humanism's view that human beings possess to a unique extent creative and communicational powers which, when liberated, enable them to exercise a degree of freedom of choice and action in shaping their lives.[44] It would be impossible to find any 'traditional' or 'liberal humanist' critic who believes that the individual is fully or even largely autonomous, much less self-creating or world creating; or who imputes such views to any Shakespearean play. The caricature, however, lends superficial plausibility to the claim that radical theorists and critics have effected a great escape from crippling error and illusion, another 'Copernican revolution'.

The combined effect of the French *maîtres* and Sigmund Freud on radical criticism has been to generate an all-pervasive determinism in the interpretation of Shakespeare and his contemporaries. The dramatists' characters are now largely the controlled subjects or 'effects' of impersonal forces, psychological, linguistic, or political. This determinist bias is particularly noticeable in work on the tragedies, where there seems to be no recognition of the fact that in any social system there will always by definition be limits to freedom, and that there will always be fatal, freely chosen courses of action and disastrous conflicts between individual will and desire on the one hand and society and circumstance on the other. The politically activist nature of radical criticism, and its utopian subtext (change the political order and all will be well), precludes awareness of the fact that a dialectical relationship between character and fate, freedom and determination, is central to most great tragedies.

The determinist bias came to prominence first in Stephen Greenblatt's seminal study, *Renaissance Self-Fashioning* (1980). Greenblatt repeatedly finds evidence to show that 'massive power structures . . . determine social and psychic reality' and concludes in his autobiographical and eminently Foucaultian Epilogue that in the sixteenth century as now 'the human subject' seems 'remarkably unfree, the ideological product of the relations of power in a particular society'. Following Foucault, too, he fatalistically sees disciplinary society producing the modes of opposition that in the end merely confirm the system from which the rebellious individual never escapes; struggle against the dominant ideology is futile.[45]

Symptomatic of the constructed and subjected nature of the self in Greenblatt's interpretation of Renaissance literature is the phenomenon of theatricality, which signifies both the formation and the undermining of identity. Given the political and religious pressures of the time (he explains), role playing was virtually inescapable; it was fostered as well by rhetoric and by manuals of gentlemanly behaviour such as Castiglione's *The Courtier*, which provided advice on 'the formation of an artifical identity' (162–9). But power itself and its instruments of oppression are also synonymous with theatricality: Iago's plot against Othello is precisely analogous to the Spanish colonists' entrapment of the Lucayan Indians, exhibiting the same empathetic and improvisatory ability 'to play a role, to transform oneself . . . into another', insinuating oneself into the ideological structures of the other and turning those structures to one's advantage (227–8). Here too (as in his essay 'Invisible Bullets'), Greenblatt's identification of Renaissance theatricality with power, deceit, and subjection extends beyond Shakespeare's characters to Shakespeare himself, who (Iago-like) uses his improvisatory skills 'in the service of Elizabethan power' (252–3).

It has always been recognised, however, that Shakespeare's plays, and especially the tragedies and histories, evince a profound and characteristically Renaissance interest in the varying and problematic relationships between freedom and necessity, nature and nurture ('art'), self and society, permanence and change. Shakespeare characteristically thinks in terms of opposites (resolved and otherwise), works dialectically, and is fertile in controlled ambiguity, ambivalence, and paradox; thus the determinist bias in radical criticism makes his plays far less open and subtle than in fact they are. It is perfectly true that religious persecution and the circumstances of court life encouraged dissembling and role-play, and that Castiglione and his like advocated the art of skilful self-adjustment to times, persons, and places. But Castiglione too thought dialectically, believed in an innate self, and was insistent that one should never cultivate a manner or style which is at variance with one's individual nature.[46] To claim that he gave advice on the formation of an artificial identity is untrue, although it is a claim that others have taken over from Greenblatt without checking what Castiglione actually said. Greenblatt's highly influential approach to theatricality, moreover, is extremely misleading, since theatrical metaphor could signify constancy and truth to self as well as discontinuity and falsity.[47]

6

The primary characteristic of radical criticism of Shakespeare is its political orientation: the title of Dollimore and Sinfield's collection of essays, *Political Shakespeare* (another major landmark in the radical 'advance'), would fit the two *Alternative Shakespeares* equally well, as would its Introduction. Radical criticism aims always to analyse the operations of power and, more importantly, to use commentary on Shakespeare's texts in such a way as to effect 'the transformation of a social order which exploits people on grounds of race, gender and class'.[48] The first aim is a perfectly legitimate specialist undertaking in itself; but single-minded concentration on the merely negative aspects of power, and especially the tendency to view all aspects of human experience from a political perspective, inevitably produces a Shakespeare drained of subtlety, variety, and humanity (one feels constrained to recall Marx's remark that 'man is more fundamental than the citizen, human life more than the political life').[49] Moreover, the master trope that 'nothing is outside politics', amounts (as Frank Lentricchia has observed) to 'a new Hegelian expressive unity of culture', a 'monological vision', something that radicalism habitually condemns.[50] The second aim (radical transformation of contemporary society) would be dismissed as ludicrous daydreaming by any conscientious and progressive politician in a democratic system. Its effect on criticism and teaching, however, cannot be taken so lightly. Although it is claimed that radical criticism has brought 'a new rigour' to the study of literature,[51] it is difficult in principle to see how a determination to make literary texts serve a political purpose is compatible with what is normally understood as rigour in intellectual discourse.

7

Another outstanding feature of radical criticism is its historical dimension. This is regarded as a major advance on traditional criticism for a number of reasons. Critics working in the New-Critical tradition allegedly ignored the historical context of the plays in order to justify treating them as documents of timeless significance; the radical critic exposes the fallacy of universalism by disclosing the embeddedness of the text in the power politics of early modern England. Moreover, traditional critics in the latter half of the twentieth century who studied the plays in relation to their historical contexts did so on the basis of an optimistic, harmonising, monological world view, devised by apologists of the Tudor regime and (according to E.M.W. Tillyard) accepted by Shakespeare and all his contemporaries; radical critics expose this world view as an ideological fiction, bring to light the socio-political conflicts and discordances which it sought to conceal, and so disqualify conservative readings of the plays. Furthermore, traditional critics all erred in their use and understanding of the relationship between the text and its historical context, treating the latter as mere background to the text and as the provider of unchallengeable, objective facts. Aiming at something more serious than passive acceptance of the plays' vision of reality, intending in fact to change history, radical critics refuse to privilege the literary text. And being trained in postmodernist versions of Nietzschean perspectivism ('Facts there are not, only interpretations'), they know that historical data are always contaminated by the ideology of those who record them: context reaches the historian in textualised form and its relationship with the literary text is one of structural similarity and mutual influence. The radical critic studies text and context, literature and history, on a basis of equivalence and interaction.

In response to these claims one might first suggest that the ahistoricism of New-Critical readings has been exaggerated and misrepresented. The best practitioners in this mode had a good sense of historical context which informed their interpretations.[52] They did not engage directly with historical context for the reason that they were reacting against the historicism of early twentieth-century scholars who felt that the academic study of imaginative literature could be made intellectually respectable only if it gave precedence to historical and scientific method and all the factuality of sources and influences. To the extent that they ignored historical context, the New Critics were claiming that imaginative literature (and not history, philology, politics, or anthropology) was their chosen subject and that there were manifest reasons for privileging it. Whether the world would be better off if the complete works of Shakespeare had survived and (say) Elizabeth I's state papers did not, or vice versa, might be difficult questions for some to decide, but in the view of the New Critics the independent study of literature as an art was beyond question and needed no apology. And if art (as Raymond Tallis has observed) is the perfection of human consciousness,[53] they had good reason to think so.

The assertion that pre-radical historical scholarship identified Shakespeare's plays with a monological, harmonious world view has been repeated so often that it has come to seem like unchallengeable truth; in fact, however, it constitutes a serious falsification of critical history. Tillyard's optimistic, monological world-view approach to Shakespeare, first promulgated in 1945, was accepted by many, but from the start (when Hiram Haydn called it 'a little naïve') it faced a challenge which grew in intensity and sophistication for a quarter of a century.[54] As noted already, too, the present writer has shown that the work of Shakespeare and some of his major contemporaries incorporates a 'theoria of the world' (the phrase is Marlowe's) in which the notions of conflict and harmony are central and interdependent – a dialectical philosophy of the natural order which was utterly familiar to their audiences and readers.[55] Radical critics, however, in spite of their obsession with conflict and contradiction, have shown no interest in this development: one reason may be that it would (at the least) complicate their imposition of a Derridean and/or Marxist conflictual paradigm on the plays (which treat contradiction as either unintended or intentionally concealed); another might be that they are dogmatically opposed to using the history of ideas (intellectual history) in historical-contextual studies, even though their own work is relentlessly ideas-driven.[56]

In practice, radical critics regularly contradict their claim to treat history as textualised, ideologically constructed, non-transparent, resistant to objective understanding.[57] In her programmatic essay offering a new model for the historicist study of literature, 'Literature, History, Politics', Catherine Belsey says: 'The claim is not that such a history [as the one she recommends], or such reading of literary texts, is more accurate, but only that it is more radical.' This candid privileging of politics over truth renders explicit what one sees as inevitable in politicised analysis and interpretation of any kind of material. But in the same essay Belsey claims that such a history would 'uncover a world of violence, disorder and fragmentation' that liberal humanist critics have failed to see, and she bases part of her general argument on a major fact about the seventeenth century which (she says) 'historians' have made 'quite clear'; while in her study of the tragedies of the period, she relies heavily on such facts.[58] In practice, she retains a partial commitment to the belief that it is possible to penetrate ideological representations of historical reality and arrive at some reasonably reliable truths about the past; she may also be aware that readers are likely to accept the strategic manipulation of textual facts when they have been provided with a measure of manifestly accurate historical information. With Terence Hawkes the same contradiction issues in an exquisitely self-refuting pronouncement. Of radical criticism, he says, 'Getting Shakespeare and early modern culture "right" is not its aim. Getting to grips with what our inherited notions of "right" conceal from us is.'[59] But discovery and knowledge of that which has been concealed has to be what Hawkes knows is right. Moreover, the scare quotes indicating that 'traditional critics' not only get it wrong but also fail to perceive that there is no such thing as 'right' is another self-refuting claim, since the clear message is that the assertions and revealings of the radical critic are right.

An unresolved conflict between respect for the regulative principles of accuracy and objectivity on the one hand, and a belief on the other hand that these should be dismissed as the strategic tools of a discredited bourgeois epistemology, is commonplace. Drakakis claims to have written 'scrupulously and disinterestedly' about critical history; he also applauds theorised critical practices which seek to 'liberate these [Shakespearean] texts from the straitjacket of unexamined assumptions and traditions', practices which are 'firmly linked to . . . the process of "making sense" of the Shakespearean text';[60] but the familiar scare quotes adroitly allow for a shift to the relativist theme that the text is what you make of it, that objectivity or neutrality in interpretation is always a pretence, and that radical critics must do openly and consciously with Shakespeare what traditional critics have always done, often unwittingly. They must 'appropriate' and 'adjust' him to political ends, bearing in mind the salutary historical fact (if they should be troubled by scruples about accuracy) that bourgeois critics and directors have made 'the holy writ of the text the dominant form of ideological oppression'.[61] This in effect is what is meant by Lisa Jardine's assertion that 'political commitment sharpens the focus of . . . historical work';[62] the sharp focus is on what you intend to find and say, even though the tone and phrasing occasionally enlist the notion of analytic and interpretive rigour as normally understood.

The radical critics' habitual claim that they reject traditional distinctions between literature and history, text and context, is also contradicted by their practice, which actually 'depends on these distinctions, since it assumes that the history of the period (or the particular aspect of it they focus on) supplies the necessary context for comprehending the literary text'; what they call contextualising always moves from historical context to text, and not vice versa. Nor do they ever adduce evidence to show that there is a reciprocal relationship between text and context in the sense that the former affects the latter.[63]

More intriguing perhaps is the conflict between theory and practice in relation to the claim to respect the historical specificity of the text and to the cognate condemnation of universalism. Sixteenth- and early seventeeth-century texts are regularly treated as analogues and allegories of present-day socio-political life; politically correct and stereotyped, and free from all suggestion of a transhistorical human nature with enduring human passions and problems, universalism enters by the back door.

8

The assumptions and intentions of radical criticism have led inevitably and demonstrably to a deterioration in standards of analysis, investigation, and interpretation in Shakespeare studies. In two papers, 'Testing the New Historicism' and 'Cultural Materialism and the Ethics of Reading', first published in 1995 and reprinted here, I sought to demonstrate this point in detailed analyses of specimen work by two highly regarded radicals, Stephen Greenblatt and Jonathan Dollimore. At this point, however, some indication of the remarkable extent and persistence of the deterioration is obviously necessary, so I would like to move to a conclusion in the present chapter by illustrating briefly the working practices of two quite different practitioners in the radical mode of political-historical criticism.

Steven Mullaney's flagship essay on new historicism in *Alternative Shakespeares*, Volume 2 (17–37) is understandably one of the best of its kind, since his monograph *The Place of the Stage: License, Play, and Power in Renaissance England* (Chicago: University of Chicago Press, 1988) is a model of that methodology at work; it has been hailed by Louis Montrose, himself a leading exponent of new-historicist theory and practice, as 'a major study not merely of selected Shakespearean plays but of the very conditions of possibility of Renaissance drama'.[64] Mullaney contends in this study that the popular drama of which Shakespeare was the chief exemplar owed its special character to its marginal location in the Liberties, where commerce, prostitution, and the theatrical flourished in a kind of homologous relationship. From this location, the drama acquired its multiplicity of voices, its wide range of alternative perspectives. In the final chapter of the book, however, Mullaney argues that towards the end of his career Shakespeare made a determined effort in one play – *Pericles* – to conceal and transcend the unseemly origins of his art. Adopting an interpretive model suggested by Frederick Jameson's *The Political Unconscious*, and influenced too by Stephen Greenblatt, Mullaney argues that Shakespeare sought here to conceal the drama's formative links with the commercial and the theatrical, de-historicising and de-collectivising it, projecting his work into a timeless, universal, aesthetic world ruled (king-like) by an authorising, individualist author (135–51).

According to Mullaney, the attempt was quite conscious on Shakespeare's part, but the evidence for it is hidden in the text's unconscious, in the 'seams', 'gaps', and 'significant lacunae' which bear witness to a process variously characterised as 'suppression', 'evasion', 'concealment', 'obscuring', and 'reduction'. Beginning with Shakespeare's alleged suppression of the commercial link, he notes that in Lawrence Twine's *The Patterne of Painfull Adventures* (1576), 'one of the play's sources', Apollonius (Shakespeare's Pericles) makes his gift of grain to the starving city of Tarsus in the market place, asking for payment first but then changing his mind and returning the money; in recognition of which generosity the citizens erect a statue in his honour in the market. In *Pericles*, however, there is no request for payment, no money is exchanged, and the commercial location of the gift and the statue is not mentioned.

As Mullaney reports it, commerce combines neatly with prostitution and the theatrical in Twine's account of the heroine's sojourn in the brothel. Instead of submitting her body to her first client, Tharsia (Shakespeare's Marina) tells him the tale of her woeful adventures, converting 'by her *performance* the man's desire for a woman into the desire of an *audience* for a story, and with profitable results'. Her first client eavesdrops on the second, 'hides behind the door to *watch* and listen to the ensuing *scene*'; after which both men remain 'to *watch the scene played* over, again and again'. Thus Tharsia 'converts the bawdy house into . . . a *playhouse*'. In *Pericles*, however, the heroine's conduct is cleansed of theatricality just as her father's gift-giving is cleansed of mercantilism: whereas Tharsia shows by her storytelling 'a shrewd sense both of business and of *theater*', pious Marina simply 'preaches divinity in the whorehouse and converts its customers' (142–3; my italics).

Shakespeare's use of Gower as the play's presenter, Mullaney argues, constitutes an 'occlusion' of both the theatrical and the historical: Gower narrates what could be dramatically enacted, presents himself as an authorial figure (Shakespeare grasping at 'professional authorship and the modern construction of the author'), and 'introduces *Pericles* as a tale of universal significance, forever timely and uncontaminated by historical and cultural contexts' (148).

The allegation that Shakespeare suppresses theatricality in dealing with the brothel episode is the most conspicuous and intriguing part of the argument. But it collapses when one looks beyond Mullaney's summary of Twine to what Twine actually wrote. First, the clients do not 'watch and listen' behind the door; they simply (says Twine) 'listen' outside the window. Nor is there the slightest hint anywhere in Twine's language of the extended theatrical metaphor which dominates Mullaney's summary of events. Furthermore the primary emphasis is not on Tharsia's storytelling ability but (as in *Pericles*) on the piety and pathos of her pleading. She begins: 'For the love of God, gentleman, take pity on me, and by the name of God I abjure you . . . to bridle your lust'; and Twine concludes: 'Thus Tharsia, through the grace of God, and fair persuasions, preserved her body undefiled.' Furthermore, there is no suggestion of theatricality when she moves to the market place, where 'her cunning in music and eloquence in speaking' (the twin Orphic arts) win fame for her and money for the brothel keeper.[65] Beyond these objections, it has to be said that the idea of Shakespeare occluding theatricality is an astonishing paradox in itself, and it is made all the more incomprehensible when one recalls that he went on to make it so notable a feature of *The Winter's Tale* and *The Tempest*, where Camillo, Paulina, and Prospero are playmakers who plot the action and distribute roles ('I see the play so lies / That I must bear a part', says Perdita [4.4.656–7]). Was Shakespeare overwhelmed there by a sense of guilt at what he had done in *Pericles*? Moreover, had he been bent on obliterating all reminders of the unsavoury Liberties, the first change he would have made would have been to reduce the brothel episode to a distant off-stage event, instead of which he gives more attention to it than does any other version of the story, presenting it on stage with 'stark and deeply etched realism'.[66] These facts are ignored by Mullaney.

In his successive mentions of Twine and Gower as 'one of Shakespeare's sources' (138, 148), Mullaney is again guilty of serious but rhetorically convenient 'occlusion'. The identical phrasing smooths out a very important difference: the consensus view is that '[o]f the two, Gower exercised by far the greater influence' (as one editor puts it), 'so that' (as another editor observes) 'his spirit is fitly chosen to act as the play's presenter'.[67] The reader should have been reminded of this, since in Gower's version of the story (which Mullaney never considers), as in *Pericles*, there is no 'mercantilism' – no request on the noble hero's part for money, no mention of the market; nor is there any hint of theatricality in the virtuous heroine's conduct in the brothel section. We can hardly attribute these absences in Gower's fourteenth-century tale to authorial anxieties caused by 'the larger social and economic contradictions' of the early modern period.

But even more remarkable perhaps is the fact that in a chapter devoted entirely to *Pericles*, and indicting Shakespeare of grave offences, including that of an individualist desire to become an 'author', the large and familiar problem of the play's authorship is never once mentioned. Shakespeare's friends Heminge and Condell apparently believed that *Pericles* was not one of his plays, since they excluded it from the First Folio. The majority of modern editors assume that he was responsible for the last three acts (perhaps half-heartedly rewriting someone else's work) but that he did not write the first two acts.[68] Like the priority of Gower's version as a source, the fact of mixed authorship is particularly relevant to what Mullaney makes of the non-mercantile allusion to the gift of grain and the location of the statue, which comes in the prologue to the non-Shakespearean Act 2 of the play; but the authorship problem is generally relevant to all the charges levelled so unequivocally against Shakespeare.

Finally there is the charge against Gower the presenter, construed as encapsulating in himself the three deadly sins of antitheatricalism, ahistoricising, and universalising. This is very unconvincing. It is Gower's specific and conventional task as Chorus (like that of the Chorus in *Romeo* and *Henry V*) to summarise in narrative form what cannot be dramatised in the two hours' traffic of the stage. He is not a fictional, representative author but a particular fourteenth-century author with an appropriately archaic manner of speech: he is historically specific. His opening assurance to those 'born in . . . latter times' that the story is very old is less a universalising ploy than a historically correct statement (*Apollonius of Tyre* being a third-century Latin composition) as well as a simple recommendation: '*Et bonum quo antiquius eo melius*' ['the more ancient a good thing is, the better it is'], he says. Furthermore, these allegedly dehistoricisng, universalising remarks occur in the prologue to the non-Shakespearean Act 1. We must conclude that Mullaney's narrative of Shakespeare's unworthy attempt in *Pericles* to escape from the contradictions of his historical moment into a timeless universal realm is pure fiction.

Aligning herself with Dollimore, Sinfield, and (especially) Greenblatt, Lisa Jardine in *Reading Shakespeare Historically* (1996) joins all those for whom Shakespeare is a reactionary dramatist busily hiding what the radical critic has to ferret out in the text's fissures, silences, and contradictions. She is a 'text reader' (her term) of daunting intellectual authority, for as she reminds us herself, her 'personal intellectual history' is one 'within which literary studies form only a part of an academically diverse collection of interests and areas of expertise', including 'history . . . history of science . . . neo-Latin studies . . . text studies . . . not to mention . . . science' (1, 158, n. 2). She is thus a striking example of the new interdisciplinary approach which radical criticism has introduced to literary studies as part of its attack on the methodological narrowness of traditional criticism. As such, her work provides an ideal focus for the question: how disciplined is the new interdisciplinarity in Shakespeare studies?

Jardine addresses *Henry V* at the beginning of *Reading Shakespeare Historically* because it seems to her to be the play best suited to answer a question which vexes her students: 'Does Shakespeare matter?' 'What is the study of Shakespeare for?' (Or as was said in the 1970s, is he relevant?) The best way to answer this question, she believes, is to employ the method of Stephen Greenblatt and other new historicists who have 'brilliantly excavated the way in which a kind of issue-grounded *explication de texte* or close reading can elucidate our own cultural assumptions', initiating with the dead author 'a conversation about burning questions in the here-and-now' (6). She promises that this method 'will produce a distinctive version of *Henry V*' (7).

The burning question which she saw as relevant to *Henry V* in 1996 was prompted by the war in Yugoslavia, where nationalism was responsible for horrendous violence against ethnic and religious minorities. She detects in Milosevic's war as in Henry's a radical contradiction between nationalist expansionism and ethnic purity. But before exploring this contradiction, and showing how Shakespeare occluded it, she takes to task the editor of the recent Oxford edition of the play, Gary Taylor, accusing him of an act of occlusion involving the word 'shame' (5–6). She notes that in his version of the textually problematic Act 4 scene 5, where he negotiates between the First Quarto and the Folio texts, Taylor edits out Bourbon's phrase 'Shame and eternal shame', his reason (given, she says, in Appendix A) being that in his view it is 'unShakespearean' and 'no longer accords with the strongly British nationalistic focus of the folio play'. 'We may be shocked' by such an editorial decision, she remarks, 'but that is material for another discussion'.

Taylor, however, gives no such reasons, nor any remotely like them, either in Appendix A or anywhere else. Moreover, since the phrase 'shame and eternal shame' is not a comment on Henry's ruthlessness, but rather a Frenchman's verdict on the humiliating defeat of the French, the sentiment is perfectly in accord with the play's nationalistic sentiment; and although the phrase is edited out, this short French scene (19 lines) still begins and ends in Taylor's edition with the French sentiment in question: 'Reproach and everlasting shame' (line 4) , 'Let life be short, else shame will be too long' (line 19). I think we are entitled to use her own word and describe Jardine's reading of Taylor as shockingly erroneous and confused. Logically, it is quite irrelevant to her argument, but its presence may have something to do with her conviction that Henry's actions and Shakespeare's alleged fudges are shameful; or it may reflect her dislike of the positive interpretation of Henry's character given in Taylor's Introduction, an interpretation with which it would be impossible to reconcile her own argument.

The argument itself has obvious flaws based on careless reading and an inadequate supply of relevant historical and historiographic knowledge. It turns heavily on the firm conviction (evident in her first book, *Still Harping on Daughters* [1983]) that in Shakespeare's plays women are rendered even more culpable and defective than many critics are inclined to believe. Thus in the French leaders' outbursts in 3.5, blame for the humiliation of their defeat is 'deftly divert[ed] on to the French women . . . it is because of cross-breeding between Norman women and English men that an English stock has been produced which is currently trouncing the French on the battlefield'; and again, 'the Dauphin rails against the loose women of France, whose sexual exploits with Englishmen have produced the doughty descendants . . . who now threaten the French with defeat' (11–12). This reading is amazingly wrong, since the Dauphin blames his male and not his female forebears for the impending disaster:

> *O Dieu vivant!* Shall a few sprays of us,
> The emptying of our fathers' luxury [lust],
> Our scions, put in wild and savage stock,
> Spirt up so suddenly into the clouds
> And over-look their grafters?
>
> (3.5.5–9)

Most editors consider it unnecessary to elucidate the obvious sense of the second line here, but one recent editor was on the lookout for a stumbling student and provided this gloss: 'the seed emptied out by our ancestors (i.e. the Norman invaders of England in 1066) in their lechery'.[69] Jardine, however, seems determined to suppress the obvious sense, for she attaches an admonitory endnote to these five lines: 'Note that there is no suggestion that Norman *men* might have hybridised their line by cross-breeding with English *women*' (161; her italics). Later in the same scene, of course, the Dauphin complains that French women in the here-and-now have been saying provocatively that they will choose these hardy descendants of their forefathers as lovers; but that, by dramatic implication, is entirely to their credit: they do not want to couple with noble 'runaways' and dancers who write sonnets to their horses (lines 29–35; 3.7.40–42); they are naturally inclined to strengthen the stock.

Jardine's interpretation of 3.5 as a familiar misogynistic jibe at the innate lasciviousness and weakness of women contributes crucially to the developing argument. Because expansionist nationalism begets sexual intercourse with the enemy, it is at odds with national purity on both sides, and this 'fundamental contradiction', which is 'a constant source of rhetorical anxiety' in the play, is 'dissolved . . . by appealing to the inevitability of female fallibility' (13). Thus Katherine is brought forward by Jardine as the play's Eve: her 'susceptibility to being "won" – willingly joining her French stock to Henry's English . . . covers for the possible illegality of Henry's seizure by force of the French crown'. Indeed it also exonerates the French patriarchy: Henry's 'verbal sleight of hand . . . shifts to her the responsibility for capitulating to England and surrendering French territory'; it is she who 'betrays the French cause' (14). More importantly, of course, she introduces impurity to the English line, creates a 'contradiction between Henry's proud boasts of "Englishmen" pure and true, and the fact that his own progeny will be hybrid Anglo-Gallic' (7).

But there is not the slightest hint in the text that anyone, French or otherwise, sees Katherine as responsible for the surrender of French territory: this is a completely intrusive idea. Furthermore, Henry's appeal to his men's patriotic sense – to love of England and pride in its history and reputation – at no point involves the idea of ethnic purity (it doesn't even refer to 'Englishmen'). Nowhere in the play is there any allusion to the notion of ethnic purity in the sense that applied in the Serbo-Kosovan conflict. The alleged contradiction is fictitious. Given Henry's Anglo-Gallic ancestry (in the line between him and the Conqueror, six of his royal forebears married French women), it would make no sense at all for him to invoke such a notion. Thus there can be no 'pathos' (7) whatever in the Anglo-French character of his own progeny. And as I shall recall in Chapter 3, a little knowledge of English history tells us that the Tudor dynasty had very good reason to be pleased with his marriage to Katherine of Valois.

Jardine asserts that in the last scene, '[a]s part of his strategic plan for shifting the audience's attention from warfare to wooing, Shakespeare alters both history and his source and tacitly erases the legitimate French heir', the Dauphin (9). But Shakespeare's chief source is Holinshed, where the Dauphin is conspicuous by his absence before and during the treaty of Troyes and the marriage of Henry and Katherine. He is not mentioned until later when he is appealed in his absence for the murder of the Duke of Burgundy.[70] Furthermore, Henry's position rests on the premise, nowhere challenged by the French, that he himself has always been the legitimate heir.

Professor Jardine's twin attempt to excavate 'thematic points of contact' between Henry V's French campaign and the Bosnian wars of the 1990s and to expose Shakespeare as deeply misogynist – and by such means to justify the study of his plays – rests on a flawed historical basis and an even more flawed reading of the text. But the point I wish to make is that this is historical criticism whose flaws derive from its political commitment and its reductive, homogenising methodology.

9

Jardine was right to recall that critics of Shakespeare should always have in mind the needs of students who see him at first at a great distance. But I do not think that students are well served by the kind of politicised and theorised work which she commends. It is joyless and constricting, a denial of the right to that imaginative entry into the author's vision which is the chief reason for becoming a student of literature in the first place. Moreover, by discouraging an intelligent appreciation of literary art, which heightens awareness of the complexities of language, and by encouraging attention only to those aspects of the text which fit the political purpose and the theorised interpretive model, it effectively diminishes the capacity to read *any* text well. Criticism of this kind does not inculcate unswerving respect in analysis and interpretation for accuracy, logical coherence, and evidential justification. It valorises performance rather than substance and unwittingly sanctions intellectual dishonesty. And it can only reflect badly on the just causes which it seeks to advertise; for justice is not well served by half-truths and error.

At the root of the problem is postmodernism's attack on notions of truth, reference, objectivity, and evidence. The effectiveness of this onslaught was powerfully demonstrated in the notorious Sokal Hoax in 1996 (the same year as the publication of *Reading Shakespeare Historically*), when the editorial board of *Social Text*, the leading American journal in cultural studies, accepted as a serious piece of scholarship a wickedly nonsensical parody of postmodernist 'argumentation', having been seduced by the author's application to physics of all the usual postmodernist mantra about the transgression of boundaries and the radical democratisation of intellectual and cultural life. Its effectiveness was apparent elsewhere in 1996 when a panel of twelve eminent members of the Modern Language Association of America met to discuss 'The Status of Evidence'. According to the printed transcript of the meeting, one of the members reported:

> When I told somebody this afternoon that I was going to a panel on evidence, she said, 'You mean they were able to find anybody left at the MLA who still believes in evidence?' [Laughter][71]

From the tenor of the discussion that ensued, the laughter was not provoked by what was deemed an amiable exaggeration. It was uncomfortable laughter; the chairperson had noted that in some circles criticising a student or job applicant whose argument is not true to the text 'decisively discredits the judge for adhering to what is regarded as an outdated and flawed standard'; and most of those present who seemed committed to belief in the possibility of objective truth were noticeably reluctant to express strong opposition to the contrary position.

Postmodernist relativism has served to license the freewheeling mode of argument and the strategic manipulation of evidence that suits the political agenda of radical criticism. In the pedagogical sphere, the manipulative tendency is ingrained at ground level. One of the most depressing features of literary study in the past few decades has been the theoretical narrowness of the manner in which 'theory' has been taught. Students in mandatory 'Theory' courses are provided with bibliographies and guidebooks which conceal from them the existence of a very substantial and sophisticated body of theoretical work exposing the intellectual inadequacies of the strange doctrines to which they are being subjected, the most recurrent theme in all such critique being that the soft-minded relativism of postmodernist theory repeatedly collapses in self-refutation. (For the benefit of the open-minded and the disaffected, I offer a select list of such writings in an Appendix.) But reasonably intelligent students may not need to challenge 'Theory' on the level of high abstraction and global interdisciplinarity which it occupies with unjustified but terrorising assurance. If encouraged to do so, they can easily see for themselves that its practical application, even by the most distinguished 'text readers', invariably entails deficiencies of the most radical kind.

Chapter 2

Testing New Historicism: 'Invisible Bullets' Reconsidered

1   The Seminal Document

Any attempt to characterise new historicism and evaluate its contribution to our understanding of Renaissance literature could legitimately confine itself to Stephen Greenblatt's 'Invisible Bullets'. He himself would probably regard this as his major Shakespearean project, having revised it three times and given it pride of place at the beginning of *Shakespearean Negotiations: The Circulation of Social Energy in Renaissance England*.[1] The essay focuses on *Henry IV* and *Henry V*, but its argument is purportedly applicable to all the histories (23) and indeed to all Shakespeare's plays (40). It is arguably the most important study of Shakespeare and of Renaissance culture in the new-historicist mode. Some have objected that it produces a view of Shakespeare which is politically unacceptable insofar as it confirms the Foucaultian stress on the futility of resistance and subversion. My own concern, however, is less with Greenblatt's conclusions than with how he arrives at them: with the coherence of his arguments, his use of evidence, and the precise nature of his methodology. Given the cult status of this essay, and given too the institutional distinction of Greenblatt himself (winner, with *Shakespearean Negotiations*, of the Modern Language Association of America's prize for An Outstanding Literary Study, President of that Association in 2002, and hailed by *PMLA*'s editor in 2003 as 'an intellectually unimpeachable source' of scholarly advice), an analysis of the kind I am offering here seems worthwhile. It constitutes in effect a localised inquiry into standards of excellence in the professional study of literature today.

2   The Argument

'Invisible Bullets' deals with Shakespeare's combination of conservative and radical tendencies, an issue which had been foregrounded by critics and scholars working in the New-Critical tradition and variously explained by them in terms of an artistry which conjoins antithetical meanings and fuses opposed attitudes.[2] Greenblatt accounts for this seeming contradiction in Shakespeare by reference to certain ideological strategies, constituting a discourse of power, which are identified by Machiavelli and operative in Thomas Harriot's *Brief and true report of the new found land of Virginia* (1588) and Thomas Harman's cony-catching pamphlet, *A Caveat for Common Cursitors* (1566).[3] Like Harriot's and Harman's, Shakespeare's subversive conservatism is the product of an unjust social order which sustains itself by means of deceit and illusion. Characteristic of the ruling class's deceitful operations is its toleration and even production of subversive ideas and action in such a way as to reinforce its hold on power. Shakespeare's plays reproduce and contribute to this process. Instead of presenting an attitude of qualified and provisional approval towards the dominant order, or a dialectic (resolved or unresolved) of contrary attitudes, they enact and justify the submission of heterodoxy to orthodoxy: subversion is both produced and contained. Rather than leaving his audience with a heightened understanding of complex political problems, or in a state of uncertainty, or divided among themselves, Shakespeare uses play and illusion to lead them through subversive thoughts to a positive acceptance of the dominant order. One might question this argument on the ground that Elizabethan history shows an extremely nervous regime consistently doing its utmost to forestall subversion. One might further object that the texts of Machiavelli, Harman, and Harriot do not provide sufficient evidence for postulating a discourse of power so pervasive that even Shakespeare could not escape it. 'Invisible Bullets' confidently sidesteps such questions, finding all its persuasiveness in the discovery of striking analogies between its selection of very different texts. It seems all the more important, therefore, to look closely at its use of these texts, the nature of the analogies, and the manner in which the resulting interpretive model is applied to Shakespeare's plays.

3   Machiavelli

The overriding aim of Greenblatt's essay is to establish the dependence of power on strategies of deceit; and in this endeavour Machiavelli is called upon as a key witness. Machiavelli's particular relevance stems from his purported interest in the origins of religion and its relation to the deceitful strategies of power. 'One of Machiavelli's arguments', claims Greenblatt, is that 'Old Testament religion . . . and by extension the whole Judeo-Christian tradition, originated in a series of clever tricks, fraudulent illusions perpetrated by Moses, who had been trained in Egyptian magic, upon the . . . credulous Hebrews'; indeed for Machiavelli 'the origin of religion' itself lay 'in an imposition of socially coercive doctrines . . . on a simple people' (24, 27). Greenblatt concedes, however, that this argument 'is not actually found in Machiavelli' (24). But, he observes, it seems to have acquired special force in the Renaissance because of the religious crises of the time. And 'here', he adds, 'Machiavelli's writings are important'. Precisely why they are important we are not told; we can only infer that they are so because they help to show that the argument really can be ascribed to Machiavelli. The *Discourses*, says Greenblatt, 'treats religion as if its primary function were not salvation but the achievement of civic discipline, as if its primary justification were not truth but expediency'. Thus in his chapters on Roman religion Machiavelli reports that Numa Pompilius, while seeking to reduce the savage Romans to civil obedience, had recourse to religion as the most assured support of any civil society, and even claimed that he had converse with a nymph who dictated to him all that he wished the people to do (24).

It should be noted that in this section of the *Discourses* Machiavelli is neither considering the origin of religion nor voicing a negative attitude to it.[4] He is emphasising its positive contribution, both past and present, to social cohesion: religion, he explains, entails good institutions, and whereas kingdoms which depend on the virtue of one man do not last long, those which possess sound institutions will endure.[5] Above all, Machiavelli is lamenting the corruption of the Roman church in Renaissance Italy and the consequent disunity of the nation. Moreover, although he notes that religion was cunningly exploited by pagan rulers to secure obedience and civil order, he nowhere even hints that religion originated in political deceit.

The manner in which Greenblatt seeks to persuade the reader that Machiavelli identified Moses and the whole Judaeo-Christian tradition with original deceit requires careful attention. There is a reference to Moses in *The Prince* (I.ii) which Greenblatt introduces immediately *before* he discusses the *Discourses*. In 'his bland way', he remarks, Machiavelli 'observes . . . that if Moses' particular actions and methods are examined closely, they appear to differ little from those employed by the great pagan princes' (24). Moving from this assertion through the ensuing commentary on the *Discourses*, we are inevitably inclined to assume that Machiavelli has treated Moses and the pagan prince Numa Pompilius as two of a kind, and has traced the origin of Judaeo-Christian religion, as well the religion of ancient Rome, to political fraud. And if we think thus, we will be untroubled when Greenblatt later conjoins 'Numa and the primitive Romans, Moses and the Hebrews' (26), and refers to the dangerously subversive 'Machiavellian hypotheses' about 'the origin of religion in an imposition of socially coercive doctrines by an educated and sophisticated lawgiver on a simple people' (27).

However, the relevant chapter in *The Prince* does not say, as Greenblatt claims it does, 'if Moses' actions and methods are examined closely', which implies the unmasking of deceptive appearances. Nor is it concerned with religion. Its theme is that leaders who endure longest are those who rely least on fortune and most on strength of mind and on armed self-defence; of whom, adds Machiavelli, 'Moses, Cyrus, Romulus, Theseus, and such like are the most excellent examples'.[6] The inclusion of Moses in this list implies no comment on religion but springs from Machiavelli's universalist conception of human nature and political history: 'men are born and live and die in an order which remains ever the same'.[7] Nevertheless, Greenblatt's circuitous and incorrect identification of Machiavelli with the juggling-Moses theory of politics, religion, and 'the origin of European culture and belief' (28; cf. 34) greatly enhances his claim that a common discourse of power is detectable in non-dramatic Renaissance texts. Machiavelli is a much more impressive witness to set beside Harriot than is the notorious spy-catcher Richard Baines, who is mentioned at the start of the essay as having accused Marlowe of saying that Moses was 'a Juggler' and that Harriot could do more than he (21).

4   Harriot

Greenblatt's initial procedure with Harriot is strikingly similar to his treatment
of Machiavelli. He concedes that Harriot 'does not voice any speculations
remotely resembling' the 'Machiavellian hypotheses'; but a few sentences later
he claims that 'if we look attentively' at the *Report* we find, 'as in Machiavelli,
a sense of religion as a set of beliefs manipulated by the subtlety of priests to
help instill obedience and authority', 'a mind that seems to be virtually testing
the Machiavellian hypotheses' (26). Greenblatt identifies in the *Report* three
discursive practices which involve the said hypotheses. They are: (a) *testing* a
subversive interpretation of the dominant culture (here, the function of illusion
in the establishment of religion, and of religion in the establishment of power);
(b) the *recording* of alien voices 'or, more precisely, of alien interpretations',
'subversive inquiries'; (c) *explaining* the underlying moral principle of the
dominant form of power in such a way as to expose its limitations to sceptical
critique (35–9). This division suggests the kind of analytical precision and
structural order one would expect from an essay which ambitiously presents
itself as the blueprint for a poetics of Elizabethan power and theatre (64).

The idea of testing obviously presupposes conscious intention; and at first
'Invisible Bullets' clearly indicates that Harriot was consciously putting to the
proof a 'most radically subversive hypothesis . . . about the origin and function
of religion' (30), one which could have led to torture and worse on the charge
of heresy. 'Harriot not only thought . . . but also evidently believed' that the
political operations of religion in Virginia revealed to him 'a simplified version
of his own culture' and 'his own civilization's past' (28). Greenblatt finds evidence
for Harriot's awareness of what he was doing in the fact that he observed a
radical change in the religious outlook of the Indians: they were, said Harriot,
'brought into great doubts' about their own 'traditions and stories' as a result
of their association with the English. Exemplifying this process is the incident
where the Indians, believing that their corn had withered because they displeased
the colonists, asked them to pray to their Christian God to preserve the corn,
promising in return a share of the crop. This incident, Greenblatt intimates,
was carefully controlled by the English as part of their determination to 'live by
the sweat of other men's brows'. 'As Machiavelli understood, physical
compulsion is essential but never sufficient; the survival of the rulers depends
upon a supplement of religious belief. The Indians *must be persuaded* that the
Christian God is all-powerful . . . that he will wither the corn and destroy the
lives of savages who displease him by disobeying or plotting against the English'
(30; my italics).

Rightly or wrongly, however, the text indicates that Harriot did not plant this
idea in the minds of the Indians but that they produced it spontaneously
themselves. Nor does the text suggest that he made any attempt to exploit it.
More important, 'if we look attentively' at its context we will see that Harriot
attaches a significance to the incident quite different from that suggested by
'Invisible Bullets'. The incident figures as part of a section on the religion of the
Indians which seems designed mainly to show that they could easily be converted
to what Harriot and his readers considered the true faith. Harriot begins by

observing that although they are polytheists they believe in 'one onely chiefe and great God'; so that although their religion 'be farre from the truth, yet beying as it is, there is hope it may bee the easier and sooner reformed' (*TR*, 372). The various incidents which chart the Indians' eagerness to assimilate the Christian God to their pantheon, as well as their fascination with the religious rituals and hymns of the English, are all for Harriot promising signs of that possible reformation. It is true of course that he sees Christianisation, 'civilisation', and colonisation as going hand in hand. But he gives us no reason to suspect him either of conscious deceit or of considering the possibility that religion in general and the Judaeo-Christian tradition in particular originate in political coercion and trickery. Nor need we doubt the impression of sincerity in the account of his own missionary efforts (*TR*, 376).[8] The often stark conjunction of religious and materialistic motives in the first colonists has troubled western liberals ever since historians such as W.H. Prescott drew attention to it; much missionary zeal was indeed no more than 'pious humbug' designed to conceal from the colonists their 'rapacity and aggression, or simply the horrible responsibility implicit in their very presence' (as Greenblatt says of Harriot and his companions [38]). But it is bad history to imply that there were no colonists in whom the religious motive was genuine: Columbus himself, as Prescott eloquently attests, is an outstanding example. It is true that on one desperate occasion (recalled by Greenblatt) Columbus saved himself and his shipwrecked crew from disaster by pretending to the Indians that his prayers caused an eclipse of the moon; but it would be naive to conclude that that in any way contradicts the sincerity of his faith.

Greenblatt clearly feels uneasy about the fact that 'testing' signifies conscious intention. It is, he concedes, 'a strange paradox' that Harriot could test and confirm a radically subversive view of religion in the process of imposing his own religion (30). An attempt is made to resolve this contradiction by abandoning the idea of intention and introducing that of the author as unconscious agent of a power which he embodies and serves, and which produces the Machiavellian hypothesis in order to establish itself. So on the following page it is said that 'Harriot's text is committed to record his confirmation' of a hypothesis whose 'potential subversiveness . . . is invisible not only to those on whom the religion is supposedly imposed but also to most readers and quite possibly to Harriot himself' (31). Thus 'for all his subtlety and his sensitivity to heterodoxy Harriot might not have grasped fully the disturbing implications of his own text' (32). And yet, adds Greenblatt reflectively, 'It may be that he was demonically conscious of what he was doing'; in which case, he concedes, this narrative of his activities would have to be characterised as a 'biographical romance'. For a while, then, the possibility of 'demonic consciousness' (33) seems to be ruled out, even though it has been taken for granted earlier.

But Greenblatt will soon reinstate the biographical romance. After all, he says later, 'Harriot was hounded through his whole life with charges of atheism' (34); and although he has admitted at the outset of the essay that 'there is no justification . . . for dismissing' Harriot's 'profession of faith as mere hypocrisy' (22), 'we simply do not know', he now insists, 'what was thought in silence' (34–5). We are returned therefore to the spy-catcher document as good reason for seeking politically and religiously subversive ideas in a text where no one has suspected them before. To dismiss Baines's document and what it implies, we are warned, is a 'perversely attractive' option; but 'the actual evidence [in favour of doing so] is tenebrous' (35). In the end, Greenblatt's way out of his impasse is simply to declare in an impressively phrased paradox that 'in Harriot's text the relation between orthodoxy and subversion seems . . . to be both perfectly stable and perfectly volatile' (35). But this does not remove contradiction and inconsistency from the argument; and it leaves us with the problem that no evidence of subversion has so far been uncovered.

Begging the question, however, Greenblatt goes on to say that 'we can deepen our understanding' of the strange relationship between orthodoxy and subversion if we consider a second mode of subversion and its containment in Harriot, namely the recording of alien interpretations and subversive inquiries (35). These derive from the Indians' attempts to explain why so many of their people died of infectious diseases introduced by the English while the English themselves were unscathed. Some Indians advanced an astrological explanation; others suggested that the English were not mortal; others that it was God punishing them for their hostility to the English; lastly, some thought they were being shot at by invisible English bullets. Although the penultimate ('moral') interpretation comes from the Indians themselves, Greenblatt identifies it as specifically Christian on the grounds that Harriot half-agrees with it: 'we ourselves have cause in some sorte to thinke no lesse' (*TR*, 380). The invisible-bullets theory, he indicates, represents the subversive voice; it is the materialist explanation – viral infection – which science will discover centuries later, and which invalidates the moral, 'Christian' explanation: 'In the very moment that the moral conception is busily authorizing itself, it registers the possibility (indeed from our vantage point, the inevitability) of its own destruction' (37).

The antithesis here of an alien (subordinate) and a Christian (dominant) view is factitious, since the moral interpretation is common to both sides. Moreover, the invisible-bullets theory is in no real sense subversive. If a puzzled reader asks how it can be construed as such the only answer he will get from 'Invisible Bullets' is that the idea of viral infection is 'present, at least metaphorically' (37). Astonishingly, the historical critic falls back here on the allegorical hermeneutics of *Ovide moralisé* (which could turn erotic tales into moral fables).

Later in the essay we are informed that the process of recording 'culminates for Harriot in a glossary, the beginnings of an Algonquian-English dictionary, designed to facilitate further acts of recording and hence to consolidate English power in Virginia' (45), a 'practical word list with its [Algonquian] equivalents for *fire, food, shelter*' (49). This information is incorrect. Included in the serial descriptions of 'merchantable commodities' given at the start of the *Report* are some vegetable and mineral items for which there is no word in English, and whose names had to be transcribed. But there is *no* glossary anywhere in the *Report*; and nowhere is there any glossing of the three words cited (or any such).[9] Moreover, only when 'recording' is diluted to mean anything uttered by anyone outside the dominant order could it be said that 'glossing' constitutes one and the same practice with it; obviously, we must question the investigative usefulness of categories so elastic and imprecise. As we shall see, however, such elasticity, and especially the alleged presence in Harriot of a politically invaluable glossary, are necessary if analogous ideological strategies are to be shown at work in writers as heterogeneous as Harriot, Harman, and Shakespeare.

An interpretive strategy akin to the allegorical is at work in Greenblatt's account of what he calls 'explaining'. The limitations of the established ideology, he observes, are most intensely exposed when its value is not merely assumed but explained. This is evident when Harriot reports that 'some of the inhabitantes which were our friends & especially . . . Wingina' (their chief), convinced that the diseases which had afflicted them were the work of the Christian God, urged the English to ask God to punish those Indians who were enemies to both their tribe and the colonists. To which request, reports Harriot, the English replied that God would not accept such prayers; that as true servants they should rather petition Him to the contrary, asking that they should all live together in peace; and that whatever happened for good or ill always happened 'as by his wisdome he had ordained best' (*TR*, 379). This orthodox account of the doctrine of divine providence and its relation to Christian ethics is, remarks Greenblatt, morally and logically coherent; but it is also 'pious humbug' which confirms for us 'the drastic disillusionment that extends from Machiavelli to its definitive expression in Hume and Voltaire' (38–9).

It is of course correct to suggest that many who have benefitted from Enlightenment rationalism would reject the doctrine of divine providence, especially as expounded in the circumstances given here. But the only evidence of a subversive hint within the text which Greenblatt can adduce is the fact that when their enemies were eventually smitten by disease the friendly Indians returned to thank the colonists, even though 'wee [had] satisfied them not in promise' (*TR*, 379). Greenblatt intimates that Wingina's mindset as revealed in this situation was perfectly Voltairean: he '*clearly thought* his lesson in Christian ethics was polite nonsense. When the disease spread to his enemies, as it did shortly thereafter, he returned to the English to thank them – *I presume* with the Algonquian equivalent of a sly wink' (39; my italics). Since there is no mention of Wingina, much less of what he clearly thought, in Harriot's account of the return visit of the natives, Greenblatt's presumption is remarkable. But it is also understandable: Voltairean subversiveness is more plausibly attached to a solitary Indian in a sixteenth-century text than to a whole group.[10]

5 Harman

The process of heterodoxy working within a containing orthodoxy is allegedly apparent also in Thomas Harman's *Caveat for Common Cursitors*; of the three practices sustaining this process, however, only that of recording alien voices seems to have been detected. This tract on the wiles of Elizabethan vagabonds is strategically chosen for a number of reasons. The relationship between the vagabonds and Harman (a middle-class justice of the peace) would seem to complement and parallel the native–colonist relationship in Virginia, and so to counteract the impression that there might be something 'slightly absurd' (45) in linking Harriot's report on events in Virginia with Shakespeare's investigation of political conflict in medieval England. Although he had earlier (26–7) noticed that the colonists saw the social arrangements of the natives in the same hierarchical terms as prevailed in England, Greenblatt now asserts, in the interest of analogical exactness, that 'middle- and upper-class English settlers regarded the American Indians less as another race than as a version of their own lower classes: one man's tinker is another man's Indian' (49). Moreover, since successive Tudor governments dealt harshly with vagabonds and 'masterless men', the *Caveat* permits emphasis on the oppression of the common people, something which Greenblatt wishes to foreground in his interpretation of Shakespeare's histories. In particular, he believes that the *Caveat* gives him some grounds for his central claim that deceit and treachery were fundamental to the way in which the dominant class exercised control: something else on which he places great emphasis in his view of the histories. Lastly, because the differences between Harman, Harriot, and Machiavelli are otherwise so great, we are to take on trust the scholarly assurance that the common discursive mode can be 'found in . . . a hundred other texts' (52).

Like other pieces of contemporary rogue literature, but far more generously, the *Caveat* provides its readers with the names of the different types of vagabonds and with a glossary of 'cant', the rogues' professional jargon. Since it was believed that cant was used for the purposes of conversing safely on criminal matters, knowledge of it was said by the pamphleteers to be a form of self-protection for the citizen and a means of detection for agents of the law. Harman improves upon this service to the community by adding to his glossary a list of the alleged names of 'the most notorious and wickedest walkers' living at the time (109).

Harman claims to have achieved some of his insider knowledge by deceitful means: 'not without faithful promise made unto them' would the rogues 'discover their names or anything they showed to me' (62; cf. 84, 101, 106). And although Greenblatt acknowledges that 'much of the *Caveat*, like the other cony-catching pamphlets of the period, has the air of a jest-book' (50), he takes this confession very seriously and gives it special emphasis. Harman, he says, '*repeatedly* calls attention to his solemn promises never to reveal anything he has been told'; he uses 'false *oaths*' and is guilty of 'ruthless betrayal' in his 'middle-class' desire to suppress 'primitive rebels against the hypocrisy of a cruel society'. In fact he is part of 'a *community* of vagabond haters' which 'seems to batten on the breaking of *oaths*' (50–52; my italics).

But this changes the nature and degree of Harman's deceit, and it gives a wholly disproportionate emphasis to its role in the book. Much of the allure of the cony-catching pamphlets was the impression they gave of penetrating the secret, complex order of a criminal society; and if one way of stressing its secretiveness was to claim that those who divulged and those who sought its secrets endangered their lives,[11] another was to claim that the secrets had been divulged in strictest confidence and extracted with enormous difficulty. Moreover Harman never makes or breaks an oath (his readers knew there was a large difference, both legal and theological, between promise and oath). Nor does he 'repeatedly' call attention to promises. Nor does anyone else make or break a promise in dealing with the vagabonds. Moreover, of Harman's four allusions to promise, one is thoroughly unconvincing, since the demand for a promise of secrecy is made by a vagrant whose hilarious tale of frustrating a lecherous citizen brings her out on the side of the angels and in no way endangers her standing with her own community. Furthermore, almost all of Harman's information comes to him from friends and casual acquaintances who have been cheated and robbed; while his infrequent and brief references to his own deceit inevitably make little impression in a collection of tales which vividly records the myriad forms of dissembling, role play, disguise, and lying by means of which the vagabond community outwits law-abiding and gullible citizens.

Nor does Harman seem a blinkered champion of the middle and upper classes; as he says (repeatedly), the victims of the wandering rogues are most often 'poor householders' (61), 'poor farmers' (109), solitary housewives and elderly travellers (68), 'the common people' (85, 113). Greenblatt claims that a powerfully but unintentionally subversive effect is obtained 'again and again' (51) in the rogue literature when the doxies and morts turn the moral tables on those who rebuke them by arguing that their lives are at worst imitations of the lives of the great. Only one example of this kind of subversion is noted, and it comes, not from the *Caveat*, but from a tract on diceplay attributed to Gilbert Walker. The rogue in question happens to be a suave, gentlemanly gambler who lives in style and comfort;[12] and his eloquently subversive speech is part of a cynical effort to recruit as his assistant a desperate young man whom he has just fleeced. Rather than credit Walker with the imagination to perceive that such a speech is dramatically appropriate to such a character in such a situation, Greenblatt represents the dice-player's argument as a potent piece of authorially unintended subversion.

The device of metaphorising bits of the text in order to fit them to the system of analogies on which the interpretive model depends is evident in comments on the significance of printing in the *Caveat*. Harman was friendly with the printer who produced the *Caveat*, and on one occasion, before the book was half printed, the printer joined him in chasing and catching a thief (85–90). With an eye to what he will make of theatricality (allegedly analogous to printing) in *Henry IV*, Greenblatt says of this incident that printing is here 'represented in the text itself as a force for social order and the detection of criminal fraud'; the incident thematises Harman's conception of the book as a powerful tool for the oppressive forces of order (50–51). To be consistent in this mode of interpretation one would have to take account of Harman's subsequent complaint: 'I had the best gelding stolen out of my pasture . . . while this book was first a printing' (*Caveat*, 80); but to read this detail on any but the literal plane would simply expose the absurdity of the imported metaphor. Moreover, if printing is to join treacherous dissembling as a characteristic means by which the lower classes are kept in order, then one should also attend to the fact that whereas printing is referred to only twice, and incidentally, there are many occasions when writing is represented as a phenomenon of major importance. This fact would normally be grist to the mill of any textualising, poststructuralist critic. But in Harman writing is identified entirely with the craftiness of the vagabonds, many of whom are supplied by expert forgers in their own community with perfect imitations of those passports and documents which licensed both travel and begging (74, 80–81, 84–5, 91–4).[13] To take this into account would be to reinforce the obvious impression that it is not the upper but the lower classes who excel in the arts and crafts of deceit. But that is a direction in which 'Invisible Bullets' cannot go, for it would subvert its argument entirely.

6   *Henry IV*

Greenblatt acknowledges that Shakespeare is a highly sophisticated playwright, fully aware of his own political intuitions. A 'relentless demystifier', he 'understood' the ideological strategies used in colonial discourse. He 'grasped' these strategies by 'looking intently' at contemporary politics and 'reading imaginatively' in the chroniclers (23, 40). But he is complicit with contemporary power, all his devastating insights into its functioning being part of his highly successful attempt 'as sovereign juggler' (64) to beguile the audience into enthusiastic acceptance of the established order. How anyone who is consciously devoted to the relentless demystification of a particular power structure could write plays designed to reinforce it, or how an audience presented with so fiercely negative a view of monarchical authority could be persuaded to glory in it, is never acknowledged as a problematic assault on common sense. The 'strange paradox' allegedly present in Harriot is here pushed to cracking point. It is noticeable, however, that when the contradiction becomes most acute it is relaxed, as in the account of Harriot, through unobtrusive replacement of the intending author by the responsible text and the mystical, Foucaultian conception of power as both ubiquitous and omnipotent.

Nevertheless, the introduction to the sections on Shakespeare promises to proceed in a consistent and systematic manner. The claim that his plays are 'centrally, repeatedly concerned with the production and containment of disorder' is to be established in terms of 'the three practices . . . identified in Harriot's text – testing, recording, and explaining', all of which 'have their recurring theatrical equivalent' (40). However, the analysis of these practices is fitful, as, apparently, is their presence in the plays. For the most part, examples of recording fail to match the initial definition of that practice: we hear the voices of the lower classes in *1 and 2 Henry IV*, but nothing they say challenges the ideology of the establishment; the only subversive voice is that of Falstaff, a knight eager to become 'either earl or duke' (*1H4*, 5.4.138).[14] The foreign voices in *Henry V*, as Greenblatt admits, are also politically disappointing. Since *Henry IV* and *Henry V* are seen as full-scale 'tests' of monarchical ideology (55–6), 'testing' becomes a redundant category, a mere synonym for interrogation or subversion.

The plays, it is claimed, show all power and authority as 'self-undermining'. As prince and later as king, Hal is the central embodiment of this self-subverting power; indeed he represents in his success the founding (no less) of the modern state. If Greenblatt, as seems likely, sees the modern state very much in terms of the government which sacrificed a generation of young Americans to the killing fields of Vietnam, we may have a clue to the extraordinary picture of Hal offered in these pages. What other critics have seen as the coolly calculating side of the prince is hugely magnified and becomes the man entire. The phrases which create this portrait call attention to the fact that the power and unity of the essay rest far more on its rhetoric than on its logic. A key figure in this rhetoric is repetition (including synonymous variation), beginning with a word which appears nowhere in the plays but which adroitly connects Hal (as it has connected Harriot and Shakespeare) with the Machiavellian Moses of Baines's document. 'We are continually reminded', says Greenblatt, that Hal is a 'juggler; a conniving hypocrite' (41). He is 'a mere pretender', 'the prince and principle of falsification . . . a counterfeit companion' who plans from the start to 'sell his wastrel friends' (48). He is 'meanly calculating' and 'reveals the emptiness of the world around him' (42, 48). His value is 'dependent on the circulation of false coin and the subtle manipulation of appearance' (42). His formal majesty is built on 'the squalid betrayals that preserve the state' (53). He is 'an upper-class Harman' whose relations with the lower class exemplify 'ruthless betrayal' (51–2). He is even 'more coldhearted' than his brother, 'the coldhearted betrayer of the rebels' (55). As conqueror of France, he is the personification of 'royal hypocrisy, ruthlessness, and bad faith' (56).

Of great importance to this interpretation is Hal's first soliloquy, from which he emerges here as the representative of a state that betrays the people and of a dramatic art that betrays its audience. In attempting to justify – to 'explain' – himself, Hal says that he will in due time throw off his loose behaviour, redeem time when men least think he will, and so 'falsify men's hopes'. The last phrase Greenblatt flexibly glosses as meaning 'to disappoint, to deceive men, to turn their hopes into fictions, to betray' (41). He thus presents the prince as practising heartless falsity upon his 'adoring' (42) tavern friends. It is surely relevant to note that Sir John is the only one who pins his hopes on Hal's kingly future, and that he has already been assured that such hopes are misplaced. More important, Hal's promise to falsify men's hopes clearly refers to the shallow minds and 'smiling pickthanks' who 'prophetically forethink' his fall and slander him at court; whom he complains about in Part 1 (3.2.23–5), and recalls at the end of Part 2: 'I survive / To mock the expectation of the world, / To frustrate prophecies, and to raze out / Rotten opinion, who hath writ me down / After my seeming' (5.2.124–8).

Analysis of the play's acts of recording, when we hear 'subversive voices' (52), 'the voices of those who dwell outside the realms ruled by the potentates' (43), also points accusingly at Hal. Falstaff's conscripts are important here. Victims of 'the established order', 'produced as well as consumed by the great', they are 'the masterless men who rose up periodically in desperate protests against their social superiors'. These voices, says Greenblatt, 'exist and have their apotheosis in Falstaff"; more importantly, 'their existence proves to be utterly bound up with Hal' (43) (which implies, without asserting, that he is responsible for their plight). However, we hear nothing at all from these voices in Part 1 and nothing even vaguely subversive from them in Part 2, their most memorable contribution being Feeble's loyal protest: 'No man's too good to serve's prince' (3.2.227). Nor can the unscrupulous way in which they are conscripted be taken as reflecting on Hal and the established order. Their presence in the army meets with instant disapproval from both the Prince and Westmorland. In what sense Falstaff can be construed as their 'apotheosis' is difficult to see. They are his victims, a comment on his cheerfully cynical rapacity

('I have misused the King's press damnably' [1: 4.2.12, 58–66]); and in both parts of the play they contribute substantially to the underlying argument in favour of what is identified in 'Invisible Bullets' as perfect treachery: the rejection.

Francis is another voice outside the established order with whom 'Invisible Bullets' associates some bitterly subversive ideas. Like Falstaff's conscripts, however, Francis himself says nothing that can be interpreted subversively. It is his treatment by Hal which is made to yield such significance: the Prince reduces him to 'the mechanical repetition of the word "Anon"', an action which 'implicates Hal not only in the apprentice's linguistic poverty ... but in the poverty of the five years apprenticeship Francis has yet to serve' (44). Unsupported by evidence or argument, this interpretation depends for its rhetorical effectiveness on a characteristically ambiguous use of 'implicates' (meaning 'involvement' but hinting at 'responsibility'); on the leap via metaphor ('poverty') and supposition from Francis's few words to his implied status as a victim of economic exploitation. More seriously, it depends on missing the scene's relationship to the complex structure of the play. Given the dependence of 'Invisible Bullets' on analogy, its failure to attend to Shakespeare's subtle system of analogies, and to perceive that these frequently define very important differences, is remarkable. The scene with Francis demands comparison with the one which precedes it, for there Hotspur's wife accuses him of babbling in military and equestrian terms while asleep, only to be answered in the same repetitive idiom (2.3.45–52). So she calls him 'a paraquito' or little parrot; which anticipates Hal's comment on Francis: 'That ever this fellow should have fewer words than a parrot.' And lest the analogy should be missed, Hal continues: 'I am not yet of Percy's mind ... he that kills me some six or seven dozen Scots at a breakfast, washes his hands, and says to his wife, "Fie upon this quiet life, I want work".' Hal would love to 'play Percy' and have Falstaff play his wife, for he is now 'of all humours': quite unlike the two men whose enslavement to one humour emphasises his own attainment of the Renaissance ideal of nobility, which combines valour with eloquence and wit. It is this fullness of nature and accomplishment which divides Hal between two worlds and accounts for his tardy response to the call of duty. Here too the scene with Francis – *'the Drawer stands amazed, not knowing which way to go'* – provides another analogy which is also a contrast; Hal delays in responding to the call of duty, but only seems not to know where he should go. His exuberant humour, too, distances the practical joke on Francis from the kind of sinister cruelty which 'Invisible Bullets' imputes to it.[15]

Just as the apprentice's linguistic 'poverty' is turned against Hal, so too is the linguistic invention of the other drawers. The drinking terms which Hal acquires from them are damningly classified with the 'practical word list ... with its Algonquian equivalents for *fire, food, shelter*' allegedly found in the colonialist Harriot, and also – 'a deeper resemblance' – with 'the sinister glossaries appended to sixteenth-century accounts of criminals and vagabonds' (49). Although Hal's easiness with drinking slang is for the drawers themselves a sign of his capacity for good fellowship, it is construed here as a treacherous quest for power and domination. Textual evidence for this is found in Hal's remark: 'They take it upon their salvation, that . . . when I am King of England I shall command all the good lads of Eastcheap' (2.4.8–15). These lines, however, suggest the idea of service spontaneously offered rather than cunningly secured (cf. 'no man's too good to serve's prince'); moreover, the clauses judiciously omitted between 'that' and 'when' undermine Greenblatt's picture of the ruthless prince and the 'adoring' Falstaff: 'They take it . . . that though I be but Prince of Wales, yet I am the king of courtesy, and tell me flatly that I am no proud Jack like Falstaff.' The purpose of Hal's consorting with the drawers, as of his joke on Francis, is no more sinister than that specified at the end of this speech (when he plans the joke): 'to drive away the time' (line 26). Only a determinedly humourless and theoretically driven response could produce the interpretation of the scene offered by 'Invisible Bullets'.

Further support for the interpretation, however, is fetched from the speech in Part 2 where Warwick assures the dying King that Hal will not be corrupted by his sojourn in Eastcheap. Here there actually is an analogy between language and political calculation: Hal studies his companions 'Like a strange tongue, wherein, to gain the language, / 'Tis needful that the most immodest word / Be looked upon and learnt' (4.3.69–71). But it is illogical to imply that the metaphoric function of language at a particular point in Part 2 can be retrospectively applied to a literal reference to language in Part 1. Moreover, Warwick's application of the analogy – like someone who has learned that certain words are obscene, Hal will 'cast off' his riotous companions in due time – does not identify language learning as a deceitful attempt to gain power over the lower classes.

An important analogy in the argument of 'Invisible Bullets' is that between Hal and John, since it allegedly confirms Hal's identification with ruthlessness, deceit, and betrayal. But here more than ever we must perceive that in Shakespeare's design likeness frequently emphasises difference. The only difference between Hal and John acknowledged by Greenblatt is that Hal is even '*more* coldhearted' than 'the coldhearted betrayer of the rebels' (55; italics added). This is remarkably at variance with the text, no matter how long we dwell on the coldness of the rejection speech. Falstaff himself has emphasised difference in similarity, remarking that the cold blood which the brothers inherited from their father has been changed in the 'very hot and valiant' Hal (2: 4.2.117). Cool and self-controlled though he is, Hal shows unquestionable signs of a warmhearted nature: in the tenderness and generosity which he extends to the dying and dead Hotspur and the supposedly dead Falstaff; in his bitter allusions to unexpressed grief when talking to Poins about his father's illness; and in the tears to which his father's savage criticism reduces him. Pointedly, it is his father who publicly emphasises the two sides of his nature: 'being incensed, he is flint', but 'he hath a tear for pity, and a hand . . . for meting charity' (2: 4.3.31–3). All of this goes unrecorded in 'Invisible Bullets'.

Hal, suggests Greenblatt, is implicated in the treachery practised on the rebels by John: 'out of the squalid betrayals that preserve the state emerges the "formal majesty" into which Hal at the close . . . merges himself' (55). No account is taken of the fact that Hal is conspicuously absent from Gaultree and that the dramatic structure of the two plays establishes a vivid contrast between John's mode of conquest in Part 2 and Hal's in Part 1. Moreover, in his determination to identify the monarchy with deceit and betrayal, Greenblatt ignores the fact that not only the King and Prince John but also the rebellious Northumberland and Worcester – and all those friends of Hotspur whose 'promises' were 'fair' (1: 3.1.1) – are guilty of lies and betrayal. In this world of lies and broken promises Hal is in fact the exception. Challenging Douglas at Shrewsbury, he identifies himself as 'the Prince of Wales . . . Who never promiseth but he means to pay' (1: 5.4.41–2). The defeat of the rebels at Shrewsbury is the fulfillment of his solemn vow to his father that with the help of God he will overcome their leader and 'die a hundred thousand deaths / Ere break the smallest parcel of this vow' (1: 3.2.153–9). The rejection, too, is the fulfillment of a promise made both to the audience (1: 1.2.196–205) and to Falstaff ('I do, I will'). And the last words spoken by him in Part 2 are a solemn, public promise which greatly moderates the effect of the rejection: he will give Falstaff an allowance for life and in addition advance him if he reforms his ways. It is highly significant that in his concluding sentence Hal asks the Chief Justice to ensure that this twin promise is honoured ('Be it your charge, my lord, to see performed the tenor of my word'), since it was axiomatic in ethical theory that 'faith or fidelity . . . is the foundation of justice'.[16] With immense care, Shakespeare presents Hal as a prince who from the start invites us to match his words against his deeds, actively repudiating the Machiavellian ethic (*The Prince*, ch. 18) of which, for Greenblatt, he is the quintessential expression.[17] Shakespeare has been implying throughout that if anyone will unify the divided nation it will be a strong ruler who keeps his word and inspires trust. This conception of Hal's character (to be further considered in Chapter 3) is reiterated in the final scene of *Henry V*, where Henry tells Kate he is 'a fellow of plain and uncoined constancy' eloquent only in 'downright oaths, which I never use till urged, nor never break for urging'; and where he ends the play with the injunction: 'may our oaths well kept and prosperous be!' (5.2.145–54, 368).

Although it is never recorded in 'Invisible Bullets', Hal's challenging and empirically validated self-definition has obvious bearing too on the claim that he is so wholly implicated in politically motivated deception and theatricality as to have no identity. He conforms, says Greenblatt, to the general rule that in the dominant order 'to be one-self means to perform one's part in the scheme of power rather than to manifest one's natural disposition . . . the very core of the self'; indeed 'it is doubtful that such a thing as a natural disposition exists' (46). There are, however, several occasions when the text calls attention to the difference between Hal's playful role and a stable inner self. These too are ignored, at least one of them deliberately. Greenblatt quotes a few lines from Hal's speech to the Chief Justice – from 'My father is gone wild into the grave' to 'raze out rotten opinion'. For no apparent reason, the clause which finishes the sentence is omitted: 'who hath writ me down / After my seeming' (2: 5.2.127–8). This conception of an essential Hal which the superficial and the slanderous fail to acknowledge is recalled in *Henry V* both by Ely, who says he obscured his reflective nature 'Under the veil of wildness' (1.1.63–4), and by the Constable of France, who identifies no compulsive role-player but a 'Roman Brutus, / Covering discretion with a coat of folly' (2.4.37–8).

Identified (like Harman's printing) as one of power's 'crucial agents' (50), theatricality is simplified and misunderstood in the essay. Ignored is the fact that theatricality covers the whole social spectrum, and that it can have a wide range of ethical implications, positive, neutral, or negative. It includes Bolingbroke's politic display of humility when an ambitious subject as well as his determination to act like royal flint with unruly subjects; Hal's carefree imitation of Hotspur as well as his uneasy donning of gorgeous majesty; Falstaff's puritanism and heroics, Pistol's Ercles vein, and Mistress Quickly's ladylike airs and graces. Given the fact that the play emerges from a culture obsessed with the idea that all the world's a stage on which everyone has a part to play in every moment of time (and on which they often affect the wrong part), the identification of theatricality with fraudulent power is historically incongruous. 'Play the man, Master Ridley', said Bishop Latimer to his friend, as they went to the stake for heresy. Just so, the woodcuts in Foxe's *Ecclesiasticall Historie* commonly represent the central figure of the martyr as stealing the state's carefully staged show of power with a final display of heroic self-definition. Kings and queens might stage themselves and their power, but they were no more theatrical than some of their powerless victims.[18]

7   *Henry V*

Greenblatt's account of *Henry V* severely exposes the weakness of his central argument. This play, he claims, 'deftly registers every nuance of royal hypocrisy, ruthlessness, and bad faith' while at the same time offering 'a celebration, a collective panegyric' to a 'charismatic leader' (56). This coexistence of quite contrary evaluations, we are told, does not mean that the play is 'radically ambiguous'; rather, 'the subversive doubts the play continually awakens originate paradoxically in an effort to intensify the power of the king and his war . . . The very doubts that Shakespeare raises serve not to rob the king of his charisma but to heighten it' (62–3). Here more than ever the figure of paradox helps to gloss over the contradictoriness and implausibility of the argument. (So absorbed is Greenblatt in his own imported paradox that he fails to notice that paradox – as we shall record in Chapter 3 – is conspicuously central to Shakespeare's mode of thought and expression in the play.)

The discussion of 'recording' in *Henry V* suggests certain limitations in the essay's historical awareness. Analogous to the relationship between the colonists and the American natives, claims Greenblatt, is that between Henry and his Irish, Welsh, and Scottish captains; they 'symbolically' represent Hal's taming of 'the last wild areas in the British Isles' (56). That one thousand 'nimble Irishmen' did wonders for Henry at Harfleur (as Holinshed records);[19] that Henry was Prince of Wales and born in Monmouth (as Fluellen, following Holinshed, emphasises); that Scotland was a dangerously aggressive neighbour of the English in the fifteenth century (as Henry reminds us: 1.2.136–54); that by 1599 Essex and others had already been favouring James VI of Scotland as Elizabeth's successor; and that unity in diversity is a conspicuous political ideal in the play: none of this is deemed relevant or allowed to qualify the categorical statement that the Irish, the Welsh, and the Scots are the recorded voices of a doomed tribalism.

The discussion of recording illustrates both the difficulty of fitting the thesis to the text and the doubtful analytical value of the category itself. Greenblatt has obvious difficulty in getting the three captains to speak as they ought. Only Fluellen, he concedes, and only then 'at one moment . . . articulate[s] perceptions that lie outside the official line'. This happens when Fluellen compares Alexander the Great, who killed his friend in a drunken orgy, and Henry V, who *'in his right wits and good judgements, turned away the fat knight with the great-belly doublet'* (4.7.45–7; my italics). The comparison, we are told, produces 'a moment [which] is potentially devastating' for the King. 'The comparison with drunken Alexander focuses all our perceptions on Hal's sober coldbloodedness' and intimates that royal authority 'as the play defines it, is precisely the ability to betray one's friends' (57–8). Greenblatt mitigates the implausibility of this reading by ignoring the significance of the italicised phrase and the fact that Alexander's drunkenness was not just carnivalesque but homicidal, and then by inserting a damning reference to Henry's 'responsibility for the execution of his erstwhile boon companion Bardolph'. It should be noted that the Bardolph allusion is taken from a later 'moment' in the play and involves textual misrepresentation as well as misinterpretation. Although Henry subsequently approved of the sentence, it was not he who condemned Bardolph for his theft of church property, but the Duke of Exeter (3.6.43, 106). Moreover, this action accords with the strict discipline – approved by Fluellen – which Shakespeare, following Holinshed, projects as an important part of Henry's stature as a military commander: 'At his first comming on land, he caused proclammation to be made, that no person should be so hardie on paine of death, either to take anie thing out of anie church . . . or to hurt or do violence to either priests or women, or anie such as should be found without weapon or armor.'[20] Shakespeare's Henry repeats this command, adding that lenity, 'the gentler gamester', is more effective in winning a kingdom than cruelty (3.6.111–12). Greenblatt supports Pistol's belief that Fluellen should have pleaded with Exeter or the king to 'Let gallows gape for dog, let man go free' (line 41), and clearly implies that the appeal should have been granted (line 56). But Pistol's attitude is surely meant to recall the kind of justice favoured by the likes of Falstaff and Davy, Justice Shallow's manipulative servant: 'I grant your worship that he is a knave, sir . . . but a knave should have some countenance at his friend's request' (*2H4*, 5.1.36–8). So neither the memory of Henry's rejection of Falstaff ('when in his right wits and judgement'), and all that Sir John represents, nor the determination of Henry and his officers to uphold strict discipline and military justice, can be reasonably construed in the given contexts as a critique, 'devastating' or otherwise, of royal authority. Nor can either warrant Greenblatt's comparison with Harman's alleged practice of betraying low-life characters with the sole purpose of benefitting the dominant minority (57–8).

Although the Welsh captain's recorded voice supposedly produces a moment which prompts us to identify the moral authority of royal power with the ability to betray one's friends, Greenblatt contradictorily goes on to admit that neither the English allies nor the low-life characters 'fulfill adequately the role of aliens whose voices are recorded' (58). And although this would seem to suggest some awareness that he has been straining unduly to fit the text to an interpretive schema which is imposed rather than derived, Greenblatt proceeds to deal in the same contradictory fashion with the alien 'voices' of the English enemies. The French say much that is contemptuous of the English; yet they voice 'remarkably little that is alien or disturbing to the central voice of authority' (58). It is indeed strange (we might add) that the French never once challenge Henry's hereditary claim to their throne. Much could be made of that, but it would not help the argument of 'Invisible Bullets'.

The discursive mode of 'explaining', unlike that of 'recording', is alleged to be powerfully disturbing in its subversive force; and what is subverted now is the King's claim that the cause was good. Greenblatt's gift for phrasemaking is at its most seductive here as he reduces the war to a disgraceful tale of violent self-interest hypocritically dressed up as 'God's triumph' with 'a deliciously favorable kill ratio' (60). In Henry's private reflections as well as his public utterances, the play foregrounds the Tudor chroniclers' conception of Henry as a Christian knight who submits himself to the will of God and who (as at Shrewsbury: *1H4*, 3.2.153–4) attributes his success to God alone. Greenblatt, however, insistently derides Henry's piety as manifestly self-subverting bad faith.

Evidence for the play's 'relentlessly subversive' (65) view of the war is found in a speech of Williams in the debate with the disguised King (*H5*, 4.1.129–86). Some critics interpret this speech as being concerned only with the questionable justice of the war and the deaths and mutilations it entails; for them, Henry's response evades the issue. An alternative interpretation would note, however, that the rhetorical structure of the speech focuses primarily on Henry's possible responsibility for the 'damnation' of those who die in battle with 'irreconciled iniquities' on their souls. In its historical context, no charge could be graver, and it is to this climactic charge that Henry responds. But Greenblatt simply dismisses his reply to the religious indictment as 'a string of awkward' and 'mutually contradictory' sentences (what the contradictions are, we are not told). He also ignores Williams's remark endorsing Henry's response and closing this part of the debate ('’Tis certain, every man that dies ill, the ill upon his own head; the King is not to answer it': lines 4.1.185–6). Nor does Greenblatt record the way in which Williams's sour claim that Henry would probably seek to escape death through ransom (line 192) is later shown to have been wide of the mark.

Although the theological climax of Williams's speech is ignored, much is made of Henry's subsequent prayer asking God not to punish him for 'the fault / My father made in compassing the crown' (4.1.290–91). With 'his marvelous talent for establishing connections' (as one respectful critic terms it),[21] Greenblatt links Henry's prayer for pardon for his dead father's sin with Claudius' 'inadequate repentance' for the fratricide he himself has recently committed (61–2). Rhetorically effective though it might be, the analogy serves mainly to confirm Greenblatt's determination to damn Henry. There are undoubtedly moral and political resemblances between Claudius and Bolingbroke, although the differences are also substantial. But the differences between Claudius and Henry V are huge. And yet coming after a previous comparison of Henry with that ultimate embodiment of ruthless hypocrisy, Marlowe's Fernese (61), this loaded comparison is slightly less than shocking.

Its power to shock too has been diminished by the lingering association of Henry with rape that bridges the sections on recording and explaining. Henry, we are told, 'repeatedly warns his victims that they are bringing pillage and rape upon themselves'; indeed he 'speaks as the head of an army that is about to pillage and rape them' (62). This powerfully subversive theme culminates in the wooing of Katherine, an interpretation of which scene Greenblatt prepares us to accept with the help of one of his more unusual analogies. Recalling the amusement of Italians when he himself unintentionally pronounced the word *coglioli*, meaning 'balls', he explains that our pleasure in hearing Katherine stumble into indecencies is intensified because she is 'by implication learning English as a consequence of . . . an invasion graphically figured as rape'. In the wooing scene, the 'sexualized violence' of Henry's invasion is 'transfigured and tamed', the fate of the other being now 'complete absorption' (59). Which means that however much she is charmed by Henry, Katherine's marriage is rape legitimised by power.

The play's subtle engagement with the subject of sexuality I shall be considering at some length in Chapter 3; here it can be dealt with briefly. That there are some allusions to both sexual potency and rape in the text is true. But we must be factually accurate about these allusions and attach to each its appropriate contextual meaning. In the first place, Henry does not 'repeatedly' warn the French about rape. He warns some Frenchmen about it once, in a special situation, and never mentions it again. With his army too enfeebled to capture Harfleur by force even if they wanted to, Henry relies on the word rather than the sword, urging the citizens to accept an offer of mercy while there is still time. In his powerful oration, he links rape with infanticide and the murder of old men as reminders of the scarcely controllable violence of soldiers when once let loose in mortal combat. We cannot disprove that Henry would have expected his men to commit such crimes, or condoned them if committed, had his oration failed; but it would have been entirely out of character if he had done so. Nor is there any evidence elsewhere that rape or infanticide or the murder of old men takes place. Henry's approval of Bardolph's execution is one of many indications (beginning with his stern reply to the Dauphin's mocking message) that a major condition of his greatness is the *control* of energy and violence. Therein lies the significance of his marriage. In the good-humoured, erotically suggestive conversation between Charles, Burgundy, and Henry in the last scene, where the bawdry is begun by the Frenchmen (at Henry's expense), Charles tells the enamoured Henry that the cities he has won are at the moment 'turned into a maid, for they are girdled with maiden walls that war hath never entered'. To which Henry immediately responds: 'Shall Kate be my wife?' (5.2.319).

In general, of course, any invasion of another nation can be figuratively spoken of as rape. But whatever we think about the motives of Canterbury when justifying this particular invasion, it is indeed remarkable that the French never once dispute or even condemn Henry's repeated, hereditary claim to their country. They do not see the English as foreigners at all. As Lisa Jardine half-reminded us, the Dauphin and Britain speak of them as 'the emptying of our fathers' luxury', bastard sons of those Normans who invaded and conquered Albion (3.5.5–10); more graciously, the French king refers to Henry as 'our brother' (2.4.75, 115; 5.2.10). The suggestion, surely, is that this war is to be conceived as a dynastic conflict in which two branches of the same family struggle for possession of their forefathers' throne. Shakespeare's audience of 1599 would have been imaginatively responsive to this notion. The Queen's father had renewed the crown's ancestral claim to France and led an army into battle for it, adding some territory to his residual medieval inheritance. During the reign of Mary Tudor the military defeat which led to the loss of Calais and its adjoining territories and fortresses ('so long possessed by the English, and now in forren tenure') was experienced as a profound humiliation by both nation and Queen ('when I am dead and opened, you shall find Calis lieng in my hart').[22] Elizabeth herself became obsessed with this 'brightest jewel in the English crown', as it was then called.[23] In the years 1559–63 and yet again in 1596 she tried her utmost, both diplomatically and militarily, to regain it. It was as if retention of Calais gave grounds for hope that a sizeable portion of France would one day return to English rule. Ludicrous though it may now seem, Elizabeth and her successors until well into the nineteenth century – as English coinage shows – were styled monarchs of England and France. Clearly, the claim to France was deep-rooted in the discourse of English nationalism. To ignore this context in a politically and discursively self-conscious interpretation of *Henry V*, while at the same time privileging Harriot's report on the Algonquins, is to offer a singularly skewed form of historical contextualisation. And yet to consider such a context would be to undo a master analogy: between Hal's French conquests (military and amorous) and the rape of Virginia.

8   'The tenor of my word'

In the last endnote to the final version of 'Invisible Bullets', Greenblatt reflects that we should perhaps 'imagine Shakespeare writing at a moment when none of the alternatives for a resounding political commitment seemed satisfactory; when the pressure to declare himself unequivocally an adherent of one or another faction seemed narrow, ethically coarse, politically stupid' (175). This recalls the New-Critical objection to Tillyard and Dover Wilson for 'taking sides between two viewpoints instead of letting both be real'.[24] But it is not the same as saying that Shakespeare is artistically and politically committed to the side which he relentlessly identifies with deceit and ruthless betrayal. Unwittingly, Greenblatt has slipped back into the critical position from which the argument of 'Invisible Bullets' largely derives. The novelty of his argument lies mainly in pushing the New-Critical position to an extreme point where ambivalence becomes a schizoid condition (on the part of both playwright and audience) represented as profound paradox.

But most of the appeal of the essay lies in its novel use of heterogeneous analogy to support the audacious argument: what allegedly happens in Shakespeare's texts is plausible because it happens in very different forms of contemporary writing. As we have seen, however, the analogical argument is radically flawed. Not only is the range of texts chosen absurdly small. The evidence for parallelism is selected and used with persistent disregard for the principles of scholarly inquiry and sound reasoning. There is an indifference to consistency which could politely be called eccentric: factual claims as well as interpretations are boldly made, then retracted (giving the impression of scholarly scrupulosity), then reasserted. When an interpretation seems too far-fetched, a strong commitment to intentionality is silently abandoned in favour of ideological and discursive determinism. An air of analytical thoroughness is induced by way of the three discursive practices; but these tools are fitfully and inconsistently applied; and the argument would not suffer in the least if they were subjected to Occam's Razor. Bits and pieces of text are put together in an entirely misleading fashion. Grave enjoinders to 'look attentively' at the texts and discount 'tenebrous' evidence are matched by additions to the texts, by factual misstatements about what the texts contain, and by fanciful speculation about the thoughts and gestures of historical persons mentioned therein. The flamboyant habit of numerical inflation – 'many times', 'again and again', 'repeatedly', 'continually', 'a community of vagabond haters', 'a hundred other texts' – cloaks the paucity of evidence and its unrepresentative nature. Evidence which we take as having a literal value in the text is the product of metaphorising, ambiguous phrasing, and insinuating collocation. Insistent repetition and elegant variation on the theme of deceit and betrayal, coupled with a tone of moral indignation, give enormous force to this rhetorical armoury and suggest to readers that disagreement will place them among the moral reprobates of history or the erstwhile Friends of Ronald Reagan and Margaret Thatcher.[25]

Eve Tavor Bannet has suggested that critical methodologies such as the new historicism which draw on the Marxist paradigm of the relations between literature, culture, history, and society are 'incapable of speaking singularity, because their premises and methods reduce everything and everyone to the same'.[26] It is one of the several ironies of Greenblatt's study that its hostility to domination and assimilation of 'the other' should be characterised by systematic suppression of difference. The relentless hunt for analogies serving the master model of economic and imperialist domination completely obscures the central fact that *Henry IV* deals with dynastic conflict between equals and with the problematic relationships between right and wrong in a kingdom where there is no indisputably legal inheritor to the throne. It induces blindness to the complex art of parallel and contrast whereby Shakespeare's characters are defined as part of the one culture and yet as individuals, so that Hal emerges from the world to which he belongs as the one man endowed with the qualities – moral as well as temperamental – which make for effective and stable leadership.

The gravely defective methodology employed in 'Invisible Bullets' is not confined to Greenblatt's readings of Shakespeare, nor, of course, to himself alone; some indication of its impact on others has already been given, and in my final chaper here I shall be examining its seriously distortive effects in Greenblatt's account of Marlowe and in the Marlovian criticism of his British admirers. Its professional acclaim, I believe, justifies some pessimistic reflection on the current state and future prospects of scholarship, criticism, and teaching in the field of English literature. At the very least, one is surely entitled to claim that the American academy has lost some of its respect for certain values which should endure through changing fashions, and without which it is impossible to lay claim to disciplinary rigour. Not, of course, that British academia has reason to feel complacent. As we shall see in Chapter 5, the two chief practitioners of cultural materialism (which they themselves have tentatively re-named the 'New Reductionism' or 'Creative Vandalism') are no less cavalier than the founder of new historicism with the ethics of reading, recording, and explaining.

Chapter 3

War and Peace in *Henry V*

True hero and 'amiable monster'; mirror of all Christian kings and Machiavellian imperialist: more than any other Shakespearean protagonist, Henry V has given rise to interpretations characterised by extreme and contrary perspectives.[1] Some critics hold that the positive image of the King which the play projects is to be understood as seductive appearance: the real Henry is a thoroughly sinister figure. Others argue that the positive and the negative perspectives are equally valid and must be integrated to any interpretation of the play which aims at completeness and impartiality; and I would include in this group the dissenter who contends that the opposed views are mutually incompatible and that we are compelled to choose between them.[2] A striking feature of readings offered by the second group of critics – readings profoundly affected by the New-Critical dedication to ambivalence, however variously that concept might be phrased – is that the search for subversive ironies is conducted with such enthusiasm and ingenuity that a predominantly negative impression of the warrior king is what emerges.[3] Neither group of critics seems prepared to entertain the possibility of an affirmative but complex picture of a hero; one which celebrates greatness while allowing for aspects of character or conduct which we would normally reprehend or rather wish away, but which are somehow intrinsic to heroic achievement or arguably unavoidable in the circumstances in which greatness is achieved. In modern times, England's great wartime leader, Winston Churchill (and I speak as an Irish nationalist!), would surely fit such a description.

1

The play evokes the horrors of war so vividly that selective quotation makes it easy to tip the balance of judgement against Henry. I hope to show, however, that if we attend carefully to both the play as a whole and the historical and cultural context from which it derives so much of its shaping thought we must conclude that it projects, as intended, an affirmative view of the King and his war. Consider first the chronicle tradition. Like Edward Hall before him, Holinshed acknowledges the brutalities of war when dealing with Henry's invasion of France. His account of the 'lamentable slaughter' of the French prisoners, for example, makes it seem like a wild orgy of violence: 'some Frenchmen were suddenlie sticked with daggers, some were brained with pollaxes, some slaine with malls, others had their throats cut, and some their bellies panched'. Yet Holinshed does not allow his awareness of martial savagery to affect his strongly held view that Henry was a great and good king and that his war in France was entirely justified; he has no doubt that Henry's 'dolorous decree' to kill the prisoners was necessary in the circumstances.[4] Unlike Shakespeare, too, Holinshed also records occasions when Henry acts with ruthless severity against besieged towns and castles which resist beyond his deadline for surrender. Side by side with his many references to Henry's chivalric and Christian virtues, Holinshed's allusions to the dark side of the campaign might seem profoundly ironical to the modern reader. But they cannot have been so intended or so perceived by Elizabethan readers. As Holinshed observes in passing, and as modern historians confirm, such acts were sanctioned 'Iure belli, by the law of arms' (131) and were the norm in medieval warfare.[5] The same non-ironic juxtaposition of the eulogistic and the grimly realistic is to be found in Froissart's account of the French campaigns of Edward III and the Black Prince.[6]

In imaginative literature, too, it was customary to acknowledge the horrific concomitants of martial heroism. Chaucer's noble knight Palamon and his nobler lord Theseus are devotees of Mars, yet within the Temple of Mars are decorations 'hidouse to biholde':

> The careyne in the busk, with throte ycorue,
> A thousand slayn, and nat of qualm ystorve,
> The tiraunt, with the pray by force yraft;
> The toun destroyed, ther was no thyng left.[7]

One might have expected Torquato Tasso to give a wholly idealised account of the Christian seizure of the Holy City from the Saracens in his great epic *Gerusalemme Liberata* (1581); yet he includes some graphic stanzas on 'the atrocious and miserable spectacle' of the sack, concluding thus:

> Mournful mothers with hair unbound
> Fled pressing their infants to their breasts,
> And the predator laden with booty and rapine
> Dragged the virgins off by their hair.[8]

In Shakespeare's *King John*, the King's 'valiant kinsman' Falconbridge urges him to 'glister like the god of war', and later says of 'warlike John' that 'in his forehead sits / A bare-ribbed Death, whose office is this day / To feast upon whole thousands of the French' (5.1.54, 5.2.176–8, 5.3.5);[9] John does not measure up to this image, but Falconbridge clearly thinks that heroic royalty should. The anonymous *Edward III* (1592–3), to which Shakespeare probably contributed and certainly knew well, includes powerful descriptions of the havoc wrought in France by the King and the Black Prince ('Great servitor to bloody Mars'). I quote one of several passages from this play which are closely paralleled in *Henry V*:

> Fly, countrymen and citizens of France!
> Sweet-flow'ring peace, the root of happy life,
> Is quite abandon'd and expulsed the land;
> Instead of whom, ransack-constraining war

Sits like ravens upon your houses' tops,
Slaughter and mischief walk within your streets
And, unrestrain'd, make havoc as they pass;
The form whereof even now myself beheld,
Upon this fair mountain, whence I came.
For so far off as I direct'd mine eyes,
I might perceive five cities all on fire,
Corn-fields and vineyards burning like an oven;
And as the reeking vapour in the wind
Turn'd but aside, I likewise might discern
The poor inhabitants, escaped the flame,
Fall numberless uppon the soldiers pikes.
Three ways these ministers of wrath
Do tread the measures of their tragic march:
Upon the right hand comes the conquering king,
Upon his left his hot unbridled son,
And in the midst our nation's glittering host;
All which, though distant, yet conspire in one
To leave a desolation where they come.
Fly therefore, citizens, if you be wise,
Seek out some habitation further off.
Here if you stay, your wives will be abus'd,
Your treasure shared before your weeping eyes;
Shelter yourselves, for now the storm doth rise.
(5.1.178, 3.2.46–76)[10]

Accepting a warrior's claim to be fighting with just cause is the first imperative if a playwright and his audience are to reconcile their awareness of such realities with admiration for his heroic achievement. On this issue, *Edward III* is doubt-proof: the play opens with a French nobleman explaining in genealogical detail the soundness of Edward's claim to the French throne (1.1.11–27); later, a French citizen (3.2.35–7) emphatically acknowledges that Edward is the true inheritor, as does the French king's son – with his father's tacit agreement (3.1.107–13). The Third Frenchman who delivers the warning quoted above clearly believes that the French king is responsible for the war which devastates their country.[11]

Many critics of *Henry V*, however, contend that the scheming of Canterbury, the cumbersome and near-comical style of his disquisition on Salic law, and Henry's doubtful legitimacy as king of England together constitute firm evidence of an authorial intent to undermine the justice of the claim to France and perhaps even the sincerity with which Henry holds to it. But it is important to see the Archbishop of Canterbury in both historiographical and historical context. Like those ardent champions of the Reformation, John Bale and John Foxe, Hall and Holinshed both had a special problem when dealing with the reign of Henry V:[12] they wished to preserve the belief that England had produced in Henry a truly great king, but they could not ignore the fact that during his reign the rebirth of 'true religion' in the form of Lollardism was ruthlessly stifled. Their solution to the problem was not to ignore but to downplay Henry's hostility to the Lollards and to emphasise instead the persecuting malice and the obstructive conservatism of the Archbishop of Canterbury and his prelatical associates. The effect of this strategy is manifest in *Henry V*. When Canterbury seeks to subvert the bill in Parliament for the confiscation of church property by offering Henry financial support for an invasion of France, he would have been seen by Protestants in Shakespeare's audience as working to frustrate the beginnings of the Reformation. His scheming constitutes one part of Shakespeare's concession to the less admirable aspect of Henry's reign as seen from the Protestant point of view. The other part of this concession is the 'killing' of Sir John Oldcastle (Falstaff) and his fictional henchman Bardolph, an ironic echo of the historical Henry's execution of his friend Sir John Oldcastle, the Lollards' great champion.[13] It is surely clear, however, that Shakespeare's Henry is not affected by the Archbishop's offer, even though the Archbishop himself seems to think otherwise. Had Henry sanctioned Parliament's proposal he would have acquired considerably more assistance (direct and indirect) for his military campaign than Canterbury was offering him.[14] Moreover, Henry makes his first move towards the recovery of England's lost French territories before (and not, as in Holinshed, after) Canterbury makes his offer.[15]

It is of course arguable that Henry believes Canterbury is prepared to favour the French campaign out of mere self-interest and is cynically exploiting his predictable support when he asks him to explain the implications of Salic law. As against that, his whole manner in dealing with the Archbishop is one of steely concentration on the legal and moral argument: he apparently has no doubts about his claim to the lost duchies, concerning which he has recently written to the French king. He has already heard some of Canterbury's views on the subject but he now wants to hear in public 'the severals and unhidden passages' (that is, 'the particulars and the indisputable courses')[16] of the claim enshrined in the royal style since the time of Edward III: 'King of England and France'. In short, Shakespeare's attitude to Canterbury's manoeuvre is identical to Holinshed's; the intention is not to question Henry's integrity or independence but to depict the prelacy of Henry's time as a Reformation audience would expect to see it.

Nor does the style of Canterbury's disquisition subvert its content. It is laborious and prosaic, but that accords with the play's partly satiric perspective on the prelate and with Henry's desire for a more detailed version of what he has already heard in part. Furthermore, the speech is Holinshed almost verbatim, and its argument is perfectly clear and coherent: French appeal to Salic law in denying Henry's right to inherit through the female line is invalid because that law was not framed by or for Frenchmen; moreover, there have been some well-known instances of French princes succeeding to the throne through the female line.[17]

The contention that Henry's claim to the French throne was invalidated by his father's deposition of Richard II may be theoretically correct, but in relation to the play it collapses before the fact that Shakespeare repeatedly emphasises Henry's right, not through Bolingbroke, but through a 'pedigree . . . derived / From his most famed of famous ancestors, Edward the Third' (2.4.90–93; cf 1.2.102–5, 146, 248–9, and 2.4.50–60). Cambridge's terse remark that he was not motivated by gold (unlike his co-conspirators) in the plot to assassinate Henry (2.2.155) is undoubtedly an allusion to his brother-in-law Mortimer, who had a better hereditary claim to the English throne than either Henry or his father. This allusion constitutes another gesture of fidelity on Shakespeare's part to the historical record; but it is so understated and oblique as to be almost invisible (Shakespeare could easily have allowed Cambridge to spell out Mortimer's claim, as Holinshed does at this point in his narrative [71], and as Mortimer himself does in *Henry VI*).[18] Furthermore, Cambridge's involvement in the plot to assassinate a popular monarch at the instigation of a foreign power rules out the possibility that he has on his side any kind of moral or political legitimacy that could reasonably challenge Henry's position; Elizabeth's loyal subjects were bitterly familiar with such plots, the last of which was uncovered a few months before *Henry V* was written.[19] And while it true that in his soliloquy before Agincourt Henry expresses a sense of guilt for 'the fault my father made', it is surely significant that the fault he refers to is not the deposition of Richard (an act endorsed by Parliament, and a complex mixture of right and wrong, necessity and choice) but rather his subsequent murder: Henry has wept and prayed to God to '*pardon blood*' shed at his father's behest (4.1.290, 297). Moreover, as Gary Taylor has observed, Shakespeare's purpose in making Henry so penitent for his father's sin was to introduce the idea that he feels spiritually inadequate when he prays for divine aid before Agincourt, 'but to permit the audience not to think so'.[20]

It is arguable, however, that any attempt to arrive at a satisfactory interpretation of *Henry V* presupposes more than familiarity with contemporary (Tudor) attitudes to Henry's war and to martial exploits in general. It requires also some broad understanding – such as Shakespeare and his contemporaries would have acquired from Holinshed – of the complex relationship existing between England and France since the reign of Henry II. Such knowledge precludes the possibility that Shakespeare viewed Henry's war as an example of pure, imperialist aggression against an unoffending, separate, autonomous people, comparable in essence to the depredations of European peoples in the New World and Africa. I have referred to this relationship already (pp. 40–41), but have touched no more than the surface of a large and problematic subject.

Since the time of Henry II (a ruler more French than English), Anglo-French relations had been dominated by the fact that the English held huge territories in France: at the beginning, more even than the king of France himself. Achieved by a mixture of inheritance, conquest, and marriage, Henry II's Angevin empire, as it was called, stretched frrom the Scottish borders to the Pyrenees. However, he and his successors held these lands as vassals of the French monarchs; they were willing to pay homage to them but resisted their attempts to exercise jurisdiction in their territories. French kings in consequence missed no opportunity to destabilise and attack these possessions in a steady process of conquest and appropriation. But when the old line of French kings died out in 1328 and Philip of Valois succeeded to the throne, Edward III contested the accession, arguing that as son to Isabella of Valois and nephew to the late king he had a better claim than Philip, who was merely a cousin: as the French Citizen puts it in *Edward the Third*, 'Edward is son unto our late king's sister, / Where John Valois is three degrees removed' (3.2.36–7). Not, however, until 1337, when he was provoked by French support for the Scots in the Anglo-Scottish war, and by French attacks on both England and the 'English' province of Gascony, did Edward initiate the so-called Hundred Years War (1337–1453), in which the French crown would be won and lost twice over for England. Before Edward died, Charles V had reneged on the treaty of Brétigny which confirmed Edward's sovereignty in France, and had reconquered much of English-held territory. But Edward's grandsons, Richard II and Henry IV, maintained the claim to the lost throne: not perhaps because they thought that its recovery and retention was a realistic possibility, but more likely because they saw it as a potential bargaining counter in relation to their existing and their lost French territories. They would also have viewed upholding the claim as a matter of honour.

For anyone fresh from a reading of Holinshed's version of the reign of Henry IV, one of the most striking features of *1 and 2 Henry IV* is the way in which Shakespeare ignores Holinshed's amply documented account of Henry's French concerns and concentrates instead on the problems presented to him by his rebellious compatriots and their Scottish and Welsh allies. But Shakespeare gives a fair indication of how much he has omitted when at the beginning of Part 2 the Archbishop of York assures Hastings that 'the unfirm King [is] / In three divided', one power against the French, one against Glendower (both '[b]aying him at the heels'), and the rest against 'us' (*2H4*,1.3.71–4).[21] Apart from the final speech, when Prince John anticipates exporting 'civil swords and native fire' across the channel (5.5.103–5), and the Epilogue, which promises us merriment with 'fair Katherine of France', York's is the only allusion to the French problem in the whole of the two-part play. Clearly, Shakespeare decided that the subject of France would overload *Henry IV* and would have to be postponed until he dealt with the reign of Henry V.

But I would suggest that the undramatised French material from Holinshed's account of Henry IV's reign was necessarily in Shakespeare's mind when he came to write *Henry V* and that it should be taken as integral to the play's interpretive frame of reference. Like Richard II before him, Henry IV was crowned 'king of England and France ' (in 1399). At the same time, and in order to affirm his commitment to the defence of his French subjects, Henry created his eldest son Duke of Aquitaine, the great duchy of which only part (Gascony or Guienne) still remained in English hands. From the first year of his reign, explains Holinshed, Henry was 'troubled with . . . the covert practises of Frenchmen' as well as with 'civill sedition' at home (16). The French sought 'with large promises, and faire sugred words' to persuade the Gascons to rebel against the English 'and to become subjects to the crowne of France' (15), a threat which Henry frustrated by a combination of military and diplomatic intervention. A truce followed in 1401, but in 1403 hostilities were renewed by the French: an army of sixteen or seventeen hundred invaded the Isle of Wight (it was repelled), and a series of castles in Gascony were seized, 'no small losse to the English nation' (22). In the following year the Duke of Orleans, brother to the French king, challenged Henry to meet him in a French field, each with a hundred knights, and there to 'fight and combat to the yeelding'. His challenge spurned, Orleans invaded Gascony with an army of 6000 and besieged the town of Vergi, but having 'lost manie of his men, without honour or spoile returned *into France'* (my emphasis) (28). In the same year (1404) the Admiral of Brittany raided Dartmouth with 30 ships and 1200 men, 400 of whom were slain and 200 taken prisoner before he made a retreat (28–9). In 1405 the French launched a fierce assault by sea and land on Calais ('so much desired of the French nation') but again were repelled after suffering many more losses than they inflicted (34–6). Also in 1405, the French king added to Henry's troubles at home by sending 12 000 men to aid the rebellious Glendower; the French attacked Hereford and Worcester before being expelled by Henry himself, who chased them back to France 'making small brags of their painfull journie' (39–40). In the winter of 1406 Orleans bestirred himself again, besieging two towns in Gascony with 'a mightie armie', but eight weeks of foul weather forced him to depart 'with dishonor, for all his brags and boasts made at his first comming thither' (43). Four years later the Duke of Burgundy's plot to seize Calais by poisoning its inhabitants was fortuitously subverted by means of an informer.

In 1411, this pattern of serial and unprovoked aggression changed because of the French king's periodic fits of madness and factional conflict between France's two leading peers, Orleans and Burgundy. On request, and because he hoped to profit by these divisions, Henry sent an army to help Burgundy, who was then left in effective control of France. In the following year, however (the penultimate year of his reign), Henry sided with the Orleanists (or Armagnacs), who were so grievously persecuted by Burgundy that they appealed for Henry's help, promising in return to acknowledge him as 'theire verie lord and sovereigne' in Gascony and elsewhere, and thereby to establish 'a firme peace betwixt both the realmes' (51–3). In response, Henry sent an army of almost four thousand which fought so fiercely in defence of the Orleanists that the Burgundians made peace with the latter; who in turn persuaded the English to depart, albeit poorly recompensed for their efforts.

Henry may have intended to resume his intervention in France, taking advantage of its internal divisions,[22] but he died in the same year. He had, however, laid the ground for his heir's major preoccupation. Given the prominence of the French connection throughout his father's reign, it is hardly surprising that the energetic Prince of Aquitaine and Gascony had (as the Earl of Westmorland perceived) 'a couragious desire to recouer his right in France' (Holinshed, 66). Any reader of Holinshed would reasonably assume that this desire would have been pursued one way or another even if Canterbury had not encouraged it for his own ends – and even if the Dauphin had not foolishly sent the new King on his accession a thoroughly provocative and insulting gift (64).

Whatever then the rights and wrongs of the English claims to French territories and the French crown (issues on which the prejudices of successive centuries of historians have played), it seems most unlikely that what Shakespeare learned from the chronicles when working on *Edward III*, *King John*, *Richard II*, and *Henry IV* would have inclined him to intimate that France was the unoffending victim of Henry's aggressive imperialism. On the other hand, his reference to Essex's mission in Ireland (5.0.30–34) has been interpreted by some critics as an oblique recognition that Henry's war is not dynastic but ruthlessly imperialistic. To this end, much emphasis has been placed on the brutal nature of the war in Ireland and the extreme reluctance of Elizabeth's subjects to serve in its bloody campaigns. However, as Irish historians themselves acknowledge, Tudor interest in Ireland was from the start primarily defensive;[23] and at no time was this more true than in the last years of the century. The relevant pages of the *Calendar of State Papers* show that from 1596 (and especially after the momentous Irish victory at the Yellow Ford in 1598) until well after the defeat of the Irish and Spanish forces by Mountjoy in 1601 the government was obsessed with rebellion in Ireland because it was seen as a strategic part of Spanish plans for an invasion of England and the overthrow of the Protestant monarchy.[24] The commoner's reluctance to vanish miserably in some Irish bog was unquestionable, but it could not match the nation's fear of invasion by Spain and the return of popery. Given such a context, too, the suggestion that there was a contemporary debate on the morality of war (sparked off by Erasmus in utterly different circumstances almost a century earlier), that this was reflected in Privy Council disagreements, and that it would have prompted Shakespeare to present *Henry V* as something of a debate on the same subject, seems entirely unconvincing.[25] The state was in grave danger in 1599, war was a continuing reality, peace talks with Spain proved a delusive distraction,[26] and Elizabeth, speaking for the Protestant nation, would write with profound gratitude and admiration to the man who defeated the Hispano-Irish force. 'Tell our army from us', she wrote (as if recalling Creçy and Agincourt), 'that every hundred of them will beat a thousand, and every thousand theirs doubled.'[27] This was not a time in which martial heroism (as distinct from Hotspurrian, bellicose pride) was likely to be devalued; quite the reverse.

2

Because of what he had learned from the chronicles, Shakespeare's conception in *Henry V* of the relationship between England and France is perhaps best expressed in Chorus's vision of 'two mighty monarchies, / Whose high upreared and abutting fronts / The perilous narrow ocean parts asunder' (Prologue, 20–22), and not as a relationship of aggressor and victim.[28] This impressive image of two barely sundered but mutually threatening nations connects in the play's design with the age-old notion of the natural order as a dynamic system of interacting and interdependent opposites; and that notion, I wish to argue, affected the play profoundly – as it did both Marlowe's *Tamburlaine the Great* and Kyd's *The Spanish Tragedy* a decade earlier.[29] Such a nexus between the historical-political and the philosophic-scientific reflects the fact that the way people thought about politics was influenced by a view of nature, both non-human and human, that was dominated by the concept of contrariety or polarity.

Given the antithetical principle which shapes so much criticism of *Henry V*, and which has been emphasised here at the start, it is surprising that no attention has been paid to the network of overt polarities with which the text itself is informed. To attend to these opposites is to come closer to the play's intended meanings and, I believe, to confirm the judgement of those critics who hold that its thrust is essentially eulogistic.[30] Unlike the contraries which dominate hostile and ambivalent interpretations of Henry, the terms in the multiple antitheses to which I refer are not inherently or permanently distinct from each other, or mutually exclusive; their relationship is a mutable one characterised by changing states of conflict and harmony, division and union, difference and sameness, duality and oneness. Their relationship may generate ironies from time to time, but most of these are intrinsic to the nature of nature and experience as understood by the play; in consequence, they lack debunking sharpness and finality. They occasion paradox and oxymoron, too, but these veer towards resolution in the figure of Antimetabole, defined by George Puttenham as 'the Counterchange' and exemplified by him in the lines: 'We wish not peace to maintaine cruell warre, / But we make warre to maintaine us in peace.'[31]

Embedded in the play are certain ideas about war and its relation to peace, friendship, and love that are largely foreign to our own ways of thinking but were commonplace in early modern culture, being rooted in its whole sense of the natural order. Tamburlaine's famous proclamation, 'Nature that fram'd us of four elements, / Warring within our breasts for regiment, / Doth teach us all to have aspiring minds', evokes a natural philosophy which held that the world and humankind are governed by the forces of Strife and Love, War and Amity – symbolised in Roman mythology by Mars and Venus.[32] Stability and continuity in this 'theoria of the world' (*Tamburlaine*, 2: 4.2.86) depend on a predominance of the unifying over the divisive force; all change and death follow from the temporary predominance of the latter. But just as fire is the 'noblest' (most aspiring) and most generative as well as the most destructive element, so too strife not only threatens the natural order but is also indispensable to its functioning, since it serves to maintain essential distinctions. The radical paradoxicality of the doctrine is apparent in the familiar conception of the elemental order as a containing system of discordant concord or concordant discord where duality becomes unity, multeity oneness.

In socio-political thinking, Nature's oppositional order helped to complicate attitudes to both peace and war. Peace, union, 'harmonious contrarietie', it was agreed, is nature at its best and is what all desire; but prolonged peace was seen as a likely cause of discontent and a seditious hunger for change, while war, the 'great corrector of enormous times', was viewed as a purgative remedy for such sicknesses in the body politic.[33] Thus peace and war were held to be potentially interactive and interdependent, neither was good or bad in an absolute sense.[34] This attitude is clearly indicated in the warrior Alcibiades' declaration at the gates of Athens:

> Bring me into your city,
> And I will use the olive with my sword.
> Make war breed peace, make peace stint war, make each
> Prescribe to other as each other's leech.
> (*Timon of Athens*, 5.5.86–90)[35]

What might be termed the controlling concept or philosophical matrix of *Henry V* is slyly located in the boastful prattle of the Dauphin, Henry's foil and polar opposite.[36] Waiting with pleasurable impatience at Agincourt for the presumed annihilation of the English to commence, he describes his horse, and by implication himself, as 'a wonder of nature', a creature of aspiration, transcendence, and majesty in whom 'the dull elements of earth and water never appear'; he is 'pure air and fire', and like these two elements, he instinctively rises heavenwards (3.7.20–40). The Dauphin returns to this notion of triumphant natural ascent two scenes later in response to Orleans' rousing call, 'The sun doth gild our armour; up, my lords!' To this he answers, '*Via, les eaux et terre!* ['Away, waters and earth!'] '*Rien puis? L'air et feu?*' ['Nothing afterwards but air and fire?'], adds his companion; '*Cieux*' ['Nothing'], proclaims the Dauphin (4.2.1–6). This vein of hyperbolical fancy might be passed over as eccentrically Dauphinesque were it not for the fact that imagery of upward and downward movement, of the four elements and their corresponding qualities, and of the sun (fire personified) is operative throughout the play.

Somewhat less obvious than the stark contrast which the play establishes between the French and the English character is the fact that elemental imagery is used to define the French conception of themselves and the English, and beyond that to evoke a vivid sense of the distinct physical identities of the two countries. England, says the Constable, is a 'nook-shotten isle' of 'sodden water' with a 'climate foggy, raw and dull'; in every 'slobbery and dirty farm' the 'sun looks pale, / Killing their fruit with frowns'. Unlike the French, whose vineyards and rich fields give them 'quick blood, spirited with wine', the English are 'a frosty people' who can derive no 'valiant heat' from their wretched 'barley broth' (that is, ale) (3.5.13–25). Their Irish allies are even worse off, hailing as they do from 'foul bogs' (3.7.53–9). Thus for the French the physical appearance of Henry's men and mounts at Agincourt is entirely predictable. '[I]sland carrions, desperate of their bones', the English '[i]ll-favouredly become the morning field' when 'the sun is high'. 'Big Mars', the fiery god, peeps faintly through their rusty beavers. Their 'poor jades . . . Lob down their heads . . . The gum down-roping from their pale dead eyes.' '[L]ife so lifeless', remarks Grandpré (on whose confident spirit the sun shines bright), cannot be described in words (4.2.38–55, 62). Although normally cautious and realistic, the French king too displays on one occasion the same loftily contemptuous attitude to the English, urging his 'High dukes, great princes, barons, lords and knights' to rush on Henry's host 'as doth the melted snow / Upon the valleys, whose low vassal seat / The Alps doth spit and void his rheum upon' (3.5.46, 50–52).

Harsh contrasts and confident polarities, however, are not permitted for long in a mode of thought based on a view of nature where the elements, although hierarchically arranged, continuously interact and interchange, each element being connected by a mean with its opposite; contrarious transformation is one of nature's characteristic wonders. In Holinshed, the English march from Harfleur to Rouen is a sickly withdrawal from combat, but Shakespeare re-writes it as a swift, triumphant march, news of which stuns the French lords and momentarily turns their view of things upside down. '*Dieu de batailles!*', exclaims the Constable, 'Where have they this mettle?' How can such a ponderous lot have 'passed the River Somme' unhindered (3.5.1, 15)? This shock prompts French recognition that the invaders are not foreigners at all but rather the offspring of England's French conquerors:

> Shall a few sprays of us,
> The emptying of our fathers' luxury,
> Our scions, put in a wild and savage stock,
> Spirt up so suddenly into the clouds
> And overlook their grafters?
>
> (lines 5–9)

The French women themselves, these lords now concede, see the English as the grafted turned grafters, potential rapists turned lovers coming to regenerate a decadent lineage: 'Our madams mock at us [as dancers and cowards] and plainly say / Our mettle is bred out, and they will give / Their bodies to the lust of English youth / To new-store France with bastard warriors' (lines 27–31). This particular instance of the play's sinuous engagement with the complex theme of sexual energy and sexual relationships impinges in turn on the French nobility's view of themselves – quite different to that now held by the ladies – as 'valiant and most expert' knights and the English as vigorous but 'fat-brained' and undisciplined fellows who 'sympathise' with their mastiffs in 'robustious and rough coming on', and who are in consequence no more effective than 'a valiant flea' (3.7.129–45). Skilful soldiers are like skilful lovers it seems, and the French nobility, with so much chivalry and sonneteering behind them, are both; it is all a matter of discipline and culture, nurture directing nature. However, the triumphant march to Rouen suggests that the bastard Normans have acquired discipline from somewhere. And the ladies are attracted – especially perhaps the princess, who has already (3.4) and cheerfully taken upon herself to learn their language.

In much polarising commentary on the play, the Chorus cuts a sorry figure, that of an enthusiastic idealist whose words serve only to establish a great gulf between his lofty view of Henry's war and the unheroic realities of the dramatised action.[37] A strikingly significant contrast is discovered, for example, between Chorus's second speech and the immediately ensuing scene. Chorus asserts that when preparations for the invasion of France are afoot 'honour's thought / Reigns solely in the breast of every man' (2.0.3–4), whereas 2.1 presents a sordid spectacle of self-interest and greed as Pistol and his companions squabble among themselves and prepare for a military venture in which 'profits will accrue' – no bidding for a royal crown here, only for shillings, a noble, and later crowns (there are crowns and crowns) (2.1.94–115; 4.4.38, 45–9). It is to be noticed, however, that Chorus himself mediates this gap between the honourable and the dishonourable when he proceeds in the same speech to lament that all England's children are not the same and that France has found among them (and at the highest level) '[a] nest of hollow bosoms, which he fills / With treacherous crowns' (2.0.21–2). Thus the argument for a deliberately subversive contrast between the heroic claims of Chorus and the baseness of the Falstaffian trio is unconvincing.[38] One might as well claim that Hal's great display of chivalric virtue at Shrewsbury (so lauded by his enemy Vernon) is diminished or invalidated by Falstaff's ignoble antics on the same battlefield. On the contrary, Harry's virtue is understood in both plays to 'thrive and ripen best / Neighboured by fruit of baser quality' (*H5*, 1.1.61–2).

To dichotomise Chorus and drama, moreover, is to miss important affinities between Chorus's sentiments and those of both Henry and the Dauphin. Chorus anticipates at the outset the Dauphin's favourite (elemental) idiom, modifying it, however, with a strain of modesty alien to the French. He begins, 'O for a muse of fire, that would ascend / The brightest heaven of invention', and then expresses the hope that his 'flat unraised spirits' will bring together two mighty monarchies whom the sea parts asunder; he wants to 'confine' and 'girdle' within his 'wooden O' the fire of Mars, 'the vasty fields of France', the 'perilous narrow ocean' and the affrighted 'air at Agincourt' (Prol.1–22). He returns to this idea in the Epilogue, where he apologises for the attempt to confine 'mighty men' in 'little room'; yet his parallel remark that the short-lived King 'greatly lived' in his 'small time' (lines 3–5) hints that he himself (Chorus-playwright) is a clone of Henry, the king who embodies pride and humility, conquest and control. 'Warlike Harry' (to go back to the beginning) promises that having 'plodded like a man for working days', an earthbound creature obscuring his majesty in Eastcheap, he will 'rise with so full glory' that he will dazzle all the eyes of France (1.2.278–80). Preparing for war, he assumes 'the port of Mars' and will employ 'famine, sword, and fire'; but, as Chorus notes, they will crouch at his heels, '[l]eashed in like hounds', to be let loose when and as he decides (Prol. 5–7). Henry is an authentic figure of aspiration and power who exercises a godlike control over the diverse elements at his disposal (a realistic version of the quasi-symbolic Prospero). Conversely, the French quickly descend into chaos and despair when the two armies meet: 'Disorder, that hath spoiled us, friend us now! / Let us on heaps go offer up our lives' (4.5.17–18).

                                      3

Central to the constellated polarities of *Henry V* is the character of the King himself and its analogous relationship to the functioning of the body politic as defined by Exeter and Canterbury. In a properly governed kingdom, says Exeter, 'high and low and lower ... keep in one concent, / Congreeing in full and natural close / Like music' (1.2.180–83). Canterbury elaborates on this idea, emphasising especially the achievement of consent in contrariety, oneness in multiplicity (the quibble on 'consent', matching Exeter's on 'concent', reinforces the idea of a polyphonic *discordia concors*):

>   many things having full reference
> To one consent may work contrariously,
> As many arrows loosed several ways
> Come to one mark,
> As many several ways meet in one town,
> As many streams meet in one salt sea,
> As many lines close in the dial's centre,
> So may a thousand actions once afoot
> End in one purpose . . .
>
>   (lines 205–13)

But Canterbury then reduces the notion of a multiplex unity to what were thought of as its basic natural forms, the quadripartite and the bipartite: he advises Henry, 'Divide your happy England into four, / Whereof take you one quarter into France'; and he concludes by saying, 'our nation [must not] lose / The name of hardiness and policy' (lines 215–21).³⁹

A conscious pairing of opposites, this last phrase ties the foregoing discourse on social order to the play's conception of Henry's character. Just as matrimonial unions were conceived in terms of *discordia concors*, so too were noble individuals. In the panegyric conclusion to his chapter on Henry's reign, Holinshed refers to the King as at all times 'wisehardie' (133), a neologism which pinpoints the traditional notion of greatness or nobility as a synthesis or balance of the qualities proper to war and peace (see below, p. 110). Henry, explains Canterbury, is master of both the 'theoric' and the 'practic part of life'. His discussion of divinity and commonwealth affairs is wonderful to hear, and his discourse on war sounds like 'a fearful battle rendered . . . in music' (1.1.41–52). The King himself declares that in peace nothing becomes a man so much as 'modest stillness and humility', but when 'the blast of war' blows he must 'imitate the action of the tiger' (3.1.3–6).

What seems to impress others most about Henry is that he has encompassed in his short lifetime the extremes of 'wildness' (1.1.26, 64; 1.2.268) and civility. Canterbury sees this 'blessed . . . change' in theological terms as a marvellous work of grace, but Exeter and the Constable of France both associate it with the dynamics of nature's oppositional order, and in consequence acknowledge the continuing presence in his reformed character of the energy and vitality associated with the notion of 'wildness':

> The strawberry grows underneath the nettle,
> And wholesome berries thrive and ripen best
> Neighboured by fruit of baser quality.
> (1.1.60–62)

> As gardeners do with ordure hide those roots
> That shall first spring and be most delicate.
> (2.4.39–40)

We catch occasional glimpses and echoes of Henry's 'wild' past. He can be playful as well as stern, merry as well as grave, or both. This duality is encapsulated in the recurrent motif of mockery. Henry's response to the Dauphin's gift of tennis balls is less a 'merry message' (1.2.299) than a grimly sardonic promise to match the Dauphin's frivolous gesture with a different kind of mockery. (Henry's quasi-comical counterpart, Captain Fluellen, will do the same to Pistol: '[I]f you can mock a leek, you can eat a leek' [5.1.38].) His second message to the Dauphin, conveyed by Exeter, returns to this motif, advising him to '[s]weeten the bitter mock' he sent him or expect a hot answer (2.4.122). There is a grim playfulness too in Henry's handling of the men who plotted to murder him. But a clearer echo of his partnership with Falstaff in 'jests, and gipes, and knaveries, and mocks' (4.7.48) occurs when he relaxes his gravity after Agincourt and tricks Fluellen into a confrontation with Williams, who had subjected the disguised king to considerable mockery (4.1.195–200). In a more obviously jovial mode, Henry mocks his own uncourtly manner and countenance when he woos Katherine and begs her to sweeten mockery with kindness: '[G]ood Kate, mock me mercifully' (5.2.199).

Henry is both daunting and amiable. 'Never was monarch better feared and loved' (2.2.25), says Cambridge, hypocritically but correctly; and like Cambridge, Shakespeare's audience would have regarded this as the highest praise one can offer a king.[40] But for many the grave, stern, hard side of his nature stays longest in the memory and gives substance to the charge of inhumanity. Henry, however, is not feared because of a tyrannical disposition but because he has the innate power proper to heroic kingship. Holinshed refers to this quality when he describes him as 'marching with his armie, and passing with his carriage in so martiall a maner, that he appeared so terrible to his enimies, as they durst not offer him battell' (75). The Dauphin has the same quality in mind when he describes his mount: 'He is the prince of palfreys; his neigh is like the bidding of a monarch, and his countenance enforces homage' (3.7.26–8).[41] Such authoritative power undoubtedly has a darkly frightening aspect. Henry, says the Constable of France, is 'terrible in constant resolution' (2.4.35), and King Charles amplifies this idea in a grim warning to his peers and the Dauphin:

> Think we King Harry strong;
> And, princes, look you strongly arm to meet him.
> The kindred of him hath been fleshed upon us,
> And he is bred out of that bloody strain
> That haunted us in our familiar paths.
> Witness our too much memorable shame
> When Cressy battle fatally was struck,
> And all our princes captived, by the hand
> Of that black name, Edward, Black Prince of Wales;
> Whiles that his mountain sire, on mountain standing
> Up in the air, crowned with the golden sun,
> Saw his heroical seed, and smiled to see him,
> Mangle the great work of nature and deface
> The patterns that by God and French fathers
> Had twenty years been made. This is a stem
> Of that victorious stock, and let us fear
> The native mightiness and fate of him.
>
> (lines 48–64)

Although this remarkable speech crystallises just what it is in Henry that prompts so many critics to pass negative judgements on him, its tone is laudatory and awed, like its original in *Edward III*, which in turn follows its source (Froissart) in accepting as natural the coexistence of ferocity and nobility in martial heroes like Edward and the Black Prince.[42] And since it is uttered by Henry's enemy, the speech is all the more impressive as praise than the older play's version. Taken as a whole, the speech is inextricably paradoxical, affirming greatness in leadership while acknowledging the destructive energy it may entail.

The action which most strongly expresses Henry's terrible self – his identity as Mars incarnate – is the order to kill the prisoners. Shakespeare mitigates the ferocity of this action by reducing Holinshed's multiple modes of slaughter to the single act of throat-cutting (ugly but swift), by preparing the audience for it by means of proleptic allusions, and by locating it off stage.[43] Of course Henry's curt command is thrown into stark relief with obvious deliberation. Coming after Exeter's heavily pathetic account of the deaths of Suffolk and York, and after his own access of sympathetic tears, the abrupt response to the alarum signalling a desperate French counterattack provokes a sense of shocking contrast (4.6.37). It can be argued that this contrast is designed to expose the savagery behind the veneer of chivalry and brotherhood with which Chorus sedulously covers Henry's campaign. I would contend, however, that it is meant to provoke awareness of a complex reality.

The first point to note is that a bold synthesis of opposites is already inherent in Exeter's description of the deaths of Suffolk and York:

> Suffolk first died, and York, all haggled over,
> Comes to him, where in gore he lay insteeped,
> And takes him by the beard, and kisses the gashes
> That bloodily did yawn upon his face.
> (4.6.11–14)[44]

What we may infer from this enacted oxymoron is a fact well known to soldiers, namely that companionship in mortal danger can generate an extraordinary bond of love. And what we may infer from Henry's ensuing command is not just that he is swift in assessing danger and taking preventive action, but also that the bond of homosocial love can generate cruel violence. Yet this is not a simple case of good contrasting with evil. Suddenly attacked by greatly superior numbers (see 4.5.19–20), and with the prisoners as an added danger to his sick and exhausted army, Henry has to decide between the lives of his own men and those of the captive French.[45] Such a situation requires us to acknowledge the realities of warfare, where in certain circumstances the grimly euphemistic order to 'take no prisoners' is inescapable, and to disobey it is to jeopardise the lives of one's companions.[46] Gower's comment on the killing of the prisoners (which he wrongly assumes was a response to the deaths of the baggage boys), 'O, 'tis a gallant king!' (4.7.11), is certainly discordant and was probably intended to challenge romantically chivalrous attitudes to warfare; but when seen from a realistic military perspective, the calm speed with which Henry delivers the order seems admirable as well as terrible. Moreover, the terrible effect of the command is almost instantly changed by Fluellen's announcement that all the baggage boys (including Falstaff's likeable young page) have been killed by a band of cowardly Frenchmen who fled from the battle (4.7.1–3).

Of course Henry's subsequent threat to kill the 'other prisoners' if the horsemen on a nearby hill refuse either to fight or 'void the field' (line 58) is by no means calm.[47] Perhaps because he has heard about the baggage boys, or simply because the horsemen are engaged in a pointless cat-and-mouse game, he prefaces his threat with the admission: 'I was not angry since I came to France / Until this instant' (lines 54–5). But not only is this a manifestation of the 'manly rage' (3.2.24) appropriate to the martial or Achillean hero, and in tune with the Henry who sent the Dauphin's envoy back to France with burning ears; it also recalls his father's remarkable analysis of his nature towards the end of *2 Henry IV* and constitutes part of a larger attempt to present him as a complex, contrariously constructed character:

> He hath a tear for pity, and a hand
> Open as day for meting charity.
> Yet not withstanding, being incensed, he is flint,
> As humorous as winter, and as sudden
> As flaws congealèd in the spring of day.
> His temper therefore must be well observed.
> (*2H4*, 4.3.31–6)

The flint in Henry's nature is indirectly evident in the deaths of Falstaff and Bardolph. The report of Falstaff's death from a broken heart, for which his friends hold the King responsible, is deeply affecting, and for many the most memorable part of the play; the comic sentimentality of the Hostess's great speech certainly emphasises Henry's hardness. But the placement of the report is highly significant.[48] It occurs in a scene which demonstrates in a comic mode the ease with which friends can become enemies and vice versa: 'Corporal Nym, an thou wilt be friends, be friends. An thou wilt not, why then, be enemies with me too' (*H5*, 2.1.103–5); and it is followed by the scene in which a shocked and disillusioned Henry passes sentence of death on 'the man who was his bedfellow, / Whom he hath dulled and cloyed with gracious favours', but whom he has discovered plotting his assassination (2.2.8–9). Apart from the pain of personal betrayal, Henry registers a grave awareness of the wider implications of his friend's hidden enmity: had the conspiracy succeeded, it would have brought his 'whole kingdom into desolation' (line 174). Falstaff would not in any literal sense have become Henry's enemy and plotted to kill him; but he did expect to command both him ('*my* royal Hal') and his laws; and as Hal's father vividly predicted, that would most certainly have spelt disaster for the 'poor kingdom' (*2H4*, 4.3.247–67). Falstaff and his associates had to be got rid of as surely as Scroop and his.

Other clues as to how we must view Henry's responsibility for Falstaff's death can be found in Nym's laconically balanced observation on the matter – 'The King hath run bad humours on the knight, that's the even of it . . .The King is a good king, but it must be as it may' (*H5*, 2.1.121–6) – and in his subsequent protest against the 'bad humours' of Fluellen (3.2.26). Beating Nym and Pistol for retreating from the breach, Fluellen combats cowardice in the same angry mood as Hal condemned Falstaff's evasive tricks at the battle of Shrewsbury. If Henry of Wales is to be a good king in all circumstances, or his Welsh captain a good officer, his hard humour 'must be as it may'.

Henry's harshness and his 'lenity' are simultaneously invoked on several occasions. The conspirators cut themselves off from his mercy completely, not only by the nature of their crime but also by their insistence, in an argument that works against them, that the pardon he extends to a drunkard convicted of railing against his person is misguided. He must beware of setting a precedent in the toleration of unruly behaviour, warns Scroop: 'That's mercy, but too much security'; he can be merciful, but he must 'punish too', adds Cambridge (2.2.44–7). Their sentiments seem designed to fit Falstaff's friends. When Pistol wilts with Nym under the Welsh captain's blows, he pleads flatteringly: 'Be merciful, great duke . . . Abate thy rage . . . Use lenity' (3.2.21–5). Pistol's plea anticipates his later intervention on behalf of the thieving Bardolph, condemned to death by the Duke of Exeter in accordance with Henry's injunction that 'lenity' rather than 'cruelty' is to be used towards French citizens and that no abuse of property or person is to occur (3.6.111).

That Henry should uphold the Duke's sentence of death on an old acquaintance in punishment for stealing a small piece of church property has seemed utterly callous to many. It may indeed have been intended to shock; but consideration of the dramatic context and of the difference between Holinshed and Shakespeare in such matters hardly permits a negative judgement on the King here. Shakespeare softens very considerably the severity of Henry's 'Iustice in warre' as recorded and admired by Holinshed (77): during a long siege, for example, Henry spied two of his own soldiers who had gone beyond the camp boundary he had clearly defined; he immediately ordered them to be apprehended and hanged 'upon a tree of great height, for a terrour to others, that none should be so hardie to breake such orders as he commanded them to observe' (102).[49] And whereas in the play Henry tells Exeter to extend mercy to all after the surrender of Harfleur, Holinshed records that he sacked the town.

Bardolph is hanged by Exeter for the theft of what Pistol dismissively calls a 'pax of little price' (3.6.44); and since in Holinshed's parallel incident the stolen object is a pyx, a more valuable object than a pax, critics have read into this difference Shakespeare's desire to emphasise the pettiness of Bardolph's crime and the cruelty of Henry's behaviour. Given the fact that Shakespeare deliberately lessens the harshness of the historical Henry's martial justice, this is unconvincing. But even if 'pax' is not a compositer's error for 'pyx', or Pistol is not characteristically muddling Latinate words, it still has to be noted that most people in Shakespeare's audience would not have known what either a pyx or a pax actually was, both having disappeared from churches after the death of the Catholic Mary Tudor almost fifty years earlier (stealing from a church, however, they would have regarded as a serious crime).[50] Moreover, Pistol's dismissive qualifier ('of little price') is only what one would expect in this thief's plea for lenity.

But more important altogether than these considerations is the fact that the one person to be caught infringing martial law in the play is Bardolph, the habitual thief on whose behalf Henry in his wildness once struck the Lord Chief Justice in his court. In consequence, Henry's response to the sentencing of Bardolph actually works in his favour. Had he interfered with the Duke's judgement for reasons of friendship (to which Pistol appeals when he asks Fluellen to intervene), the notion of the King as a marvellously reformed character would have been instantly undone; and the irony of such a reversal would not have been missed in critical commentary. Given the reformed Hal's specific identification with justice and law, Fluellen's insistence (backed by the reliable Gower) that in this case 'discipline ought to be used' (3.6.55) is of crucial significance.

Henry's hardness is especially evident in his threats. Here we see martial fury on the verge of explosion: leashed in with a terrible coldness (as in his response to the Dauphin's mocking message), or put on display in controlled rhetoric imaging uncontrolled violence, as in the address to the Governor of Harfleur. Stephen Greenblatt was neither the first nor the last critic to take the Harfleur threat in its entirety as a genuine statement of intent and the most telling piece of evidence supporting the case against Henry. A distinguished editor has even intimated that one of its most horrifying images constitutes Shakespeare's overall conception of the campaign: 'The war is imaged as dog-hearted soldiers raping the daughters of France, an image which culminates in Henry's own depiction of himself as a plain dog-soldier raping Katherine from her father.'[51]

To get the Harfleur speech in correct focus one should recall that late-medieval warfare was characterised far less by pitched battles than by prolonged sieges, and that the speech or message warning the besieged leaders of the terrible consequences of their refusal to capitulate, combined with an offer of life and property if they submitted, was a common and all-important weapon of assault.[52] It was a means to limit terror, and the more terrifying it was, the better. A simple example is the threat delivered by Henry VIII in 1513 when besieging Touraine (during *his* attempt to recover some of the lost French inheritance). Henry warned the defenders that they must 'render up to him this citie or else that he would put it . . . to the sword, fier, and bloud' – adding, however, 'he that asketh mercie of us, shall not be denied' (Holinshed, 588–9). Shakespeare's Henry uses the same tactic, but far more impressively. In his oration, he gives terrible force to the antithesis governing all such speeches, while invoking and fusing at the same time natural and supernatural polarities: he invites the Governor and his councillors to choose between 'the cool and temperate wind of grace' and 'impious war, / Arrayed in flames like to the prince of fiends' (3.3.90–110). What is most notable in his development of the antithesis is a realistic awareness of the limits to a commander's control of his foot-soldiers when all-out aggression begins, an awareness based on simple recognition of the inherent savagery of undisciplined human nature (cf. 5.2.55–60).[53] And as I have argued already (p. 40), the idea that he would not try to prevent, or would in any way tolerate or condone, the 'wildness' of infanticide and rape is wholly incompatible with his character as a leader whose rule demands execution even for the theft of a pax. The hideous images in his speech function as hyperbole of a kind that derives much of its effectiveness from the brutal facts of military history.[54]

Perfectly crafted for the task in hand, the Harfleur speech is rhetorically superb. It powerfully extrapolates from the destruction/mercy antithesis the play's central antithesis of wildness and discipline. It also issues in a recognition of both the Dauphin's inadequacy (he has failed to 'repair our towns of war / With men of courage and means defendant') and Henry's twofold character: 'Therefore, dread King, / We yield our town and lives to thy soft mercy' (2.4.7–8; 3.3.47–8).[55] With the Governor's confirmation of the King's twofold identity we might compare Hamlet's description of his father as possessing '[a]n eye like Mars, to threaten and command', yet so loving to his wife '[t]hat he might not beteem the winds of heaven / Visit her face too roughly'.[56] The comparison helps to bring out the insinuated relation between the Henry who besieges and parleys with Har*fleur* and the one who besieges and parleys with 'my fair flower-de-luce' (5.2.207); between the warrior who asks the Governor, 'What say you, will you yield?' (3.3.42), and the wooer who asks Katherine, 'What sayst thou then to my love? Speak my fair, and fairly, I pray thee' (5.2.166–7), and later persuades her to accept his kiss 'patiently, and yielding' (line 272). The siege metaphor for wooing was of course a literary commonplace, and in the purportedly Shakespearean part of *Edward III*, as here, a meaningful relationship between the two kinds of siege is employed.[57]

Speech as a unifying agent is a major element in Shakespeare's characterisation of Henry and of others with whom he is implicitly compared and contrasted. A fundamental issue is the concordant or discordant relationship between words and deeds (conceived as potential opposites). This is manifest in a pervasive concern with boastfulness, verbosity, and inconstancy, qualities which militate against cohesion and efficiency. The bragging of the French nobility is repetitive and intensified by their rhetorical self-consciousness: 'we speak upon our cue, and our voice is imperial' (3.6.122–3). Their 'fluent' and 'eloquent tongues' (3.7.33–4) underscore a humiliating contrast between what they promise and what they perform, and serve not only to distinguish them from the English nobility but also to set them quarrelling among themselves in petty rivalries – the chief point of contention being the Constable's claim that the Dauphin's big talk is never matched with appropriate action (3.7.90–117).[58]

But if the English peers are free from French vices such as these, some of their subordinates are not. At the bottom of the ladder there is Bardolph, who according to the perceptive Boy 'faces it out but fights not'; Pistol, who has 'a killing tongue and a quiet sword'; and Nym, whose 'few bad words are matched with as few good deeds' (3.2.28–40). And these three old Falstaffians are as unreliable in friendship and love as they are in battle. 'Holdfast is the only dog', declares Pistol (2.3.50), 'oaths must have their course' (2.1.103); but because he marries Mistress Quickly, who was troth-plight to Nym, the two 'sworn brothers' are threatening each other with furious words and brandished swords when they first appear. Bardolph, of course, plays the peacemaker and the two friends-turned-enemies become friends again with the help of a nice antimetabole from Pistol's rhetorical armoury: 'friendship shall combine, and brotherhood, / I'll live by Nym and Nym shall live by me . . . Give me thy hand' (2.1.101–13). However, Pistol's subsequent remark to Quickly, 'oaths are straws, men's faiths are wafer cakes' (2.3.49), casts doubt on the durability of this bond. Yet it is clear from the extreme contempt in which the Falstaff trio is held by the likes of the Boy and Gower that they are not representative of the common soldier in the English army. Like that other 'malady of France' (5.1.83) to which Pistol's wife has succumbed, this one is not widespread on the English side.

But there is also Captain Fluellen, who is taken in by Pistol's 'prave words at the bridge' because he is so verbose himself (3.6.62). His boastful enthusiasm for military discourse (albeit 'in the way of argument, look you, and friendly communication') infuriates the choleric Macmorris, who protests: 'It is no time to discourse, the town is besieched, and the trumpet call us to the breach, and we talk and, be Chrish, do nothing' (3.2.98–110). Just as Fluellen mistook Pistol, so do he and Macmorris mistake each other (line 136), and a quarrel is narrowly averted by the mediating efforts of their moderate English comrade, Captain Gower. Pointedly, Fluellen's unproductive talk on 'the disciplines of war' is ended when '*A parley* is sounded' (SD, line 137) and the King whose 'discourse of war' is already famous for its eloquence (1.1.43) enters to speak to the Governor of the town.

Speaking to Montjoy, Henry identifies bragging as a French disease and apologises for being momentarily infected by it: 'Yet forgive me, God . . . This your air of France / Hath blown that vice in me. I must repent' (3.6.149–51). It is significant that he does not apologise to his men or Montjoy but to God, for the outstanding feature of all his promised and accomplished actions is that he makes them contingent on divine aid. This habit not only serves to sharpen the English/French contrast, it also fits Henry's historical reputation as a pious Christian prince. It is consistent, too, with a well-known ideal in Christian chivalry (exemplified by both Edward III and the Black Prince in Froissart and the anonymous play)[59] as well as with Henry's character as delineated in *Henry IV*, where his modesty contrasts with Hotspur's boastful pride and where he solemnly recognises that he will defeat Hotspur at Shrewsbury only if God so wills it (*1H4*, 3.2.153–4).[60] His humility is part of his piety and neither are mere show: the man who is shown praying in private and with intense earnestness at the end of 4.1 is no Machiavellian prince who cultivates only the appearance of both piety and fidelity (*The Prince*, ch.18).

Henry is a man in whom words and deeds are one, a leader whose resolute constancy daunts his enemies and inspires his friends and followers: the root sense of the word 'constant', meaning to 'stand together' – Pistol's 'Standfast' – is pertinent, as is the intimate connection in Renaissance iconography between Constancy and Concord, each of which was held to include the other.[61] *Semper eadem, semper una* ('Always the same, always one'), was Elizabeth's personal motto; it laid claim to a virtue which was held in supreme regard by her subjects, not least because it was often conspicuous by its absence in the troubled waters of contemporary politics. Chorus's image of Henry's 'fleet majestical' dancing on 'th' inconstant billows' and '[h]olding due course to Harfleur' (3.0.15–17) epitomises his character as a ruler who (in the wavering Hamlet's phrase) is constant to his purposes, determined and able to keep his word and to control the unstable and changing elements over whom he holds sway. His constancy is conspicuously tried in the matter of ransom, the tempting offer which Montjoy makes to him when all seems lost, and which could of course divide him from his men in a more than physical sense. 'I myself heard the King say he would not be ransomed', says the disguised Henry to Williams. A constitutional sceptic, Williams is convinced that when it comes to the crunch Henry will not do what he said (4.1.189–93). Williams's distrust gives added force to the sombrely defiant speech in which Henry – in front of all his men, and just before battle commences – responds to Montjoy's final offer of ransom: 'Bid them achieve me, and then sell my bones . . . They shall have none, I swear, but these my joints' (4.3.91–123).

The manner in which Henry triumphs in the ensuing conflict must also be taken as evidence of his constancy, a fact emphasised by the contrast drawn between his methods and those adopted by the French at the outset of the conflict. When first 'advised by good intelligence' of Henry's 'dreadful preparation', the French '[s]hake in their fear, and with pale policy / Seek to divert the English purposes' by means of the assassination plot (2.0.12–22).[62] Outnumbered and fearful as he and his men are at Agincourt, Henry might understandably have abandoned his initial stance of heroic defiance and resorted to some guileful trick in the manner of Prince John at Gaultree Forest; instead, he conquers (the point is stressed) 'without stratagem . . .in plain shock and even play of battle' (4.8.109–10). To associate Shakespeare's version of England's most renowned king with Machiavelli (who held that 'it is a glorious thing to use fraud in the conduct of war')[63] flies in the face of a clearly marked authorial intention.

Although the assassination conspiracy is an early warning that he will always have to contend with the threat of inconstancy in others, Henry is characterised not only as a figure of unity in himself ('always one'), but as an inspiring unifier; in him is realised his father's dream that his subjects, 'All of one nature, of one substance bred', would turn their 'opposèd eyes' away from civil butchery and 'in mutual well-beseeming ranks, / March all one way' (*1H4*, 1.1.9–15). Their own conduct apart, there is nothing to contradict and much to support the conspirators' smooth assurance that all his subjects are in 'fair consent' behind his government (2.2.22–8).[64] He has overcome 'Hydra-headed wilfulness' (1.1.35) in himself and his subjects, created oneness in duality and multeity. Shakespeare's distribution of the captaincy between representatives of the four neighbour nations, men whose 'friendly communication' survives temperamental clashes, is clearly symbolical of an army which mirrors the effective functioning of the natural order. The French peers are never once seen with their officers and footmen ('our superfluous lackeys and our peasants'), and are distressed when they learn after Agincourt that their nobles lie 'drowned and soaked' in the blood of commoners and mercenaries – for them, an assured guarantee of their own shameful descent from on high (4.2.25; 4.7.73–80).[65] Shakespeare's Henry, by contrast, in his first and most famous military speech, addresses his men collectively, calling them all 'dear friends' ; and although that friendship and its warmth of feeling are severely tested, they survive: York's dying claim for himself and his friend Suffolk, 'We kept together in our chivalry' (4.6.19), is basically true for the army as a whole.[66]

Henry's capacity to hold his men together is given its severest test in Act 4 when the exuberant force that left Southampton has been transformed by illness and fatigue into '[s]o many horrid ghosts' (4.0.28). Fortitude and fidelity are the twin constituents of constancy; but fear, begetting doubts and despair, affects all alike in Henry's sick and outnumbered army, and gravely threatens its unity. The threat, however, is contained within an overall and finally triumphant sense of comradeship. Given the ease and openness with which Henry talks to the likes of Fluellen, we must take Chorus at his word when he tells us that on the night before the battle he 'visits *all* his host', calling them 'brothers, friends, and countrymen', so that 'every wretch, pining and pale before . . . Plucks comfort from his looks'. The stress is on the King's sun-like capacity not only to shine on 'mean and gentle all' but also to renew life by dispelling fear: 'A largess universal, like the sun, / His liberal eye doth give to everyone, / Thawing cold fear' (lines 32–4, 43–5). Throughout Act 4, homosocial love between the English commanders and between them and their men is emphasised: even the truculent Williams praises Sir Thomas Erpingham as a 'good old commander and a most kind gentleman' (4.1.95). Bedford says of Salisbury, to whom he has just bidden farewell, 'He is as full of valour as of kindness, / Princely in both' (4.3.15–16). Pointedly, this is followed by the stage direction, '*Enter the* King'. The friendly spirit emanates from Henry, his thoughtful exchanges with Gloucester, Clarence, and Erpingham being noticeable for their quiet cordiality. All this is in conspicuous contrast to the relations which have been seen to exist in the French camp (a fact invariably ignored in hostile readings of Henry's character, and even in some ambivalent, positive-and-negative readings).

Pistol's pompous and French-sounding address to the disguised Henry, '[A]rt thou officer, / Or art thou base, common and popular' (4.1.37–8), throws the King's own easiness with all ranks into relief. This easiness is apparent in the amused tolerance with which he reacts to Pistol's obscene comment on his professed friendship with Fluellen, against whom Pistol is planning revenge.[67] And although strained, the same tolerance and humour are detectable in the encounter with Bates and Williams. Henry, it should be stressed, does not belong to the category of stage-kings who 'adopt disguise as a caprice', furtively seeking to discover what their subjects really think of them (as Anne Barton and others have claimed).[68] He has borrowed Erpingham's cloak because he is in a deeply reflective mood, wants to be left to 'debate' with himself, and 'would no other company' (4.1.24–40);[69] he does not enter to (much less 'visit') Bates and Williams, they enter to and accost him. And when he is drawn into debate, he makes the same point that he will brood on in his subsequent soliloquy, namely that the appurtenances of kingship cannot alter the fact that 'the King is but a man' (something which Richard II and Lear grasp too late). He is understandably irritated by Williams's allegation that he will seek ransom when most of his men have died for him; and having just been remarking to Gloucester on the need to 'dress us fairly for our end' (line 10), he is especially disturbed by the charge that he is responsible for his men's dying spiritually unprepared. But where another king might not have taken the trouble to do so, he gives a carefully argued reply to the main charge, and Williams is won over.[70] And despite Williams's caustic mockery and quarrelsomeness at the close of the encounter, Henry responds to Bates's peace-making plea – 'Be friends, you English fools, be friends! We have French quarrels enough' (lines 219–20) – sufficiently to part from the two men with an amiable jest at the expense of the French. By means of his trick on Fluellen, too, he subsequently manages to turn the effects of this difficult encounter into a demonstration of what he guesses to be the tough-minded Williams's characteristic virtues: 'I judge / By his blunt bearing he will keep his word' (4.7.172–3). Just as he accepted Fluellen's patronising verbosity, perceiving that '[t]hough it appear a little out of fashion, / There is much care and valour in this Welshman' (4.1.84–5), so too his bitterness at being subject to the criticism of Williams and his like (lines 231–3) does not alienate him from this common soldier or prevent him from handsomely rewarding him for possessing precisely those virtues that he claimed the King lacked, courage and truth.

4

Henry's reflective mood before the battle of Agincourt gives rise to a number of paradoxes which serve to anticipate the great transformations involved in the successful conclusion to his invasion of France. First comes the memorable axiom, 'There is some soul of goodness in things evil, / Would men observingly distil it out', a paradox characteristically associated with nature, which permits the extraction of 'honey from the weed' (4.1.1–12). It is prefaced appropriately by an exclamation ('God almighty'), paradox being the figure of wonder.[71] What follows when Henry moves from reflection ('the theoric') to action is clearly intended as wonderful verging on the miraculous.

The general paradox of good-from-evil comprehends two others of a more specific nature. The first of these focuses on the opposites of life and death. Henry remarks to Erpingham that the good example of others can make men 'love their present pains' to such an extent that 'the mind is quickened' and '[t]he organs, though defunct and dead before, / Break up their drowsy grave and newly move / With . . . fresh legerity' (4.1.18–23). And when Montjoy warns him that the bodies of his men will fester on the field of battle, he retorts that many of them will find native graves 'and live in brass', while those who perish on French soil,

> though buried in your dunghills,
> They shall be famed, for there the sun shall greet them,
> And draw their honours reeking up to heaven,
> Leaving their earthly parts to choke your clime . . .
> Mark then the abounding valour of the English,
> That being dead, like to the bullets crazing,
> Break into a second course of mischief,
> Killing in relapse of mortality.
>
> (4.3 99–107)

The death–life paradox points to Henry's transformation of '[y]on island carrions, desperate of their bones' (4.2.38), into the band of brothers who triumph over the vastly superior numbers of glittering, super-confident Frenchmen: ' 'Tis wonderful', exclaims Exeter when it is all over (4.8.113). Holinshed dismisses the report that only 29 Englishmen were killed in the battle (as against 10 000 Frenchmen), noting that 'other writers of greater credit' say that over a hundred of Henry's men were killed in the first encounter. Shakespeare chooses the unrealistic version, and for the same reason as he refrains from staging a battle scene and omits to mention the historical Henry's supremely effective use of archers ringed by pointed stakes: for he is intent on making Henry's transformation of his army just as amazing as the 'noble change' which he himself showed 'th'incredulous world' when he 'died' to 'wildness' and rose to wisdom, becoming, in the words of all the chroniclers, 'a new man' (*2H4*, 4.3.282–4).[72] The astonishing victory at Agincourt is less the product of his warrior skills than of his unifying, inspirational character.

The second of the more specific paradoxes is Exeter's pathos-ridden account of the deaths of York and Suffolk. Himself an image of violent bloodshed 'espoused to death', but sealing 'with blood ... A testament of noble-ending love', York momentarily effects an analogous transformation in Exeter and Henry. 'I had not so much of man in me, / And all my mother came into mine eyes, / And gave me up to tears', says Exeter, and Henry confesses to be affected similarly (4.6.25–34). This looks to the final scene's 'noble-ending' concordance of male and female, Mars and Venus, war and peace.

Signalled by stage directions, the structure of the last scene is visibly expressive. Henry and seven English lords enter at one door, Queen Isabel, the French King, Katherine, Alice, Burgundy (the political go-between) and 'other French' enter at another. After friendly greetings are exchanged, the stage is cleared to leave Henry alone with Katherine and their largely superfluous interpreter. Finally the couple are rejoined by 'the French power and the English lords', who enter as one, having reached a political agreement whose effect is contingent on the success of Henry's meeting with Katherine. That the Queen should lead the French party on stage at the start, and pronounce the hope that 'this day / Shall change all griefs and quarrels into love' (5.2.19–20), is of obvious significance, for as she herself intimates, the 'woman's voice' (line 93), in both the literal and the metaphorical sense, is now crucial in the process of turning war into peace.

The opening exchanges between the two royal parties are remarkable for their gracious and amiable tone; although the historical situation at the treaty of Troyes might have been far otherwise, here (as in Holinshed's account) there is no trace of reluctant and embittered submission to the inevitable on the part of the French, nor even the kind of hypocritical acquiescence evident in a comparable scene in *1 Henry VI* (5.6.116ff.). The French King too bears no resemblance whatever to the historical Charles, whose mental illness (as Holinshed makes clear) prevented him from making any contribution to the treaty negotiations. Shakespeare's Charles is a dignified and authoritative figure, and neither here nor earlier does he question the legitimacy of Henry's claim to the throne. Thus his endorsement of Henry's demands at the end implicitly suggests that the French have simply been resisting a claim which they could not refute.

The diplomatic role of the Duke of Burgundy (historically an ally of the Lancastrian kings) is much more important here than in Holinshed and contributes to the sense of mediation and moderation in the negotiation of opposites. His lengthy speech urging peace, often cut or omitted in production, paints a powerful picture of the baleful consequences of war and has frequently been construed as a weighty indictment of Henry's campaign. But it is addressed to both kings and the speaker is careful to avoid apportioning blame: an Elizabethan audience could undoubtedly infer for itself that the disorders which Burgundy describes are the result of French intransigence, and it would have recalled that they were properly forewarned of war's effects by Henry himself. Moreover, the speech doesn't establish a simple antithesis between war and peace but subtly indicates affinities between the two. In the absence of 'gentle peace', says Burgundy, all that grows in the 'best garden of the world', including its citizens and their children, has degenerated from kind. 'Unpruned', 'disordered', 'uncorrected', and idle, everything 'grow[s] to wildness', 'as soldiers will / That nothing do but meditate on blood'. To 'deracinate such savagery', the coulter, the scythe, and the knife are all needed. Thus Burgundy's description of the effects of war tallies with what happens in peacetime when discipline is lost and nature without nurture runs amok (peacetime England under the King's careless rule is described in identical terms in *Richard II* [3.4.30–67]).[73] Moreover, the description emphasises the essential severity – the controlled violence – of the measures that are necessary to maintain peace. The speech recalls the 'barbarous licence' of which Henry accused his youthful self and for which he was disciplined by the Chief Justice, as well as the conduct of those men whom he refers to as having 'gored the gentle bosom of peace' and 'defeated the law and outrun native punishment' before being punished by war, God's beadle (1.2.272; 4.1.164–70). Burgundy does not explicitly say that war is 'the great corrector of enormous times' and a potential partner to peace, but that mode of thought is near and is part of the *discordia concors* enacted in the conclusion.

Burgundy's phrase, 'my speech entreats' (line 64), is a reminder that in his appeal for peace he is employing the one discipline which Shakespeare's age regarded as by far the most important in the process of regulating wild nature, namely rhetoric, the art of persuasion. In peace, love, and friendship, as in war, Henry is the play's great persuader: herein lies the essence of his transforming power, his ability to overcome and unite opposites. His marriage to Katherine was first proposed by her father, but now she has become his 'capital demand' in the negotiations. Marriage was a customary method of securing alliances and treaties, and the historical reality is that a princess would normally have to accept the proposed union whether she was greatly inclined to or not (Henry VIII, however, had to stomach several refusals). But it is very clear that Henry wants Katherine's consent and her love and does his utmost to win both; and it is equally clear that he is successful in this double aim. Shyly or coyly interested at first, Katherine is captured by his eagerness, his vigour, his charm, and the manifest genuineness of his attraction to her.

Yet Henry's successful wooing has been called lubberly and compared to that of a butcher. The butcher comparison, however, is introduced by Henry himself, and he does so as part of his artful claim (designed to put the Princess at her ease) that he is an artless and inarticulate soldier; in this he might be compared to Othello, who declares himself 'little blessed with the soft phrase of peace' before he overwhelms the senate with his tale of how he overwhelmed the 'inclining' Desdemona. Henry's calling the Princess 'Kate', too, has been read as a damning echo of Hotspur. But if it was intended as such by Shakespeare (which I doubt), it can only have been designed to suggest superiority: for Hotspur's manner with his wife was one of roughly affectionate heartiness declining at times into crudeness; and he it was who sent his men into battle without the benefit of an inspiring address, not having 'the gift of tongue' to 'lift the blood up with persuasion' (*1H4*, 5.2.77–8). Moreover, Henry's shift from 'Katherine' to plain English 'Kate' signifies tenderness and closeness, and is part of his developing claim that they will merge national identities when he becomes king of France and she queen of England (just how intimate a part of England's history she will become I shall note later). Furthermore, simple 'Kate' is only one of the garland of names in which his charm ensnares her: 'Fair Katherine, and most fair', 'most fair Katherine', 'my fair', 'good Kate', 'gentle princess', 'my fair flower-de-luce'.

Henry clearly conceives their encounter as 'a persuasion to love'; his style and attitude are utterly remote from any suggestion that she will have to accept him willy-nilly. He begins the meeting with a modest and winning appeal for rhetorical assistance: 'Will you vouchsafe to teach a soldier terms / Such as will enter at a lady's ear / And plead his love-suit to her gentle heart?' (lines 99–101); and he ends by praising the wordless eloquence of her kiss, the 'witchcraft' of her lips: 'Kate: there is more eloquence in a sugar touch of them than in the tongues of the French Council' (line 275).

He speaks in prose, a choice determined by his self-presentation as a soldier whose simple, solid virtues compensate for his unhandsome exterior and uncourtly manner. His disavowal of any ability to gasp out his eloquence in verse, like 'those fellows of infinite tongue that can rhyme themselves into ladies' favours' (lines 144–57), contains not only a claim to constancy and truth but also an appeal to the belief already held by the ladies of France that their own super-refined countrymen (who even write sonnets for their horses) are much less valuable as lovers than the home-again 'bastard Normans'. Apart from its adroit argumentative strategy, Henry's persuasion glitters with puns, paradoxes, antitheses, parallelisms, and antimetaboles which correspond collectively with its sprightliness of tone and the central attempt to bring about a true union of opposites: Katherine will not have to love the enemy of France, for '[w]hen France is mine, and I am yours, then yours is France, and you are mine' (lines 175–6).[74]

The merging of the two as lovers begins in tentative fashion when each embarrassedly confesses inadequacy in the other's language, expresses fear of being mocked, and is reassured. Henry's gracious and witty reassurance of Katherine initiates his variations on the paradox of eloquent inarticulacy, which in turn leads to the great paradox of *discordia concors*. Spoken by her and from the heart, he protests, broken English is 'broken music' (lines 104–6, 240–43), music arranged in parts for more than one voice and for instruments of different kinds; not discordant but richly concordant.[75] His rhetoric is at its most artful when Katherine acknowledges that he speaks her language better than she his (he has just translated his antimetabole into correctable French), and he responds: 'No, faith . . . thy speaking of my tongue, and I thine, most-truly falsely, must needs be granted to be much at one' (lines 189–91). They are flawed speakers of each other's language whose incipient love makes defect perfection, division oneness.[76]

Henry's siege on Katherine's 'gentle heart' combines delicacy and urgency, modesty and confidence; and she in turn yields with a gradualness and indirection which enhances her attractiveness and protects her dignity. Guided by the subtly changing tone of her replies, he moves from 'Do you like me, Kate?', to 'Canst thou love me?', to the humorously teasing 'Come, I know thou lovest me' (lines 106–7, 192, 195). But then, skilfully, and as if he has gone too far, he retreats to, 'If ever thou be'st mine, Kate, as I have a saving faith within me tells me thou shalt . . . What sayst thou, my fair flower-de-luce?' (lines 200–208). And when in response to his assurance that the union will please her father, she says, 'Den it sall also content me', he knows he has triumphed, and declares: 'Upon that I kiss your hand, and I call you my Queen' (line 240).

He has already begged her twice to take him by the hand and declare she is his (lines 130, 234), and because she here protests that he should not so abase himself as to kiss her hand, attention is drawn to the gesture. His taking her hand – which should be done with conspicuous tenderness and grace – is a gesture of substantial symbolic significance. Shakespeare always uses the handshake as a visible and emphatic token of amity and concord; but in this play, as in *Romeo and Juliet* and *Macbeth*, he employs the hand as an image of humankind's twin potentialities, our two-handedness.[77] Exeter speaks of the 'armed hand [that] doth fight abroad' and which, working in partnership with 'th' advised head', functions as part of the well-ordered kingdom which 'doth keep in one concent' (1.2.178–81). And Pistol, in a grotesque anticipation of Henry, twice asks Nym to give him his hand in token of restored 'friendship . . . and brotherhood' (2.1.68, 109–13). But in his siege oration at Harfleur, Henry warns of 'the bloody hand' of 'the rough soldier', 'the hand of hot and forcing violation', the 'blind and bloody soldier with foul hand' who defiles 'the locks of shrill-shrieking daughters' and by implication deflowers them (3.3.12, 20, 34–5).

It is a measure of Shakespeare's daring that he should not only introduce these images of blind and violent sexuality to Henry's oration but also echo them at the end, when Burgundy, seeking to engage him in the equivalent of stag-night banter, plays with the idea of sexual penetration. For several reasons, however, the procedure is rather less daring than it seems and certainly it does not reflect badly on Henry. In the first place, the intent has been to show Henry's successful determination to both limit violence and make war a means to unity and peace, confirmed by his verbal winning 'the white hand of a lady' (3.7.94). Moreover, the shift from the negative to the positive sense of the sexual imagery, from the hand of deflowering war to that of peace and love (gently taking the fleur-de-lys), is facilitated by the two metaphoric traditions – one amorous and one military – which associated sexual union with strife, conflict, and conquest.

Being ultimately a derivative of the procreative union of male and female, the notion of universal *discordia concors* (often in conjunction with the Mar–Venus myth) was commonly invoked in masques and epithalamia to magnify the significance of aristocratic marriages. In lyric tradition, too, it underpinned the ubiquitous metaphor of love's creative or delightful war; this figure is literalised in *A Midsummer Night's Dream* when Theseus tells his Amazon queen, 'I wooed thee with my sword, / And won thy love doing thee injuries' (1.1.16–17);[78] it is present in Henry's 'I get thee with scambling [struggling]' (*H5*, 5.2.202); and it was commonly extended to the metaphor of wooing and seduction as a siege.[79] In Marlowe's *Hero and Leander*, the love–war nexus is explicitly connected with the idea that the formed world emerged from primal Chaos when Strife functioned as a differentiating agent, separating the confused elements prior to their necessary conjunction in acknowledged complementarity. Hero's struggling against Leander's first embraces is essentially desirous and creative: 'She trembling strove, this strife of hers (like that / Which made the world) another world begat / Of unknown joy' (2.291–3). The resistance of the lady figures primarily in this tradition as her cautious or coy resistance to the urgent wooing of the impatient lover; he, being an aristocrat and so a warrior by profession, quite naturally sees the prolonged ritual of courtship as the besieging of a castle or walled city which he hopes will capitulate to his display of male determination. Even the entry into the bridal chamber and the woman's body after she has publicly yielded her consent can be figured in epithalamic literature as a continuation of 'Hymen's war'.[80]

Conversely, the town or city with its protective walls and its gate (its most vulnerable point) was imaged by defending inhabitants as an unviolated maiden and by the aggressor as a woman who should yield her consent to the embraces of a superior suitor or rightful lord. The motto of Tournay, 'written on the gates grauen in stone', was *La pucelle sans reproche*; according to its Provost, the town had never lost its maidenhead until it surrendered to Henry VIII.[81] The same metaphor could be extended to any uninvaded or 'unplanted' country, and the occupation of such a country in turn might serve as a metaphor for the excitement of sexual union: 'O my America, my new found land!'

These metaphoric traditions inform the light exchange initiated by Burgundy's query as to how Henry has fared with Katherine (5.2.280–308) and the much more serious exchange which follows when Henry asks whether the King has agreed terms in the treaty negotiation. Responding to Burgundy's query, Henry modestly intimates that he has not been persuasive enough to win from Katherine a forthright expression of her love for him. In a series of quibbles on the blindness and nakedness of Cupid, Burgundy reassures and instructs him, intimating that 'a maid yet rosed over with the virgin crimson of modesty' cannot admit to herself, let alone to a lover, the reality of her desire, but that she will acknowledge her love, will 'wink and yield' and 'endure handling', when she is aroused and entered in the dark. The difference between the 'blind hand' of the rapist soldier and the hand of the soldier–lover who admits to needing some tuition in blind Cupid's art is confirmed by antimetabole and the iteration of 'consent' in the exchange which follows:

> KING HENRY. Then good my lord, teach your cousin to consent winking.
> BURGUNDY. I will wink on her to consent, my lord, if you will teach her to know my meaning.
>
> (lines 301–2)

Advancing skilfully to the other part of his mission, Henry remarks to King Charles that some have good reason to rejoice at his blindness in love, since it has distracted him from the conquest of many a fair French city which he intends to have; to which Charles responds that when Katherine becomes his wife these cities will all become his by consent: 'Yes, my lord, you see them perspectively, the cities turned into a maid; for they are all girdled with maiden walls that no war hath entered . . . We have consented to all terms of reason' (lines 313–24).

In the conclusion, too, the English premise that what Henry demands is reasonable, and a fit prelude to harmonious union, is resoundingly endorsed by the antiphonal prayers of all the French. Following the King's prayer, the Queen celebrates the twin paradoxes of two as one and of English as French and French English:

> God, the best maker of all marriages,
> Combine your hearts in one, your realms in one!
> As man and wife, being two, are one in love,
> So be there 'twixt your kingdoms such a spousal
> That never may ill office or fell jealousy,
> Which troubles oft the bed of blessed marriage,
> Thrust in between the paction of these kingdoms
> To make divorce of their incorporate league;
> That English may as French, French Englishmen,
> Receive each other. God speak this amen.
>
> (lines 353–62)

5

From the time of Richard I to Edward II, England's royal coat of arms consisted of three leopards or lions. Edward III quartered the arms, combining the English lions and the French fleur-de-lys in token of his claim to the French throne: 'No king of England, if not king of France!' (*H5*, 2.2.194). And when the reigning French king reduced the number of fleur-de-lys on the French arms from 'five flower-de-luces' (*1H6*, 1.2.78) to three, Henry IV followed suit, so that until the end of Elizabeth's reign the quartered English arms consisted of three lions and three fleur-de-lys (two sets each).[82] The lily and the lion probably seemed to the English symbolically apt in relation to what were often regarded as the characteristic attributes of each nation: vigour (or coarseness) and refinement (or effeminacy). Furthermore, the quadruple conjunction of opposites carried the suggestion that England and France, although very different, were also naturally one. There is a hint of this in *Edward III* when a French mariner excitedly reports seeing a 'majestical' fleet in whose 'streaming ensigns wrought of coloured silk . . . The arms of England and of France unite / Are quartered equally by herald's art' (3.1.68–76). Similar hints occur at the beginning of *1 Henry VI* when the funeral of Henry V is interrupted by a messenger from France who tells the English lords that because of their factionalism '[c]ropped are the flower-de-luces in your arms; / Of England's coat, one half is cut away' (1.1.80–81); and later, when Talbot, facing defeat at Orleans, cries out: 'Hark countrymen: either renew the fight, / Or tear the lions out of England's coat. / Renounce your style' (1.7.27–8).[83] In *Henry V*, there should be a final sense of heraldic fitness: Henry was twice reminded at the outset that 'the blood and courage' of England's 'former lions' runs in his veins (1.2.109, 117–24), and now he has won the 'fair flower-de-luce'. Verbally, the impact of heraldic symbolism is very slight in this play; but references to flags (1.2.101), silken streamers (3.0.6), pennons (3.5.49), and banners (4.2.60) suggest that such symbolism must have made an important contribution to the visual language of the play on Shakespeare's stage. Certainly everything else in the final scene serves to confirm what the quartered arms signified.

'Thus far . . . the story' (Epil. 1–2); after which, as seen in *Henry VI*, the fleur-de-lys in the English arms is reduced to an accusing image of lost glory. It is commonly observed that the future as already shown on Shakespeare's stage, and invoked in the Epilogue, not only casts a dark shadow on the sense of achievement and the high hopes expressed in the last scene but also reduces Henry's French conquests to a tale of futile destruction. I would suggest, however, that Shakespeare quietly builds into his play the notion that Henry cannot – and knows he cannot – fix the future; what matters is what he has done and the firmness of his own intention to do what he can in an uncertain world where ultimately 'God' alone can 'dispose the day' (4.3.132; cf. 3.6.168). No one has missed the fact that Henry's buoyant suggestion that he and Katherine might 'compound a boy, half French half English that shall go to Constantinople and take the Turk by the beard' is much at variance with the disastrously feeble nature of their only child. Henry, however, introduces the idea of a crusading son interrogatively ('Shall not thou and I . . . Shall we not?'); and when Katherine answers, 'I do not know dat', he endorses her realism. Characteristically, however, he adds that the commitment is what matters: 'No, 'tis hereafter to know, but now to promise' (5.2.204–11).

Involved in the last scene are two interrelated promises with 'firm proposed natures' (line 328): one political and one marital. The political promise is made by the French king in the treaty of Troyes and is to be completed later by the peers of the realm, as signalled by Henry in the play's concluding speech:

> Prepare we for our marriage; on which day,
> My lord of Burgundy, we'll take your oath,
> And all the peers', for surety of our leagues.
> Then shall I swear to Kate, and you to me,
> And may our oaths well kept and prosperous be!
>   *Sennet. Exeunt*

Burgundy is with good reason singled out as the representative French peer. Historically, he was a lynchpin in the Anglo-French alliance and so in Holinshed 'The oth of the duke of Burgognie' is printed in full in both Latin and English, with the addition that 'the like oth a great number of the princes and nobles . . . received at the same time'. In this oath, Burgundy swears upon the holy evangelists that he and his heirs will obey Henry and his heirs 'as faithful liegemen . . . for ever' (114). But Shakespeare's audience would not have to be reminded that in *1 Henry VI* Burgundy's oath was not well kept: they could hardly forget Joan's triumphant sneer when he defects to the Dauphin, 'Done like a Frenchman . . . turn and turn again' (3.7.85), or Gloucester's outrage: 'O monstrous treachery! Can this be so? / That in alliance, amity, and oaths / There should be found such false dissembling guile?' (4.1.61–3)

The Queen prays that the union of the two nations will not be undone by discord in the marriage (the effect of Henry VIII's divorce on Spanish–English relations comes to mind); and for the short period that Henry survives, that hope is realised. What the Queen does not reckon for is that discord among the English nobility, so powerfully presented in *Henry VI*, will serve with French 'turning' to undo Henry's achievement. To read the Epilogue's allusion to the disasters of Henry VI's reign as advancing an anti-heroic view of the play is to miss the Epilogue's key point, one which ties in with the play's governing mode of thought. France was lost because England was disunited: more specifically, because it lacked a leader who could manage 'hydra-headed wilfulness' in himself and his subjects. It fell because '*so many had the managing*' (Epil. 11) of the kingdom (my italics). But the calamity of Henry's early death, his son's unfitness to rule, and the consequent loss of France does not alter the fact that in 'small time . . . most greatly lived / This star of England'. The intrinsic instability in the natural order of all unions and all structures of identity, the susceptibility of every human achievement to sudden destructive change (or swings of Fortune), is axiomatic for Shakespeare. But neither for him nor for Samuel Daniel (who lamented the huge misfortune for England in Henry's early death) does it invalidate heroic endeavour; if it did, nothing great, they assume, would ever be attempted.

But apart from the 'turning' of Burgundy and the disunity of the English in the reign of Henry VI, there is yet another historical fact which might serve to challenge a negative view of Harry's French conquests. This fact also does much to explain the surprising prominence given to Katherine in the play as a whole (compare the dramatic invisibility of Elizabeth of York in the politically all-important betrothal announced at the end of *Richard III*).[84] As Shakespeare and his contemporaries knew from their reading of Hall and Holinshed, the Tudor dynasty itself would never have been born but for Henry's French marriage; was in fact descended from Katherine of Valois and dependent for its very existence on her remarkable character. Two years after Henry's death his young widow fell in love with a handsome Welsh nonentity attached to the English court, one Owen Tudor; and although forbidden to do so by Council and Parliament, 'being yoong and lustie' she married this gentleman – in secret. They had three sons, one of whom entered the Church. The other two were generously made earls by Henry VI when he came of age, 'because they were his brethren and of one wombe descended'.[85] Edmund, the eldest, became Earl of Richmond, and with such a title was just about noble enough to marry Elizabeth Beaufort, last of the Lancastrians and great-granddaughter of John of Gaunt. With such a title, too, Edmund's son Henry Tudor (Katherine's grandson) was about noble enough to marry Elizabeth of York, daughter of Edward IV, and so could claim to have united the two warring houses of Lancaster and York in that much vaunted *discordia concors* celebrated at the end of the play which follows *Henry VI* in the Shakespearean cycle ('We will unite the white rose and the red'). Thus far the story. It is perhaps unsurprising that Tudor propaganda kept quiet about Henry VII's feisty grandmother. But it would be very surprising indeed if her coming to England as a war bride, together with her first husband's premature death, did not distil in Shakespeare's mind yet another thought on the wondrous paradoxes and mutations of human history and experience.

Attempts to resolve the contrary perspectives on Henry, argues Graham Bradshaw in his brilliant and witty analysis, serve to 'defeat those energies which make the play work'.[86] My own view is that the extreme prominence in the play of paradoxical and oxymoronic expression, combined with forceful allusions to *discordia concors*, constitute clear signs of thinking in terms of resolved opposites while retaining full awareness of the grim realities involved – an awareness which provides much material for negative and radically ambivalent criticism to work on. Failure to recognise this mode of thought not only induces interpretive error but also restricts awareness of the play's artistic complexity.

Yet for all its dialectical subtlety, *Henry V*, unlike *1 Henry IV*, does not represent Shakespeare at his best. He committed himself to dramatising a national myth of heroic kingship, but for whatever reasons, the subject did not engage his imagination fully. Henry is seen too much from the outside; there is insufficient recognition of the inner stress which should accompany or precede some of his most decisive actions; he moves too easily and too quickly from success to success. This combination of opaqueness and facility is what has led so many to view him as a ruthlessly effective Machiavellian prince rather than the embodiment of virtuous and heroic leadership: as Moody Prior puts it in one of the play's most level-headed interpretations, 'Since it is hard to believe in the paragon, it seems sensible to look for the smart operator.'[87] Like Prior, however, I believe that in doing so we are looking in quite the wrong direction.

Chapter 4

Perfect Answers: Religious Inquisition, Falstaffian Wit

1

Few would now deny that in *Henry IV* the character of Falstaff constitutes a deliberate and audacious caricature of a Protestant hero, the fourteenth-century champion of Wycliff's doctrines, Sir John Oldcastle, the first Lord Cobham, 'Lollardus Lollardorum'.[1] Shakespeare's wicked joke, as Ernst Honigmann has called it,[2] gave offence in his own time not only to Cobham's distinguished titular descendants but also to earnest Protestants such as John Speed (1611), Richard James (*c*.1625), and Thomas Fuller (1655),[3] to the authors of the anti-Catholic response play *The first part of the true and honorable historie, the life of Sir John Old-castle, the Good Lord Cobham* (1599), and no doubt to many playgoers of like persuasion. Defying the hagiographic efforts of John Bale and John Foxe, Shakespeare in effect took the Catholic side in a sectarian dispute about the character of the nobleman who was burned as a heretic shortly after his friend, the Prince of Wales, became Henry V; and although in Part 2 he changed his reprobate knight's name from Sir John Oldcastle to Sir John Falstaff, his contemporaries would still have recognised his original intention and treated the Epilogue's denial ('this is not the man') as tongue-in-cheek.

Apart from his friendship with the Prince of Wales, there are a number of parallels between the historiographic and the Shakespearean Sir John, some obvious, some teasingly oblique, most of them already noted by critics. The first Sir John was a reformed sinner who publicly confessed that in his youth he offended grievously in pride, wrath, gluttony, covetousness, and lechery. The second Sir John, 'my old lad of the castle' (1: 1.2.40), is a lecherous glutton and thief who repeatedly promises to reform and so is nicknamed 'Monsieur Remorse' (line 107).[4] The first Sir John based all his religious beliefs on the Bible and according to Bale and Foxe had a masterful knowledge of both the Old and the New Testament; the second specialises in a Puritan idiom whose chief characteristic is an abundance of biblical quotation and allusion (no other Shakespearean character quotes so liberally from the Bible). The first Sir John was condemned for supporting Lollard preachers; the second flaunts his understanding of the godly art ('Well, God give thee the spirit of persuasion, and him the ears of profiting, that what thou speakest may move, and what he hears may be believed' [lines 143–5]). One of the heresies for which the first Sir John was condemned was his denial of the value of pilgrimages, whether to Canterbury or to Rome; the second Sir John waylays pilgrims en route to

Canterbury. Henry V tried hard to get his friend to renounce his Wycliffite beliefs, but he proved righteously immoveable; the second Sir John protests to the Prince that he will 'be damned for never a king's son in Christendom' (line 93). The first Sir John was executed for treason as well as heresy; in the play the Prince initially refuses to become a thief, and Sir John threatens: 'By the Lord, I'll be a traitor then, when thou art king' (line 137). The first Sir John was executed in a singular manner, being hanged in chains as a traitor and burned as a heretic; the Prince not only teases the second Sir John about being hanged but also calls him a 'roasted manningtree ox' (1: 2.4.436). After he was found guilty, the first Sir John escaped from prison and eluded the authorities for four years before being apprehended and executed; the second Sir John spends the whole of Part 2 engaged in a similar relation with the fangs and snares of the law.

To miss these parallels and the large parodic intention which they underscore is to miss the outrageously satiric dimension and some of the socio-political implications of Shakespeare's greatest comic character. The argument for parodic intent will be reinforced here, for my purpose is to show that a central feature of Falstaff's complex comic art was probably inspired by Protestant hagiography's treatment of the way in which Oldcastle answered his theological accusers. As so often happens, parody will be seen as having metamorphosed the object of its mockery into something beguilingly attractive and even admirable. We shall move thus (unfashionably) from history, politics, and origins to openly aesthetic considerations.

What is the essence of Falstaff's comic character, what is it about him that most commands admiration and delight? Dryden was the first critic to address the question. 'That wherein he is singular', he explained, are 'those things he says *praeter expectatum*, unexpected by the audience; his quick evasions when you imagine him surpriz'd'; and he added that Falstaff's unwieldy mass seems to intensify the unexpected and extremely diverting nature of his verbal evasions.[5] Subsequent attempts to define the essential Falstaff endorse this explanation and elaborate on it in ways which are useful for my purposes. In the nineteenth century, Henry Hudson emphasised the immense self-confidence with which Sir John handles himself when cornered by Hal and Poins; indeed he infers from Falstaff's incomprehensible lies that he deliberately invites being cornered, 'partly for the pleasure he takes in the excited play of his faculties, partly for the surprise he causes by his still more incomprehensible feats of dodging'.[6] In the twentieth century E.E. Stoll distinguished between Falstaff's evasions and those of other braggart soldiers such as Bobadill, noting that the latters' are 'mere excuses and subterfuges' whereas Falstaff's are 'gay, aggressive, triumphant . . . Falstaff carries things with a high hand, and expects to bear down all before him.'[7] H.B. Charlton asked, 'What then is . . . the ruling passion, the distinctive quiddity of Sir John Falstaff?', and in his answer he too stressed the immense self-confidence with which Falstaff courts and triumphs over the threat of censorious entrapment. 'Fundamentally, it is his infinite capacity for extricating himself from predicaments . . . So adept is he in this art of extrication that he revels in creating dilemmas for himself to enjoy the zest of coming triumphantly out of them.'[8]

There is no obvious model or archetype for Falstaff's primary characteristic and its associated tendencies. Critics looking at antecedents have variously and correctly noted that there is something in him of the mythical buffoon, the Vice, the picaro, the braggart soldier, and the Elizabethan clown, all of whom are adept in evasive trickeries of one kind or another. Nevertheless, as an extremely quickwitted and intelligent knight, equipped with a sumptuous store of biblical, theological, mythological, and literary knowledge, and majestically confident of his ability to confound his moralising accusers, Shakespeare's Sir John seems remarkably unlike these prototypes. Nor do I detect his genius for the self-justifying smart answer either in Martin Marprelate, with whom he has also been compared, or in the colourless figure who shares his original name in the earlier *Famous Victories of King Henry the Fifth* (1594). So let us return to the first Sir John, or more precisely, to one of the first Sir Johns.

2

The most comprehensive account of Oldcastle's life and death, and the one we might assume was of most use and interest to Shakespeare, is that given in the expanded 1570 edition of John Foxe's *Actes and Monuments*. Together with much material from other sources, this account incorporates most of John Bale's pioneer treatise, *A brefe Chronycle concernynge the Examinacyon and death of the blessed martyr of Christ, Sir Johan Oldecastell the lorde Cobham* (Antwerp, 1544).[9] But what was of most interest to Bale, namely the interrogation of Oldcastle on the charge of heresy, constitutes less than a quarter of Foxe's lengthy account; moreover, as in the shorter narrative contained in the 1563 edition, where Bale's contribution is proportionately greater, Bale's explicitly defined *conception* of Oldcastle's examination is obscured.[10]

As he himself indicates, Bale's version of the examination is based partly on the brief and anonymous *Examinacion of the honorable knyght sir Jhon Oldcastell Lorde Cobham* (Antwerp, ?1530),[11] but mainly on the official report of the process made for Thomas Arundel, the Archbishop of Canterbury.[12] His own editorial hand, however, is at work from the start, guiding his readers' responses to question and answer in accord with an interpretation of the whole procedure which he provides in his Preface. He refers briefly in the Preface to Oldcastle's career as a distinguished servant of the crown in Wales: 'In all adventurous acts of worldly manhood was he ever bold, strong, fortunate, doughty, noble, and valiant' (7). And after he deals with the examination, condemnation, and execration of Oldcastle he pays tribute to the great fortitude with which he met his cruel death. But his purpose is not to exalt the passive heroism of the martyr over the active courage of the soldier, nor even to focus intently on his final torment in the usual hagiograhic manner. In his interpretation, Oldcastle's great triumph is oral, rhetorical, intellectual. Oldcastle, he says, was 'never so worthy a conqueror as in this present conflict with the cruel and furious frantic kingdom of antichrist' (7); and by this present conflict he means primarily the inquisition in which Oldcastle stands alone against a team of theologians led by the Archbishop of Canterbury: four bishops and twelve doctors of the church in all. In the end, Oldcastle allows his interrogators to prove him a heretic; but as Bale makes clear, he triumphantly demonstrates in his responses that what they call heresy is the true Christian faith as grounded in the scriptures. 'His courage was of such value that it gave him the victory over them by the clear judgment of the scriptures, what though the world's judgments be far otherwise' (13). It is they who are outwitted and defeated, not he. Says Bale: 'He that hath judgment in the spirit shall easily perceive by this treatise . . . what influence of grace this man of God had from above concerning his answers' (6). In other words, prepare to read inspired answers to questions which are top-heavy with learning, authority, and malicious intent. Nevertheless, suggests Bale, Oldcastle's surprising victory in this ostensibly one-sided battle of wits is exactly what the scriptures should lead us to expect.

> Most surely fulfilled Christ his promise in him which he made to his apostles: 'Cast not in your mind aforehand . . . what answer ye shall make when these spiritual tyrants shall examine you in their synagogues . . . For I will give such utterance and wisdom in that hour, as all your enemies shall never be able to resist you.' (6)[13]

Bale is here adapting and giving central significance to one of the secondary topoi of Christian hagiography, the wisdom derived from sanctity. The most famous example of this topos occurs in the legend of the virgin martyr St Katherine of Alexandria, whose spectacular triumph over the physical torments with which pagans seek to break her faith in Christ is preceded by a display of divinely inspired eloquence in response to the arguments of a team of philosophers aimed at getting her to renounce her faith.[14]

Before Oldcastle is even brought to examination, the Archbishop publicly denounces him as 'that seditious apostate, that schismatic, that heretic, that troubler of the peace, that enemy of the realm and great adversary of all holy church'. But he is undeterred by these 'hateful names' (19) and, like St Katherine, answers his inquisitors with an air of serene and often disdainful self-confidence. His first response is a written exposition of what he believes, composed in reply to the official accusation of heresy. Before being examined by the theologians, he presents this document to the King as proof that he is a true Christian, assuring him that if he is taught a better belief he will most reverently and at all times obey it (22); thus from the outset he seems to shift defiantly from defence to attack. When confronted by the theologians, he refuses at first to go beyond what he has written and state 'more plainly' his position on the eucharist, penance, pilgrimages, and the power of Rome. The implication is clear: anything not dealt with in his scripturally grounded confession of faith is irrelevant. Thus he informs them that he will gladly both believe and observe whatsoever the holy church instituted by Christ has determined, but he denies that popes, cardinals, and prelates have the power to determine such matters as stand not with God's word. With this aggressively evasive strategy, says Bale, the bishops and prelates 'were in a maner amazed and wonderfully disquieted' (26).[15]

At the end of the first examination he is dispatched to the Tower, the frustrated bishops having determined to pin him down by giving him a precise list of the church's teaching on the disputed matters and requiring him to affirm or deny belief in each of them. Reading the document, 'he marvelled greatly of their mad ignorance . . . and deep errors' and perceived their malicious intent 'purposed against him howsoever he should answer' (28). He now decides, however, to put his trust in God and engage fully with their questions and accusations; and a few days later, says Bale, he is led from the Tower 'as a lamb among wolves, to his examination and answer' (29). But his assurance does not desert him and he matches thrust with counter-thrust. The Archbishop begins by telling him he stands accursed for his contumacy. 'Then spake the Lord Cobham with a most cheerful countenance, and said: "God saith by his holy prophet, *maledicam benedictionibus vestris*".'[16] Which may be construed as a succinct way of saying, 'I would rather be cursed by you and blessed by God than vice versa.' His Lordship is apparently discomfited by this retort, for he chooses to ignore it and tries a softer approach; but with no more success. Says Bale, 'The archbishop made then as though he had . . . not heard him' but 'continued forth in his tale', saying: 'Sir, at that time I gently proffered to have assoiled you, if ye would have asked it. And yet I do the same, if ye will humbly desire it in due form and manner as holy church ordained.' Adding injured innocence to audacity, Oldcastle responds, 'Nay, forsooth, I will not, for I never yet trespassed against you' (29).

He then proceeds to evaluate the Archbishop's offer of absolution in a surprising manner, and in so doing strikes obliquely at both the spiritual arrogance of his accusers and the sacrament of penance, one of the doctrines at issue. He gets down on his knees, raises his hands to heaven, and shrives himself loudly to the eternal living God, confessing that in his frail youth he offended most grievously in pride, wrath, lechery, and so on. This confession of a very sinful past is regularly noted by Shakespearean scholars (usually as a parallel with Falstaff's lifestyle), but its purpose and the spirit in which it is made are never remarked on. It is in fact a theatrical move in a rhetorical contest; and by no means does it signify defensiveness. For having made his public confession to God Himself (who alone, he implies, can absolve him), Oldcastle rises and turns to all those who have assembled to witness the inquisition, pointing out – 'Lo good people, lo' – that his accusers have condemned him for breaking their own laws and traditions but not for his grievous violation of God's great laws and commandments.[17] Whereupon, says Bale, 'the archbishop and his company were not a little blemished' (29–30).

They fare even worse when they try to catch him out on the the eucharist and transubstantiation. Questioned on this, he summarises correctly all the relevant passages from the New Testament and on this basis affirms his belief that the consecrated host is Christ's body in the form of bread. But is it still bread? Yes he answers, it is visible bread; the body of Christ is seen only by the eye of faith. 'Then smiled they each one upon other . . . And with a great brag divers of them said: "It is foul heresy"' (31). Some among them, however, feel it necessary to ask if he believes the bread to be material bread or not. 'The Lord Cobham said unto them: "The scriptures make no mention of this word material, and therefore my faith hath nothing to do therewith"' (32). When one of the bishops insists that after the sacramental words are spoken it is bread no longer, he replies: 'Saint Paul the apostle was (I am sure) as wise as ye be now, and more godly learned: and he called it bread writing to the Corinthians'. 'Paule must be otherwise understood', they protest; to take him literally would be heresy. How can they justify this claim?, he inquires. Because, they reply, it has been so determined by Holy Church and its holy doctors. 'I know none holier than Christ and his apostle', responds the knight drily. 'A most Christian answer', exclaims Bale from the margin; but it is too much for the holy doctors: when Oldcastle proceeds to amplify his provocative point,'Then asked they him, to stop his mouth therewith' (32).

When the interrogation resumes, the Carmelite prior engages with Oldcastle and makes the mistake of saying that Matthew 7 forbids judging one's superiors. But 'the same-self chapter of Matthew', explains Oldcastle, warns us against false prophets, appear they never so glorious; as does John 7 and 10, Deuteronomy 1, and Psalm 61! The Prior foolishly persists: 'Unto whom the Lord Cobham thus answered. It is well sophistried of you forsooth. Preposterous are your judgements evermore. For, as the prophet Esay saith . . .' When Oldcastle completes this crushing rebuttal, John Bale, as it were, is unable to contain himself, and applauds once more from the margin: 'A perfect answer', he writes (34).

Repeatedly subjected to Oldcastle's masterful command of the Bible, the leaders of the English church are thus, says Bale, 'confounded in their learning'. In desperation, one of them plucks out of his bosom a copy of the document they had sent with him to Tower, 'thinking thereby to make shorter work of him. For they were so amazed with his answers . . . that they knew not well how to occupy the time, their wits and sophistry . . . so failed them that day' (37). They demand brief responses to what is written in this bill of belief. His answers are calm and sardonic; he knows they will inculpate him, but before his accusers condemn him he makes sure to treat them in kind. One of the last questions put to him asks his view of the pope; and in attending to his answer we must note that his examination has been moved from the Chapter House in St Paul's to the Dominican Friary:

> The Lord Cobham answered . . . he and you together maketh whole the great antichrist. Of whom he is the great head, you bishops, priests, prelates, and monks are the body, and the begging friars are the tail, for they cover the filthiness of you both with their subtle sophistry. (38)

Before bringing the proceedings to a conclusion, the Archbishop understandably accuses Oldcastle of having 'spoken here many wonderful words to the slanderous rebuke of all the whole spirituality'. Injured innocent to the last, Sir John loftily responds: 'Much more have you offended me than ever I offended you, in thus troubling me before this multitude' (40).

3

'You have misled the youthful Prince', says the Lord Chief Justice to Shakespeare's Sir John. 'The young Prince hath misled me', retorts the knight. 'Well, God send the Prince a better companion!', continues the Chief Justice. 'God send the companion a better prince! I cannot rid my hands of him', answers Sir John (2: 1.2.140–41, 193–6).

This encounter provides a convenient point of return to *Henry IV* for a more exact reminder of Falstaff's characteristic comic procedure. In Part 1 as in Part 2, he is under attack from the outset, enduring Hal's good humoured but energetic denunciation of his sinful way of life, a diatribe prompted by his opening question about the time of day. By way of response, Sir John slides into a distractingly graceful conceit about Phoebus and the moon, but then counterattacks Puritan-wise with an accusation that will resonate in a two-part play dense with ideas about sin, redemption, and the lost grace or sanctity of kingship: 'God save thy grace – majesty I should say, for grace thou wilt have none . . . No, by my troth. Not so much as will serve to be prologue to an egg and butter' (1: 1.2.12–20). Pertinent here is the fact that Falstaff not only poses from time to time as a godly, bible-quoting, and self-righteous Protestant, but is also endowed with a secular form of the extraordinary grace which, according to Bale, inspired the first Oldcastle's responses (because of its concern with the nature of kingship and true nobility, there is in fact a notable continuity in *Henry IV* between theological and secular notions of grace). Says Sir John to the Chief Justice concerning one of his aggressively defensive rejoinders: 'This is the right fencing grace, my lord – tap for tap' (2: 2.1.187–9).[18]

The scene in Part 1 which opens with Hal's indictment of Falstaff – 1.2 – concludes with preparations for the Gad's Hill escapade; and the whole purpose of that adventure is to create a situation in which Sir John will be compelled to admit that he is a coward and a liar. Occurring in most editions in 2.4, the scene of accusatory ensnarement – Falstaff on trial, as it were – constitutes the climax of the play's comic action. The gloating conviction of Hal and Poins that they can at last extract from him an abject confession of guilt, together with the presence of an excited on-stage audience (cf. 'Lo good people, lo'), generates suspense and focuses all our attention on the moment when Falstaff produces the answer that frustrates his accusers. The answer is too well known to quote here, but what I must quote is his answer when accused a second time in this same scene. In the playlet, Hal as King rebukes Falstaff as Prince: ' Swearest thou, ungracious boy? . . . Thou art violently fallen away from grace. There is a devil haunts thee in the likeness of an old fat man . . . Why dost thou converse with that trunk of humours, that bolting hutch of beastliness, that swollen parcel of dropsies, that huge bombard of sack, that stuffed cloak-bag of guts . . .' And so on, at length: Hal's demonising invective, his catalogue of what Bale called 'hateful names' (cf. 'that seditious apostate, that . . . that . . . that . . .') is relentless. Nevertheless, Falstaff deflates it by responding with an air of exquisitely polite incomprehension which is innocence itself: 'I would your grace would take me with you. Whom means your grace?' (lines 443–4).

The centrality of this scene's chief comic procedure to Shakespeare's conception of Falstaff is confirmed in Part 2, where the same pattern of accusation and response is repeated with slight variation. As in 1.2 of Part 1, Falstaff in 1.2 here is under attack, this time from the Lord Chief Justice, Hal's mentor-to-be; and once again he relies on a general air of self-righteousness together with the right fencing grace of counter-thrust. The attempted shaming and condemnation again constitutes the climax of the comic action and occurs in the same position as before – 2.4 in most editions. Once again, too, the moralistic hubris of Hal and Poins and the presence of an eager audience maximise the effect of Sir John's responses to accusation. The charge of degeneracy, 'Why, thou globe of sinful continents, what a life dost thou lead', is cheekily deflated in one sentence (with a mock-contemptuous glance at Hal's disguise): 'A better than thou: I am a gentleman, thou art a drawer' (lines 283–6). His answer to the more damaging accusation of slandering a prince – a crime for which, as Hal points out, the statutory punishment was the loss of both ears – involves a wily assumption of both childlike innocence and adult wisdom, its effectiveness being greatly enhanced by Hal's sneering expectation that it will be a mere repetition of the cocksure answer given after the Gad's Hill affair:

> FALSTAFF (*to Prince Henry*) Didst thou hear me [abusing you]?
> PRINCE HENRY Yea, and you knew me as you did when you ran away by Gad's Hill; you knew I was at your back, and spoke it on purpose to try my patience.
> FALSTAFF No, no, no, not so; I did not think thou wast within hearing.
> PRINCE HENRY I shall drive you then to confess the wilful abuse, and then I know how to handle you.
> FALSTAFF No abuse, Hal, o'mine honour, no abuse.
> PRINCE HENRY Not? To dispraise me, and call me 'pantler' and 'bread-chipper', and I know not what?
> FALSTAFF No abuse, Hal.
> POINS No abuse?
> FALSTAFF No abuse, Hal . . . No abuse, Ned, i'th'world, none . . . I dispraised him before the wicked that the wicked might not fall in love with thee; in which doing I have done the part of a careful friend and a true subject, and thy father is to give me thanks for it. No abuse, Hal; none, Ned, none.
>
> (2.4.303–21)

Sir John's puritanism – dissociating himself from 'the wicked' – is not forgotten as he adroitly converts his sin to virtue.

In the end, of course, Falstaff's chief accuser, now the supreme figure of authority, condemns and passes sentence upon him. But there is a suggestion that he succeeds in doing so, not because he wins the argument, but because he prudently denies the accused the right of response. The new king's 'Reply not to me with a fool-born jest' (5.5.54) recalls what the holy doctors said in desperation when overcome by the sardonic fluency of the first Sir John: '[S]top his mouth.'

We are so familiar with Falstaff that it is difficult to imagine him other than he is. And yet if we had been in at the start of his creation and knew that Shakespeare intended to debunk the godly-Protestant view of Prince Henry's executed friend, our best guess would have been that he would caricature Oldcastle's biblical babbling (as Thomas Hoccleve conceived it in 1415)[19] and would present him as a Puritan hypocrite and a cowardly soldier;[20] which he does. But we would not have anticipated Falstaff's characterisation as a reprobate who habitually wrongfoots his interrogators and accusers with incomparable rejoinders, perfect answers. That dominant characteristic, I suggest, follows from the felicitous marriage of Shakespeare's parodic imagination and John Bale's conception of the first Oldcastle as an apostle of truth whose answers had such 'influence of grace from above' that all the cunning and malice of his accusers was brought to nought. What results then is not a simple piece of anti-Puritan satire but a form of comedy which turns a Puritan butt into an exceptionally appealing character with a quicksilver mind and tongue.

Chapter 5

Cultural Materialism and the Ethics of Reading: or, the Radicalising of Jacobean Tragedy

1   The Seminal Work

It is apparent by now that cultural materialism has achieved both diversity and growth. But there can be little doubt that Jonathan Dollimore's pioneer study *Radical Tragedy*: *Religion, Ideology and Power in the Drama of Shakespeare and Its Contemporaries* is the most important and representative product of this critical movement.[1] Since its first edition, there has appeared a large body of work in the cultural materialist vein, yet *Radical Tragedy* remains the most engaging and substantial as well as the most influential example of its kind. As the 68-page Introduction to the second edition indicates, its author is fully conscious of his own and his book's cultural importance. Beginning with the question, 'Why did I write this book?', he embeds the genesis and significance of *Radical Tragedy* in a spiritual and intellectual autobiography stretching from his experience as an unhappy school leaver in a car factory to that of an internationally successful academic brooding in Moscow on the theme of high culture and state power: 'So why that night did I have a dream in which two soldiers had become Shakespeare?' (xi, lii). This autobiography in turn is centrally located in a larger history which encompasses the history of tragic theory and, more importantly, the development of Renaissance studies, literary theory, and cultural analysis during the 1970s and 1980s. But even without the benefit of this Introduction, no one could nowadays fail to perceive that *Radical Tragedy* is a key work in the history of radical Shakespearean criticism.

It is not my purpose in this essay to challenge on the purely theoretical level the Marxist paradigm which underlies the cultural-materialist reading of literature. As in dealing with 'Invisible Bullets', my purpose is the more pedestrian one of attempting to characterise and evaluate the given mode of reading Renaissance literature by examining at close hand the relationship between the critic's interpretive paradigm and some of his chosen texts: trying to determine the extent to which theory illuminates text and text supports theory; or, more bluntly, considering Dollimore's use of evidence and the reliability of his claims and conclusions.

2   The Argument

Dollimore would undoubtedly reject the charge that he is an interpreter who selectively manipulates texts to fit his own ideological position; on the contrary, he advocates criticism whose theoretical and political perspective is supported by 'diligent historical research' and rigorous 'textual analysis';[2] indeed, one reason why his book will continue to command the attention of those who do not share his political views, or his conviction that criticism should serve a political purpose, is its apparent commitment to these orthodox hermeneutic principles. In *Radical Tragedy*, he argues that Jacobean drama has to be completely reinterpreted precisely because the 'founding fathers of twentieth-century criticism of Jacobean drama' (276) were blinded by their liberal humanist ideology to the true nature of the period and its literature. He believes that he himself does not need to distort the texts in order to elicit radical views on human nature, society, and history; he simply has to read them carefully and produce corroborative evidence for the plausibility of his readings from contemporary non-dramatic and mostly non-fictional texts. Unlike some later cultural materialists, he is seldom hostile to the plays; almost all his hostility is towards the long line of critics and scholars who have thoroughly misread them. His purpose, he explains, is to establish a critical perspective which 'recovers an historical understanding' of the period and its plays and 'counters the incorrect procedure', the 'thoroughly anachronistic perspective', the 'fundamental misrepresentation of literature and history' characteristic of a criticism which 'insists on reading the early seventeenth century through the grid' of its own post-Enlightenment conceptions of human nature and society (xxxii, 155–6, 168). Put thus, Dollimore's is an entirely laudable academic project: the elimination of error and the advancement of knowledge by scrupulous re-examination of all known evidence and the discovery of fresh and relevant evidence.

Dollimore argues that the more important tragedies of this period demystified and subverted two beliefs which were fundamental to the dominant ideology of the time: God's providential ordering of human affairs, and the existence of an essential human nature which is fundamentally the same throughout history. Dollimore contends that scepticism about divine providence necessarily begot a loss of faith in the essentialist notion of a universal human nature. This is a questionable claim; but that may not be a matter of great importance. For the second type of scepticism is what matters most in *Radical Tragedy*, and it is assumed to be demonstrably and centrally present in the plays. Its importance to Dollimore derives from the twin assumptions that: (a) a radical transformation of society is possible only when it is recognised that human nature is constructed, not given; (b) belief in an essential human nature invariably functions as an ideological stratagem for maintaining the political status quo. Dollimore's central attack on what he calls essentialist humanism has had a profound effect on cultural-materialist criticism of the Renaissance: if the texts of this period cannot be shown by straight reading to endorse an anti-essentialist view of human nature, then their essentialist ideology has to be exposed and their texts read 'against the grain' in order to produce a politically acceptable interpretation.

Among recent works openly committed to this doctrinal position, the most important perhaps is Alan Sinfield's *Faultlines: Cultural Materialism and the Politics of Dissident Reading* (1992).

Following an anti-essentialist critical approach to Shakespeare originally suggested by Bertolt Brecht and Raymond Williams,[3] Dollimore insists in *Radical Tragedy* that the tragedies of Shakespeare and his contemporaries are not expressions of timeless truths about universal human nature and great individuals; rather, they are historically specific, politically acute works which subvert the prevailing ideology of their own time, and in so doing anticipate the revolution of the mid-seventeenth century. These plays reflect an awareness not only that human nature is fundamentally malleable but also that personal identity itself is 'a fiction or construct' (176): more specifically, and in the words of Foucault (whose extreme anti-humanism is omnipresent in *Radical Tragedy*), 'The individual is an effect of power ... The individual which power has constituted is at the same time its vehicle' (154; cf. 177). Where all previous criticism has gone wrong is in imposing its own secularised, post-Enlightenment form of essentialist humanism on texts which severely interrogated 'the essentialist view of man' inherited 'from sixteenth-century Christianity and its Stoic and humanist derivatives' (160–61).

3   Contextual Evidence

The persuasiveness of *Radical Tragedy* derives in part from its sheer conviction, but mainly from the way in which it amasses evidence from carefully chosen play-texts and reinforces this with an abundance of citation from contemporary sources allegedly showing that many of the major thinkers of the sixteenth and seventeenth centuries shared the tragic dramatists' anti-essentialist outlook. Chief among contemporary thinkers who are said to have voiced an explicitly radical, anti-essentialist conception of human nature are More, Castiglione, Machiavelli, Bacon, Montaigne, and Hobbes: the list is impressive and merits close attention.

Sir Thomas More

More, says Dollimore, 'omits the idea of a fixed human nature, depraved or otherwise, of which society is an inevitable and unalterable reflection. On the contrary, More believed many if not all evils to be generated by social institutions' (170).

That More believed many evils to be the effects of an unjust social order is beyond question, but to impute to him disbelief in an essential human nature, and a belief that possibly all evils are explicable in social terms, is incorrect. The beautiful place where altruism prevails and divisive egoism is unknown, is, according to More, Utopia, that is, Nowhere: 'In other places ... every man procureth his own private gain'; and every man does so because of a 'hellhound ... so deeply rooted in men's breasts, that she cannot be plucked out'. That hellhound is Pride.[4] More shows that it is possible to hold to an essentialist conception of human nature and yet entertain the possibility of social and moral amelioration.

Castiglione

Following Stephen Greenblatt, Dollimore says that in *The Book of the Courtier* Castiglione, like all the writers of manuals on rhetoric and courtly behaviour, takes up and develops the idea of 'the protean self, artificially constructed' and with no 'fixed nature or commitment to anything' (179).

It is certainly true that the courtesy writers and rhetoricians had a common preoccupation with the need to adjust speech and conduct to the variable demands of circumstance in a complex hierarchical society. But Castiglione, like Cicero (his master both in behavioural and speech matters), was continuously emphatic on the need to avoid affectation and to balance versatility with truth to one's own individual nature, 'because every thing is not fitte for every man . . . Therefore it is meete eche man know him selfe, and his own disposition, and apply him selfe thereto, and consider what thinges are meet for him to follow, and what are not.'[5] For Castiglione, as for Spenser (*Faerie Queene*, Book 6), this whole question of the artful and the 'naturall and proper' in individual behaviour is intrinsic to the great dialectic of nature and nurture. What he says on the matter clearly disproves the cultural-materialist axiom that the autonomous, unified self is an invention of the Enlightenment.

Sir Francis Bacon

Dollimore couples Bacon and Machiavelli 'on the issue of human nature' (171) and on two occasions quotes the same passage from Bacon's *Essays* as strikingly persuasive evidence of a constructivist view of the human subject. Dollimore writes (171):

> It is, says Bacon in a passage already cited in an earlier context and worth repeating here, custom and education rather than human nature which are the crucial determinants of human behaviour: 'His [that is, Machiavelli's] rule holdeth still, that nature, not the engagement of words, are not so forcible as custom'. Men behave, he adds (with a strikingly deterministic simile), 'as if they were dead images and engines moved only by the wheels of custom'.

The quotation from Bacon certainly supports a determinist theory of character; but it could hardly escape a reader's attention that the essay in question, 'Of Custom and Education', is one of a pair (38 and 39), the other being 'Of Nature in Men'. In the other essay, Bacon says:

> Nature is often hidden in men, sometimes overcome, seldom extinguished; let not a man trust his victory over nature too far; for nature will lie buried a great time, and yet revive upon the occasion or temptation . . . A man's nature is best perceived in privateness, for there is no affectation; in passion, for that putteth him out of his precept; and in a new case or experience, for there custom leaveth him.[6]

What Bacon has done in this (for him) unusual coupling of essays is to reconstitute the familiar dialectic of nature and nurture/culture in the form of a perfect *coincidentia oppositorum.*

Machiavelli

Dollimore concedes that Machiavelli 'appears to posit an unchanging human nature', since in *The Discourses* he says that 'in constituting and legislating for a commonwealth it must needs be taken for granted that all men are wicked' (171). But, Dollimore contends, such statements conceal 'the increasingly apparent' fact that 'Machiavelli is concerned not with man's intrinsic nature, but with people in history and society'. This fact is apparent, for example, when Machiavelli remarks (what follows is Dollimore's rewording of Machiavelli) 'that in coming to power a leader will often realise he was mistaken in thinking particular individuals rather than political and social forces are responsible for social disorder'; and again when 'he account[s] for man's acquisitiveness not in terms of his nature, but the individual's relative position in society' (171).

Dollimore's position on Machiavelli is initially surprising, since it has long been an axiom in historiographic scholarship that Machiavelli believed the study of history to be politically useful in the present precisely because human beings are fundamentally the same in all ages. Machiavelli has given scholars good reason to impute this belief to him: 'If the present be compared with the remote past', he says, 'it is easily seen that in all cities and in all peoples there are the same desires and the same passions as there always were. So that, if one examines with diligence the past, it is easy to foresee the future of any commonwealth, and to apply those remedies which were used of old.'[7]

In fact, if the two passages rephrased by Dollimore and adduced as evidence of an anti-essentialist Machiavelli are considered in context, it becomes obvious that each is part of an argument designed to show the uniformity of human nature throughout history. The first passage comes from a chapter dealing with plebeian government, where Machiavelli generalises on the behaviour of plebeian leaders by reference to both ancient Rome and fifteenth-century Florence. 'It has often happened', he says, 'that a man of this sort' having risen to highest office, quickly saw that he was wrong to ascribe social disorder to certain powerful citizens: 'Realizing that it is circumstances [*i tempi*, the times], not men, that have brought the disorders about, he has quickly changed his mind and his line of conduct; for acquaintance with things in detail has removed the wrong impression that had been taken for granted when only general considerations were taken into account.' Concerning this transformation in the populist leader, Machiavelli adds: 'It is the sort of thing that happens to many and on many occasions' (228). The second passage comes from a chapter asking who has the stronger reason for creating disturbances in a republic, the 'Haves' or the 'Have-nots'. While acknowledging that 'the appetites of both might easily become the cause of no small disturbance', he continues: 'Actually, however, such disturbances are more often caused by the "haves", since the fear of losing what they have arouses in them the same inclination we find in those who want to get more, for men are inclined to think that they cannot hold securely what they possess unless they get more at others' expense' (117–18). It should be added here that Machiavelli's uniformitarian view of human nature, and its corollary, the political usefulness of history, were not peculiar to himself: they were commonplace assumptions among Renaissance historians.[8]

Hobbes

Being a materialist, Hobbes is assumed by Dollimore to have an anti-essentialist view of man. He admits that Hobbes does say: 'I put for a general inclination of all mankind, a perpetual and restless desire of power after power, that ceaseth only after death', but this, argues Dollimore, does not signify essentialism, since here 'we are confronted not with essence but with the more malleable notion of instinct or passion' (172).

Leaving aside the opinion shared by Machiavelli and others that instincts and passions are major components in the basically unchanging nature of humankind, one has to say that the sentences which follow the quoted fragment from *Leviathan* 1: 11 give no hint of malleability:

> And the cause of this, is not alwayes that a man hopes for a more intensive delight, than he has attained to; or that he cannot be content with a moderate power; but because he cannot assure the power and means to live well, which he hath present, without the acquisition of more. And from hence it is that Kings, whose power is greatest, turn their endeavours to the assuring it at home by Lawes, or abroad by Wars: and when that is done, there succeedeth a new desire; in some, of Fame from new Conquest; in others, of ease and sensuall pleasure; in others of admiration, or being flattered for excellence . . . Competition of Riches, Honour, Command, or other power enclineth to Contention, Enmity, and War.

'For such is the nature of men', such is 'the nature of man' (1: 13): Hobbes does not qualify his magisterial generalisations on universal human nature. His only remedy for man's intrinsically restless and competitive nature is rigid control by authoritarian government: control accepted because of 'the passions that encline men to Peace' ('Feare of death' and 'Desire of commodious living'), and always liable to collapse because of 'the nature of man'.[9] What Hobbes offers is a cheerless version of the nature/culture dialectic.

Montaigne

With his ingenious insistence in his longest essay on the similarity and possible inferiority of men to beasts (*Essays*, 2: 12), and his frequent meditations in other essays on the inconstancy and contradictoriness of human nature, Montaigne offers much more promising material for the anti-essentialist argument. As incontestable evidence of Montaigne's anti-essentialism, Dollimore quotes and italicises his assertion that man is 'without any prerogative or *essentiall pre-excellencie*' over the beasts (174).

However, the context of this assertion is the lengthy 'Apologie of Raymond Sebond', which is quite exceptional among the essays: its sustained onslaught on human self-regard is conducted in the manner of a rhetorical exercise which makes its point by witty and audacious exaggeration.[10] Moreover the object of attack is seen in the end as the identifying human attribute, the source of all man's fantastic follies and self-deifying fancies: 'Christians have peculiar knowledge, *how curiosity is in man a naturall, and originall infirmity*. The care to encrease in wisdome and knowledge was the first overthrow of mankinde: It is the way whereby man hath cast himselfe downe to eternall damnation. Pride is his losse and corruption. Pride leadeth him from the common waies; that makes him embrace all newfangles' (1: 199; Florio's italics, here and below).

Dollimore does not quote this passage from the 'Apologie'. But he does acknowledge that Montaigne elsewhere contradicts himself in his restless search for self-knowledge. On the one hand, Montaigne seems to deny the possibility of a continuous, essential self. 'Whosoever shall heedfully survey and consider himselfe, shall finde this volubility and discordance to be in himselfe, yea and in his very judgement' (2: 12). On the other hand, he says: 'Naturall inclinations are by institution helped and strengthened, but they neither change nor exceed ... *Those which in my time, have attempted to correct the fashions of the world by new opinions, reforme the vices of apparance; those of the essence they leave untouched*' (3: 29–30). Dollimore quotes these three sentences, but attaches serious significance only to the first. He simply dismisses the second and third as Montaigne's retreat into 'a rather smug conservatism' (173); in addition, he fails to quote the intervening and following sentences, which make it clear that Montaigne's 'smug' conviction cannot be lightly dismissed:

> A thousand natures in my time, have a thwart a contrary discipline, escaped toward vertue or toward vice. These originall qualities are not grub out, they are but covered, and hidden ... Looke a little into the course of our experience. There is no man (if he listen to himselfe) that doth not discover in himselfe a peculiar forme of his, a swaying forme, which wrestleth against the institution, and against the tempest of passions, which are contrary to him.
>
> (3: 30)

The last sentence had to be ignored in *Radical Tragedy*, for it resolves the apparent contradiction in Montaigne's view of the self; the self is fluid and unstable, but is still itself: it has an individual form or essence, albeit a swaying one. This particular essay, of course, recalls Bacon's pair on the same theme. Characteristically, Bacon reformulates the familiar dialectic with considerably more emphasis on the power of nurture and culture than Montaigne allows.

What Dollimore has done, then, is to construct, outside the plays, a subversive, anti-essentialist tradition where none existed. In every case he has been confronted with an author whose view of the relationship between the individual and society, nature and culture, is basically but variably dialectical, and in every case, by means of adroit selection and omission (and a little dismissive dogmatism), he has reduced a dialectical position acknowledging interdependence and interaction to a simple determinist view. Each author is forcibly conscripted to the anti-essentialist cause.

4   The Exemplary Text

The chapter on '*King Lear* and Essentialist Humanism' is the centrepiece of *Radical Tragedy*; as its reprinting in critical anthologies suggests, it has been taken as the most characteristic and expressive example of Dollimore's cultural materialism, if not of cultural materialism per se. Dollimore himself seems to have felt that no other play exemplifies his thesis so well. From my own point of view, too, the *Lear* chapter is exemplary: the reading procedures which I find repeatedly at work in the accounts of other Shakespearean and non-Shakespearean plays are especially obvious here.[11]

Central to the chapter is a rejection of the humanist critical tradition which sees in *Lear* a particularly powerful expression of the idea that in a cruel and unjust universe human beings can redeem themselves by virtue of certain innate and indestructible human qualities. Through suffering, the tragic victim grows in stature and discloses what is best about man's intrinsic nature: (1) pity or human kindness; (2) fortitude; (3) the capacity for growth in consciousness, an ability to learn or 'apprehend' the nature of things. According to *Radical Tragedy*, *Lear* actually repudiates all claims for the value and importance of pity, fortitude, and knowledge, together with the concomitant belief in an essential human nature. The humanist interpretation, we are told, is misguided because it mystifies suffering and invests man with a quasi-transcendent identity when in fact the play does neither of these things. Man here is decentred 'in order . . . to make visible social process and its forms of ideological misrecognition' (189–91). Let us consider this argument in detail.

Pity

Because '"pity" is a recurring word in the play', explains Dollimore, humanist critics have assumed that the quality itself should be taken as something of major significance and value. However, a close look at the text, he suggests, dictates only a negative view of this emotion and its larger manifestation, human kindness. His evidence is as follows: (a) Lear's prayer for 'houseless poverty' (3.4.26) simply shows that 'where pity for "houseless poverty" is the prerequisite for compassionate action, where a king has to share the suffering of his subjects in order to care, the majority will remain poor, naked and wretched' (191). (b) When Poor Tom tells Gloucester he is cold, and Gloucester responds by telling him to go into the hovel and keep warm (3.4.148–77), this might seem 'callous' to us but is in fact no more than the type of 'casual unkindness that is built into social consciousness' in such a society; it does, however, show 'the woeful inadequacy of what passes for kindness' in that society (192). (c) Gloucester has to undergo intense suffering (blinding) before he can identify in a properly compassionate way with the deprived (192). (d) Lear's pity is both self-regarding and short-lived. He does not empathise with Poor Tom so much as assimilate him to his own grief. And 'his preoccupation with vengeance ultimately displaces his transitory pity; reverting from the charitable reconciliation of 5.3 to vengeance once again, we see him boasting of having killed the "slave" that was hanging Cordelia' (193). (e) Cordelia may embody or symbolise pity but her pity alters nothing significantly. Her death shows that 'Pity, like kindness, seems in *Lear* to be precious yet ineffectual': it cannot generate justice. In short, *Lear* demonstrates both the failure and the destruction of such values as pity and kindness (192–3). I consider these points in turn.

(a) The suggestion that social justice is contingent on the disappearance of monarchy is reasonable enough in itself, but it is an imported idea which is never once hinted at in the text; indeed, it is totally contradicted by the play's ending. Edgar, whose 'very gait did prophesy / A royal nobleness' (5.3.175–6) in the trial by combat with Edmund, becomes king. He is characterised as a man fit for this role. Not only is he Lear's godson, he learns by experience and is wise before he is old; he is also valorous and compassionate. His carefully planned political intervention saves Albion from the ruthless tyranny of King Edmund and Queen Goneril, and his care for his father has focused attention continuously on the need for active compassion, 'the art of known and feeling sorrows' (4.6.223). Shakespeare has thus shaped plot and character so as to provide for a reconstitution of the existing social order on a wise, strong, and humane basis. It cannot be claimed that this conclusion is an abrupt and pusillanimous withdrawal from subversion to recuperation; it is integral.

(b) Even as reported in *Radical Tragedy*, it is hard to construe Gloucester's response to Poor Tom as casually unkind, let alone callous. A look at the context makes the suggestion seem preposterous. Gloucester at this point is in a state of extreme distress and fear. He has been shocked by the 'discovery' that his son planned to kill him; he has discovered that Goneril and Regan seek Lear's death; he is now intent on protecting Lear and knows that he is risking his life in doing so; he is appalled to find Lear out in the storm, his wits gone, and in the company of a gabbling madman. But neither his personal distress nor his concern for the King makes him ignore the Bedlam beggar who has entered the scene: 'In fellow, there, into the hovel; keep thee warm' (3.4.178). Later, too, we perceive that Poor Tom's plight affected him far more deeply than these words suggest: 'In the last night's storm I such a fellow saw, / Which made me think a man a worm' (4.1.33–4).

(c) It is untrue to say that Gloucester has to be blinded before he can identify with the deprived. Lear is deprived of all power and property, and to identify with him requires much more unselfishness than identification with an ordinary vagabond. Lear is now like the Jew in the posters and persecutions of Nazi Europe: 'Whoever helps a Jew helps Satan' and forfeits his life.[12] Gloucester understands his own situation in the new regime very well: 'When I desir'd their leave that I might pity him, they . . . charg'd me, on pain of perpetual displeasure, neither to speak to him, entreat of him, nor any way sustain him . . . If I die for it, as no less is threatened me, the King, my old master, must be reliev'd' (3.3.2–6, 18–20). And indeed while he is still in the process of helping Lear, Gloucester is deprived of property and title; a punishment arguably worse than death will soon follow.

(d) Lear's compassion for the poor is not obliterated by his own griefs; rather, it develops into a preoccupation with the cruel injustices perpetrated by corrupt law officers on the poor and the defenceless (4.6.151–70), and so into a general awareness of corrupt 'Authority'. This preoccupation with justice and injustice is undoubtedly companion to a desire for vengeance on Goneril and Regan. But the play charts a profound change in Lear's attitude to the two evil daughters that is causally connected with his feelings of remorse and pity towards Cordelia. Before he meets her in Act 4, he is filled with a 'sovereign shame' at the thought of the 'unkindness / That stripp'd her from his benediction, turn'd her / To foreign casualties' (4.3.43–5). When he wakes from his restorative sleep and is reunited with her, 'the great rage . . . is kill'd in him', and Goneril and Regan are no more than a parenthesis in his thoughts:

> I pray, weep not:
> If you have poison for me, I will drink it.
>   . . . your sisters
> Have, as I do remember, done me wrong.
> You have some cause, they have not.
>   (4.7.71–5)

When he and Cordelia are being despatched to prison, he will not allow her even to think of them: 'No, no, no, no! Come, let's away to prison; / We two alone' (5.3.8–9). It is of course true that he shows no pity for the soldier who hangs Cordelia in return for Edmund's promise of a rich reward (corrupt Authority at work): this is where 'the old rage' returns, kills justly, and reminds us that the old king is a man of heroic stature. To suggest that by killing the murderer of his daughter he somehow invalidates his earlier compassion for the poor is absurd.

(e) Although intense, Cordelia's pity for Lear is not unique; both in words and in deed, others show pity for him from the beginning of his downfall to the very end. As outcast father, remorseful sinner, suffering old age, and a shatteringly bereaved parent, he is the main focus for pity in the play. To obscure this fact by trying to find fault with his pity for others is to get the tragedy quite out of focus.

Anyhow, it is demonstrably wrong to claim that pity here is ineffectual, produces no significant alteration, is not redemptive. Cordelia's pity for Lear makes it easy for her to forgive the immense injustice he has done her, and for him that forgiveness means everything: it turns imprisonment into intense happiness. Moreover, like the reaction of the Third Servant to Gloucester's anguish ('I'll fetch some flax and whites of eggs / To apply to his bleeding face' [3.7.105–6]), the partnership between Cordelia, with her 'aidant and remediate' tears, and the gentle Doctor, with his 'simples operative' to 'close the eye of anguish' (4.4.14–15), shows that medicine itself originates in human compassion.

The servant who kills his 'great master' Cornwall at the cost of his own life does much to redeem human nature from the depths to which it has sunk with the party in power. More pertinent to Dollimore's thesis, he also demonstrates the political value of pity, having rebelled because he was *thrill'd with remorse* ('pierced [ME *pirlian*] with pity'), when he saw the piercing of Gloucester's eyes (the notion of sym-pathy / com-passion / feeling-with is finely suggested). The first effect of this action is to deprive the evil party of its masterful leader and set the two evil sisters on the path of mutual destruction. The second effect involves Albany: he is already appalled by the cruelty of Goneril to Lear, but when he hears about the blinding of Gloucester and the servant's heroic action he decisively changes sides (4.2.30–50, 73–97). A more exalted figure than Albany, too, is moved to political action by pity: 'great France' led an army to the defence of Lear because, says Cordelia, 'my mourning and importun'd tears [he] hath pitied' (4.4.26). Even Regan begins to realise that pity has political consequences, remarking to Oswald that it was stupid not to kill off the blinded Gloucester, since 'where'er he arrives he moves / All hearts against us' (4.5.10–11).

In fact a central idea of the play is that people commit and tolerate injustice precisely because (as Gloucester says) they 'will not feel' (4.1.69); and feeling, as Edgar indicates in his own self-definition, means pity: the man destined to rule after Lear is one who 'by the art of known and feeling sorrows' is 'pregnant to good pity' (4.6.223–4), a man who will not (in Brutus's key phrase) 'disjoin / Remorse from power' (*JC*, 2.1.18–19). Goneril's expression of contempt for compassion might in itself make us reluctant to see it as politically insignificant in the *Lear* world, but the circumstances and the manner in which she expresses that contempt show how closely entwined is pity with ideas of justice, injustice, and arbitrary power: 'Fools do those villains pity who are punish'd / Ere they have done their mischief' (4.2.54–5) Thus to investigate *Radical Tragedy*'s claims for the insignificance of pity in *Lear* is to perceive how profoundly correct is the reverse (and very familiar) assumption.

Fortitude

Radical Tragedy's manifest distaste for the stoicism which the major Jacobean tragedians so conspicuously admire reflects a belief that endurance and patience are symptomatic of political quietism; this distaste generates a latent hostility to the tragic genre itself. The audacious stoicism displayed by Webster's Flamineo and Vittoria when facing their killers in the final scene of *The White Devil*, a stoicism which no audience could take as anything but heroic and redemptive, is summarily dismissed as 'futile defiance', a 'stubborn defiance born of a willed insensibility' (245). There are chapters on *Mustapha* and on *Sejanus* but none on *The Duchess of Malfi*, arguably the greatest Jacobean tragedy outside Shakespeare, a play in which the heroine, in scenes of protracted suffering, becomes the epitome of a noble, Christianised stoicism: 'Necessity makes me suffer constantly, / And custom makes it easy' (4.2.29–30). Ignored too is the well-known fact that in writing *Sejanus*, Jonson, despite all his reverence for historical accuracy, departed from his historiographic sources in order to introduce characters who confront the might of tyranny with stoic fortitude, heroically asserting their moral identities.[13]

Consistent with all of this is *Radical Tragedy*'s claim that *Lear* actually repudiates stoic fortitude, exposing it as a mystification of suffering which simply supports the notion that the human condition cannot be alleviated (194–5). More specifically, Lear's madness and Gloucester's near-madness are said to constitute 'an ironic subversion of neo-stoic essentialism'. Like other plays of the time, *Lear* thus 'confirms Edmund's contention that "men / Are as the time is" (5.3.31–2)': that is, they are unable to transcend by fortitude the material circumstances that make and unmake them (195–6). For '*King Lear* is, above all, a play about power, property and inheritance', and the cherished values of kindness and fortitude, as well as human relations and 'even identity itself', are all dependent upon, informed by, this dominant ideology (199, 201).

Very little textual evidence is actually adduced in support of the claim that *Lear* demystifies fortitude: nothing beyond what I have cited so far. Perhaps for that reason Dollimore turns to Montaigne and Bacon to provide support, if not for his interpretation of this aspect of the text, at least for its historical plausibility. Apropos Edmund's view that 'men / Are as the time is', he remarks: 'Montaigne made a similar point, with admirable terseness: "I am no philosopher: Evils opresse me according as they waigh" (*Essays*, 3: 189).' And the play's 'ironic subversion of neo-stoic essentialism', he observes, 'recalls Bacon's essay "Of Adversity", where he quotes Seneca: "*It is true greatness to have in one the frailty of a man, and the security of a god*", only to add, dryly: "This would have done better in poesy, where transcendences are more allowed"'. Bacon, continues Dollimore, was dismissive of 'idealist mimesis, that is, an illusionist evasion . . . of historical and empirical realities' (196). Before examining the alleged devaluation of fortitude in Shakespeare's text it will be helpful to look more closely at these citations from Montaigne and Bacon.

The point made by Montaigne is in no sense 'similar' to Edmund's, and the 'terseness' with which it is made is the product of Dollimore's characteristic economy with quoted material. What Montaigne says, in his leisurely fashion, is that trivial inconveniences can trouble us more than matters of substance: 'The least and slightest hindrances, are the sharpest . . . A multitude of slender evils offendeth more, then the violence of one alone, how great soever . . . I am no Philosopher: Evils oppresse me according as they waigh; and waigh according to their forme, as well as according to the matter, and often more' (3: 188–9).

The quotation from Bacon constitutes lines 8–12 of a 42-line essay whose meaning is unmistakable. It begins thus:

> It was a high speech of Seneca (after the manner of the Stoics): *That the good things which belong to prosperitie are to be wished; but the good things that belong to adversity are to be admired. Bona rerum secundarum optabilia, adversarum mirabilia.* Certainly if miracles be the command over nature, they appear most in adversity. It is a higher speech of his than the other (much too high for a heathen): *It is true greatness to have in one the frailty of a man, and the security of a god. Vere magnum, habere fragilitatem hominis, securitatem dei.* This would have been better in poesy, where transcendences are more allowed. And the poets indeed have been busy with it; for it is in effect the thing which figured in that strange fiction of the ancient poets, which seemeth not to be without mystery; nay, and to have some approach to the state of the Christian: that *Hercules, when he went to unbind Prometheus* (by whom human nature is represented), *sailed the length of the great ocean in an earthen lot or pitcher:* lively describing Christian resolution, that saileth in the frail bark of the flesh through the waves of the world. But to speak in a mean [that is the mean or middle style more appropriate to prose]. The virtue of prosperity is temperance; the virtue of adversity is fortitude; which in morals is the more heroical virtue.
>
> (15–16; Bacon's italics)

The essay does not proceed to qualify, much less to subvert, any of these ideas. So it concludes: 'Certainly virtue is like precious odours, most fragrant when they are incensed and crushed: for prosperity doth best discover vice; but adversity doth best discover virtue.' It is perfectly clear that Bacon is not ironising Seneca here, but that on the contrary he is praising him for approximating to the imaginative eloquence of poetry and the moral wisdom of Christianity. The essay provides a perfect introduction to *Lear*'s engagement with the paradoxes of adversity and the heroism of fortitude.

One aspect of classical Stoicism, it must be conceded, is glancingly ironised in *King Lear*: its recommendation of *apatheia*, indifference, emotional detachment in the face of misfortune. This is made to seem foolish when Edgar's self-consciously philosophical acceptance of proscription and poverty is shattered by the spectacle of his blinded father: pierced with pity, Edgar miserably acknowledges that 'the worst is not / So long as we can say "This is the worst"' (3.6.105–16; 4.1.1–28). This, however, does not debunk fortitude (which Edgar never loses). It is a dramatic device, one of many such, designed to intensify the sense of shocking extremity which characterises the play's vision of tragic reality. It is also an intimation that the most unbearable pain may not be worldly misfortune, or any kind of personal hurt, but rather witnessing the affliction of a loved one. Cordelia's observation, 'For thee, oppressed King, I am cast down. / Myself could else out-frown false Fortune's frown' (5.3.5–6), renders this idea explicit.

Unlike emotional detachment, fortitude is nowhere devalued. What it signifies is not political quietism, but rather the capacity to endure what cannot be changed or avoided for the time being. The play shows two characters stretched on 'the rack of this tough world' and compelled to endure the unendurable. Gloucester does long for madness as an escape from his misery, and then for extinction, but he is helped by his son, a compassionate Stoic, 'to bear / Affliction till it do cry out itself, / "Enough, enough", and die' (4.6.75–7); to endure his going hence even as his coming hither (5.2.9–10). In the sense that he continues to execrate his daughters, Lear fails totally to become, as promised, 'the pattern of all patience' (3.2.37). Yet despite his great age he does, as he boasts, 'endure' all in a storm which has no equal in Kent's experience: 'man's nature cannot carry / Th' affliction nor the fear' (3.2.48–9; 3.4.18). It is not exposure to 'this extremity of the skies' (3.4.104), nor the loss of power and property, that drives Lear out of his wits, but the assault on his heart. Yet we do not sense that he loses his identity in madness; if anything, he is then in a state of heightened consciousness, more intensely himself. And when, having regained his sanity, his mind cracks once more under the final assault on his feelings, it is not his weakness but his astonishing endurance that is registered. Says Kent: 'The wonder is he hath endur'd so long: / He but usurp'd his life'; and Edgar reiterates this idea in the play's concluding sentence: 'we that are young / Shall never see so much, nor live so long' (5.3.316–17, 326).

For more reasons than one, the Folio is right to give the final speech to Edgar, the future king. Unlike Kent, he has endured evil without loss of self-control and in consequence was able to act against it all the more effectively when the opportune moment presented itself ('When time shall serve' [5.1.48]). His *sententia*, 'Ripeness is all', is quintessential Stoicism, and very pointedly, its wording connects him with Cordelia, in whom is focused with singular poetic force the play's supreme, and by implication complementary, values: compassion and patience, feeling and the control of feeling. Cordelia wept when she read Kent's letters about her father's sufferings, but 'it seem'd she was a queen / Over her passion; who, most rebel-like, / Sought to be king o'er her'. She was moved, but

> Not to a rage; patience and sorrow strove
> Who should express her goodliest. You have seen
> Sunshine and rain at once; her smile and tears
> Were like, a better way; those happy smilets
> That play'd on her ripe lip seem'd not to know
> What guests were in her eyes; which parted thence,
> Like pearls from diamonds dropp'd. In brief,
> Sorrow would be a rarity most belov'd,
> If all could so become it.
>
> (4.3.10–25)

A point of major significance not noticed by *Radical Tragedy* is that fortitude and endurance in *Lear*, as in Shakespeare's thought generally, is intimately connected with loyalty. Constancy (so important in the characterisation of Henry V) is Shakespeare's comprehensive ethical and psychological ideal, and it implies truth both to self and to others in times of change and misfortune. In Stoic tradition, constancy, which subsumes fortitude, was the supreme virtue (Lipsius's *De Constantia*, 1594, was the major neo-Stoic text of the Renaissance). But Shakespeare's notion of constancy as twofold is a reflection of his conception of identity as relational:

> I cannot be
> Mine own, nor anything to any, if
> I be not thine. To this I am most constant,
> Though destiny say no.
> (*Winter's Tale*, 4.4.43–6)

From the outset, *Lear* raises questions about constancy-as-loyalty in very concrete form. These questions are rendered explicit in the sardonic reflections of the Fool. Who but a fool would defend one that's out of favour (1.4.104)? Or stay with a great man when he is on the way down (2.4.70–85)? What children are kind to their father when he has nothing to bequeath, being deserted by 'Fortune, that arrant whore' (lines 47–55)? If *Radical Tragedy* is to believed, the play's answer to such questions is 'No one', since the cherished norms of kindness and fortitude are dependent on the dominant ideology of power, property, and inheritance. But even if one applies the old King's crassly materialistic criterion of number and quantity, one perceives that more than half the inhabitants of the *Lear* world are not subjects of the dominant ideology: Cordelia, France, Kent, the Fool, Edgar, Gloucester, Cornwall's three servants, Albany, and the blinded Gloucester's kindly tenant – an Old Man who is

Constancy itself: 'O my good Lord! I / have been your tenant, and your father's tenant, / These fourscore years' (4.1.12–14).

Of special significance in this group is the King of France, who has arrived in England to see his prospective bride abruptly stripped of fortune and favour and mockingly offered to him as a hated pauper. In the materialist code, nothing would be more intelligible than that he should instantly obey the ideology of power and property which has presumably made him in every sense what he is. But instead of abandoning Cordelia, he acknowledges and cherishes her essential self ('Thee and thy virtues' [1.1.252]), a self hitherto concealed behind the public image of a quiet and dutiful daughter; an identity constituted of reticence, sincerity, courage, and a hatred of hypocrisy. This self she has abruptly revealed in the act of resisting her father's materialism and dismissing the suitor whose love is 'respect and fortunes' (line 248). To the faithful France, 'she is herself [her *self*] a dowry' (line 241). The King of France and the Duke of Burgundy are presumably products of the same ideology, as Cordelia and her sisters are the children of the same parents. Clearly, this text forces upon our attention *from the outset* the often startling autonomy of the self; its baffling individuality; its resistance to environmental 'subjection' and formulaic explanation.

No opening scene, then, could signal more clearly the fact that all men and women are not 'as the time is'. But even if we were to ignore France and all the ensuing instances of heroic constancy in spite of the world's 'strange mutations' (4.1.11), we have only to relocate Edmund's maxim in order to perceive that it is meant to be rejected and condemned outright. Sanitised as it is in *Radical Tragedy* by complete dissociation from its context, the fragment might well strike the unwary reader as an axiom from the philosophic musings of a justly embittered and understandably disillusioned man; as such, it might command some respect. But it is uttered by a ruthless egoist who has been richly favoured by those in power and is now poised for supremacy: 'Fortune led you well', remarks Albany (5.3.42). More exactly, it is one of two principles invoked by Edmund to justify anarchic ambition and the murder of Cordelia and Lear:

> *Edm.* Come hither, captain; hark.
> Take thou this note;   [*Giving a paper.*]
>   Go follow them to prison.
> One step I have advanc'd thee; if thou dost
> As this instructs thee, thou dost make thy way
> To noble fortunes; know this, that men
> Are as the time is; to be tender-minded
> Does not become a sword; thy great employment
> Will not bear question; either say thou'lt do't,
> Or thrive by other means.
> *Offi.* I'll do't, my Lord.
> *Edm.* About it; and write happy when thou hast done.
>
>   (5.3.27–38)

That neither Edmund nor his captain achieves happiness by being 'as the time is' is clearly an important part of the play's meaning.

Knowledge

Very little evidence either is offered in support of the categorical denial that suffering is redeemed in *Lear* by the sufferers' growth in knowledge and understanding. There is simply the claim that although Lear achieves a kind of knowledge in the sense that he learns to demystify authority ('A dog's obey'd in office'), and acknowledges his own abuse of it, this insight is succeeded by the delusion that he still has power: 'Take that of me, my friend, who have the power / To seal th' accuser's lips' (4.6.161, 171–2). This, says Dollimore, simply shows that 'power itself is in control of "justice"'; it reminds us (and here the issue of knowledge is suddenly abandoned) that *Lear* is 'above all' about power, property, and inheritance (196–7).

As an attempt to refute a long-standing interpretive position, this is extraordinarily unconvincing and offhand. It is not just a case of insufficient evidence but, again, of evidence either wholly misunderstood or wilfully misrepresented. The scene alluded to is very relevant to the question of knowledge, for here, at the height of his insanity, Lear confesses that a lifetime of flattering subservience led him to believe that he possessed godlike wisdom and power: 'To say "ay" and "no" to every thing that I said! . . . was no good divinity . . . they told me I was every thing; 'tis a lie, I am not ague-proof' (4.6.100–108). From this (prompted by Gloucester's respectful naming of 'the King'), he passes to a satiric acting out of the ruler at whose mere 'stare . . . the subject quakes' (line 111), and who will always protect and reward his corrupt officials:

> None does offend, none, I say, none; I'll able 'em:
> Take that of me, my friend, who have the power
> To seal th' accuser's lips.
>
> (4.6.170–72)

It is difficult to see how anyone could read this ironic self-identification with corrupt authority as a reassertion of the will to power. The tone of 'None does offend, none I say' should of itself prevent such literalism, but the immediately following comment of Edgar puts the dramatic significance of Lear's behaviour in the scene as a whole beyond all doubt: 'O! matter and impertinency mix'd; / Reason in madness' (lines 176–7).

The paradoxes of *King Lear*, wholly ignored by *Radical Tragedy*, bring us to the heart of the matter: they focus our attention alike on the 'miracles' that 'appear most in adversity' and deprivation and 'the more heroical virtue' of fortitude (to recall Bacon); on the often astonishing independence of the self, and on the growth of understanding. Edgar's comment on Lear's mad wisdom is exclamatory, paradox being the figure of wonder, and throughout this play the principal characters express what they learn from experience in tones of amazement verging on incredulity. It all begins with France's 'Gods, gods, 'tis strange', reinforcing his recognition that Cordelia's true self, her stubborn virtue, is revealed only when she is stripped of property and inheritance, that his love for her is augmented by her loss, that she is 'most rich, being poor', and that she 'losest here, a better where to find' (1.1.250, 261). The wonderment of discovery reappears on the bare heath with Lear's 'Where is this straw, my fellow? / The art of our necessities is strange, / And can make vile things precious' (3.2.69–71), with blind Gloucester's 'I stumbled when I saw. Full oft 'tis *seen*, / Our means secure us, and our mere defects / Prove our commodities' (4.1.19–21; my italics), and of course with Edgar's reason-in-madness paradox. The heroic endurance of the 80-year-old protagonist is itself a paradox to those who witness it, and who in so doing learn much about what Kent called 'man's nature': 'The wonder is he hath endur'd so long.' This mood of wonder at 'man's nature' is the characteristic mood of tragedy from ancient times: 'Wonders are many, and none is more wonderful than man' (Sophocles, *Antigone*, Chorus 2, str. 1). It is not something which is ever encompassed by the interpretive template of the cultural materialists.

5 'Report me and my cause aright / To the unsatisfied'

Clearly, then, the central argument of *Radical Tragedy* collapses when its bristling apparatus of supportive quotation and historical scholarship is examined with moderate care. What we are left with is repetitive assertion, a seriously distorted view of the period, and a collection of readings which strip great tragedies of their semantic complexity and rich humanity.

The difficulty of making the tragedies of Shakespeare and his contemporaries fit the anti-humanist paradigm by means of straight reading has inevitably been perceived by other cultural materialists, most notably perhaps by Dollimore's colleague Alan Sinfield. In his essay on *Macbeth*, instead of presenting Shakespeare as the ally of radical thinkers, he treats him rather as the mouthpiece of James I's authoritarian ideology; no disagreement with Dollimore is registered, nor is there any attempt to explain Shakespeare's ideological somersault from *Lear* to *Macbeth*; clearly, what matters is not the text and its interpretation but the political end in view.[14] In Sinfield's reading, the liberal and conservative critics who for centuries have misread Renaissance drama are no longer the source of error, merely the victims and purveyors of a great ideological fiction which he himself easily unmasks. Shakespeare's text, we are told, is characterised by 'most cunningly' executed 'moves', 'manoeuvres', and 'strategies' (99–100) whose whole purpose is to blacken Macbeth and sanctify his opponents, and by means of this extreme contrast to obscure the fact that there is no fundamental difference between the violence of a murderous usurper and the violence exercised by an authoritarian ruler such as Duncan or James in defence of his regime. (There is no reference to the centrally significant and tragic contrast in Macbeth himself between the brutal infanticide and the man of sensitive imagination who was once full of the milk of human kindness: 'Can such thing be, / And overcome us like a summer's cloud, / Without our special wonder?' [3.4.110–12].) This shift from Dollimore's 'hermeneutic of re-enactment' to a 'hermeneutic of suspicion' (to use Paul Ricoeur's terms) is not as radical as it seems; it is already implicit in Dollimore's often startling freedom with the words on the page. In fact, a casual mixing of the two interpretive modes is often encountered in radical criticism.

Sinfield acknowledges that his reading of *Macbeth* is 'by conventional standards . . . perverse' (108), but seems to have no doubt that it is educationally justified. As part of his cultural-materialist commitment to the dissemination of proper political attitudes through 'writing, teaching, and other modes of communicating' (108), he reprints the essay in his critical anthology on *Macbeth* with the intention of alerting students to the manoeuvres of 'state violence' today. In *Faultlines: Cultural Materialism and the Politics of Dissident Reading*, he applies the same method of reading even more forcefully to *Julius Caesar* in the belief that he will thereby 'check the tendency to add Shakespearean authority to reactionary discourses' (21). But there is a fundamental and insidious confusion at the heart of his whole critical project: on the one hand he uses the methods and materials of historical research to give authority to his readings (consider the use of writings by Buchanan, Gerard, and James VI in the *Macbeth* essay), and on the other he allows himself complete liberty of interpretation as and when he chooses, anticipating the Hawkesian principle that 'Shakespeare doesn't mean: *we* mean *by* Shakespeare.'[15]

Somewhat jokily, Sinfield offers a choice between two names for the seemingly perverse mode of reading, the first his own coinage, the other borrowed from Jonathan Dollimore: the New Reductionism, and Creative Vandalism (20, 22). The first term is preferable and deserves widespread acceptance. It tacitly acknowledges that political criticism which sees its end as justifying its means cannot claim to be a form of serious academic study characterised by consistency of principle, analytical rigour, and intellectual honesty. Such criticism inevitably slides into the propagandist mode.

'*Ethics*', it has been said (in 1993), 'is an embarrassing word which the literary academy has been reluctant to let into our discourse.'[16] This embarrassment stems from Marxist, structuralist, and poststructuralist rejection of the idea of the individual as a conscious agent capable in principle of moral discrimination and choice.[17] For the Marxist in particular, moral discourse is a bourgeois phenomenon which must give way to revolutionary politics.[18] However, since Marxist criticism is avowedly devoted to unmasking the injustices committed and legitimised by the dominant classes, and since ethics might be said to begin and end in justice, there is a certain contradiction here. But the contradiction in cultural materialism which concerns me most is the failure to perceive that justice is not divisible. Justice is due not only to the oppressed and the marginalised but also to the dead authors whose texts merit considerably more respect than those of the critics who feed off them. It is due also to those educable young readers who will lead better and richer lives if their minds are opened to the full variety and complexity of great literature, instead of being told that texts, if they mean anything at all, mean only subjection, oppression, and deception.

Chapter 6

Shakespearean Tragedy

1

A distinguished Shakespearean scholar famously remarked that 'there is no such thing as Shakespearean Tragedy: there are only Shakespearean tragedies'. Attempts (he added) to find a formula applicable to every one of Shakespeare's tragedies, defining and distinguishing them from those of other dramatists, invariably meet with little success. Yet when challenging one such attempt he noted its failure to observe what he termed 'an essential part of the [Shakespearean] tragic pattern';[1] which would seem to imply that these plays do have some shared characteristics peculiar to them and familiar to informed students of Shakespeare.

Nevertheless, objections to firm definitions of 'Shakespearean Tragedy' are well founded. They tend to ignore the uniqueness of each play and the way it has been structured and styled to fit the particular source-narrative. More generally, they can obscure the fact that what distinguishes Shakespeare's tragedies from every one else's and prompts us to consider them together are not certain common denominators but rather the power of Shakespeare's language, his insight into character, and his dramaturgical inventiveness.[2]

Uneasiness with definitions of Shakespearean tragedy is of a kind with the uneasiness generated by definitions of tragedy itself; these often give a static impression of genre and incline towards prescriptiveness, ignoring the fact that 'genres are in a constant state of transmutation'.[3] There is, however, a simple argument in defence of genre criticism, namely that full understanding and appreciation of any piece of literature is dependent on knowledge of its contexts, literary as well as intellectual and socio-political: in its relation to the author and his work, context informs, assists, stimulates, provokes. Thus knowledge of generic context helps us recognise not only authorial dependence but also authorial intention, experimentation, and originality. So too, familiarity with Shakespeare's tragedies as a whole enhances understanding of the meanings and the special nature of any one of them.

2

As practised in Renaissance England and in classical Greece and Rome, tragedy is an intense exploration of suffering and evil focused on the experience of an exceptional individual, distinguished by rank or innate quality or both. Typically, it presents a steep fall from prosperity to misery and untimely death, a great change occasioned or accompanied by conflict between the tragic character and some superior natural or supernatural power. Many have agreed with Brunetière's axiom that the essence of drama is conflict, others believe that its essence is change. In fact, however, these two phenomena are scarcely separable, the second being a natural consequence of the first; although in any one play either may be more conspicuous than the other. But the rival theories are worth noting insofar as they help in combination to explain why tragedy is the most intense and absorbing kind of drama. Tragedy, and Shakesperian tragedy above all, is conflict-and-change in extreme and violent form.

Much emphasis has been placed on conflict – and the concomitant notions of contradiction, ambivalence, and paradox – as a major characteristic of tragedy. Most of this emphasis has been due to the philosophers Hegel and Nietzsche. According to Hegel, the characteristic conflict in tragedy is not between right and wrong but between the personal embodiments of a universal ethical power, both of whom push their rightful claim to the point where it encroaches on the other's right and so becomes wrongful. The resolution of this conflict restores a condition of natural justice and confirms the existence of an essentially just and divine world order.[4] Nietzsche rejected the idea of such an order, but he too saw 'contrariety at the center of the universe' and tragedy as the conflict and reconciliation of opposites: these opposites are Apollo and Dionysus, the first symbolising reason, control, and art, the second, passionate destructive energy, orgiastic abandon, and the self-renewing force of life itself.[5] Both thinkers were inspired by the pre-Socratic philosophers who held that the natural world is a system of 'discordant concord' animated by the forces of Love (Sympathy) and Strife (War).[6] Despite very substantial differences between their theories of tragedy (and their general philosophies), both Hegel and Nietzsche were prompted by their attraction to pre-Socratic cosmology to locate tragic events in a natural dialectic of destruction and renewal, and so to emphasise a positive dimension in tragedy. But obsessed as they were with Greek culture, neither philosopher took note of the fact that the day-to-day thinking of Shakespeare and his contemporaries was rooted in that ancient and essentially paradoxical view of nature.

A.C. Bradley rightly criticised Hegel for underestimating in the tragic process the action of moral evil and the final sense of waste;[7] but he concurred with him by making conflict a central issue in his account of Shakespearean tragedy. He contended, however, that the distinguishing feature of Shakespearean tragedy is not conflict between the tragic hero and someone else, or between groups, but rather conflict within the hero, who is a man divided against himself. Bradley also adapted Hegel's dualist metaphysics, arguing that Shakespearean tragedy demonstrates the existence of an ultimate power which reacts violently against evil but in the process contradictorily and mysteriously destroys much that is good.[8]

In later versions of the conflict theory, tragedy (both Shakespearean and non-Shakespearean) has been construed as a genre which projects mutually incompatible world views or value systems;[9] and then again as one which exposes 'the eternal contradiction between man's weakness and his courage, his stupidity and his magnificence, his frailty and his strength'.[10] Shakespeare's tragedies have been seen as characterised by a disturbing conjunction of the lofty and the comic-grotesque, something which emphasises the coexistence in the hero of nobility and pettiness and reinforces a largely pessimistic view of the way in which Nature produces and destroys greatness.[11] The tragedies of both Shakespeare and his contemporaries have also been read in the light of Marx's materialist Hegelianism as embodying the contradictions and incipient collapse of feudalism and heralding the bourgeois revolution of the seventeenth century.[12]

Attention to the contradictory thrust of tragedy arguably began with Aristotle in the fourth century BC, though his concern in this respect was not with plot, meaning, or characterisation but with emotional effect. Commenting on Aristotle's claim that the success of a tragedy depends on the extent to which it arouses the emotions of pity and fear, thereby effecting a 'catharsis' of these emotions, some theorists have observed that Aristotle's pity and fear signify the contrary responses of attraction and repulsion: pity draws us sympathetically to the protagonist, regretting his or her suffering as unjust or disproportionate; fear denotes an attitude to the protagonist of dissociation and judgement and acknowledges the rightness of what has happened.[13] What Aristotle meant by catharsis has been the subject of much disagreement, but in contemporary usage the term usually implies a state of mind in which the powerful, contradictory emotions generated by the spectacle of great suffering are reconciled and transcended through artistic representation, so that a condition of exultant but grave understanding remains.

3

The models of tragedy which influenced Shakespeare and his contemporaries were not Greek (the great tragedies of Aeschylus, Sophocles, and Euripides) but Roman and late-medieval: that is, the sensational and highly rhetorical plays of Seneca (apparently written for recitation), and the tradition of narrative tragedy represented in England by John Lydgate's *The Fall of Princes* (*c*.1431–9) and the popular, multi-authored collection known as *The Mirror for Magistrates* (1569). Written in the shadow of the emperor Nero, Seneca's tragedies are characterised by a preoccupation with horrific crimes and the tyrannic abuse of power. His protagonists are driven to murder by inordinate passions such as vengeful rage, lust, and sexual jealousy; most of them, too, unlike most of Shakespeare's heroes, are conscious wrong-doers. But they are driven by passions which seem humanly uncontrollable (ghosts, Furies, and meddlesome divinities spur them on) and are often cursed by the consequences of evils rooted in the past; thus they seem more the victims than the responsible agents of their fate. Another common characteristic is their compellingly assertive sense of selfhood; this may exemplify the Stoic notion of an indestructible personal identity (as in *Hercules Oetaeus*) but more often it is a perversion of that ideal (as in *Thyestes* and *Medea*). They see their crimes as defiant expressions of self and unfold this impassioned selfhood in long, declamatory monologues and soliloquies to which Seneca brings all the resources of classical rhetoric. Like their victims, they regularly hyperbolise their feelings by projecting them on to the 'sympathetic universe' and by calling in rage, grief, or despair for Nature to revolt against earth, for primal Chaos to come again.[14]

The Fall of Princes narratives shared Seneca's fascination with power and its abuse. Like him too they emphasised the insecurity of high places and the rule of Fortune or mutability in mundane life. But Fortune and its capricious turns were now explained in Christian terms as a consequence of the Adamic Fall, which brought change and misery into the world. Thus the treacheries of Fortune are afflictions which everyone is liable to, irrespective of his moral condition. The main concern of the *Mirror* authors, however, was to show that Fortune is an instrument of divine justice exacting retribution for the crimes of tyrannical rulers and over-ambitious or rebellious subjects.

Tragic theory in the sixteenth century prescriptively underwrote what was learned from Senecan and Fall of Princes practice. Tragedy, it was emphasised, is 'high and excellent' in subject and style, does not meddle with base (that is, domestic and plebeian) matters or mingle kings and clowns. It uncovers hidden corruption and shows the characteristic conduct and the deserved punishments of tyrants. Dealing with 'the dolefull falls of infortunate & afflicted Princes', it 'teacheth the uncertainty of this world, and upon how weak foundations gilden roofs are builded'. It excites feelings of 'admiration and commiseration', wonder and pity.[15]

4

Shakespeare's affinities with Senecan and Fall of Princes tragedy, and with contemporary tragic theory, will be apparent as we proceed. But I must begin by emphasising difference. Like almost all contemporary playwrights who wrote tragedies for the public stage, Shakespeare departed strikingly from classical practice and neoclassical prescription by his inclusion of comic elements and plebeian characters. This characteristic was due to the influence of the native dramatic tradition (the mysteries and the moralities) which habitually conjoined the sublime and the homely and made its devils and villains either ludicrous fools or mocking comedians. It seems unlikely, however, that Shakespeare's inclusion of the comic in his tragedies signifies a reluctant pandering to popular taste; although he never overtly justifies this practice, the self-reflexive aspects of his art show that early in his career he reflected deeply on the nature of tragedy and evolved a sound rationale for his mixed practice. *A Midsummer Night's Dream* and *Romeo and Juliet*, written at approximately the same time, and strikingly similar in plot and style, insinuate that in real life comedy is always on the verge of tragedy and vice versa, and that each genre must acknowledge that fact by the controlled inclusion of its generic opposite. Theseus' reaction to Bottom's comical tragedy – 'How shall we find the concord of this discord?' (5.1.60)[16] – draws attention to the extraordinarily mixed nature of *A Midsummer Night's Dream* itself and implies by its phrasing that justification for the mixed mode will be found in the correspondence of the play's art to Nature – that unstable order of discordant concord constituted of opposites (the four elements, qualities, and humours) whose changing relationships are governed by Love and Strife. In *Romeo and Juliet*, what seems like a romantic comedy in the making suddenly hurtles towards tragedy with the violent death of the great jester Mercutio; for this defiantly unclassical procedure Friar Lawrence's discourse on the contrarious and paradoxical dynamics of Nature offers a lengthily explicit if oblique justification (2.2.1–30).

Apart from contributing to a more inclusive kind of tragedy than anything attempted in Greece or Rome, Shakespeare's comic element serves as a safety valve which forestalls the kind of inappropriate laughter that scenes of great tension and high passion are likely to provoke.[17] It is woven into the fabric of the drama, too, being psychologically consistent with the satiric, mocking, or deranged aspects of the tragic and villainous characters, and functioning always as thematic variation and ironic counterpoint in relation to the tragic narrative. It may even (as in *King Lear*) intensify the effect of heroic suffering.

A comic safety-valve was particularly desirable, for Shakespeare not only followed Senecan tradition by focusing on passion-driven protagonists but also departed from classical practice by presenting scenes of violent passion on stage instead of confining them to narrative report in the classical manner. His tragedies abound in spectacular scenes where rage and hatred, long festering or suddenly erupting, explode in physical conflict and bloodshed. From the beginning (in *Titus Andronicus*, *Romeo and Juliet*, and *Julius Caesar*), he sought to present in the opening scene a state of conflict either between the protagonist and his community, or between two sections of the community (one associated with the protagonist, the other with his chief antagonist); and as Bradley intimated, these conflicts relate to a conflict of loyalties, values, or conscience within the protagonist himself.

Open antagonism, however, matters less to the mature Shakespeare than hidden: evil masquerading as good, sinister betrayal, and cunning manipulation are outstanding features of his major tragedies. Thus an essential part of the hero's experience is the horrified discovery that the world he knows and values is changing or has changed utterly. Hamlet expresses his sense of overwhelming change in eloquently cosmic terms whose imagery merits attention: '[T]his goodly frame, the earth, seems to me a sterile promontory. This most excellent canopy, the air, look you . . . this majestical roof fretted with golden fire – why, it appears no other thing to me than a foul and pestilent congregation of vapours' (2.2.300–305). Based on the four elements, the imagistic pattern here shows that Hamlet construes change in terms of the pre-modern model of contrarious nature; in consequence, he tends to see change antithetically, from one extreme to the other. Hamlet's mode of thinking here is entirely characteristic of the tragedies. The great storm passages in *Julius Caesar*, *Othello*, and *King Lear*, where 'the conflicting elements' (*Tim.*, 4.3.231) are thrown into wild disorder, function as central symbols for a pervasive sense of violent change and confusion, a technique reinforced by sustained use of elemental imagery elsewhere in each play. Whereas Seneca's tragedies invoked a general correspondence between disorder in the human and the natural world, in Shakespeare's tragedies the instabilities, ambiguities, and contradictions (as well as the fruitful harmonies) of human nature and history are precisely coextensive with those of Nature.[18]

The extent to which the principle of polarised transformation affects Shakespeare's tragedies can be gauged if we consider the link and parallels between his first and his last tragedy. In *Titus Andronicus* (4.4.62–8), a comparison is made with the historical hero of *Coriolanus*, and for obvious reasons. In each case Rome suddenly becomes so hateful to its great champion that he joins forces with its enemies. Identified during the Renaissance as the archetypal city of order and civility, and associated specifically with law and oratory, Rome becomes in *Titus* a 'wilderness of tigers' where justice is mocked and the pleading tongue ignored or brutally silenced; and this decline into barbarism is comprehensively symbolised by the marriage of the Roman emperor to a barbarian queen. As in *Coriolanus*, too, it is apparent that the disaster which befalls Rome stems from the fact that its respect for the humane qualities which underpin its civility is no greater than – is in fact dependent on – its famed regard for martial valour. Each play depicts the collapse of an order in which these ethical opposites have hitherto been kept in balance; in the elemental terms used throughout *Coriolanus*, fire, signifying martial rage, eclipses water, signifying pity: 'I tell you, he doth sit in gold, his eye / Red as 'twould burn Rome' (5.1.63–4).

Transformation of the community and its representative hero are intimately and causally connected. But the overriding emphasis is on that of the hero: it is the primary source of that 'woe and wonder' which Shakespeare acknowledges at the close of *Hamlet* to be the characteristic emotional effect of tragedy. In play after play, the extreme and unexpected nature of the change which overtakes the hero is underlined by the bewildered comments of those who know him best. And even the unreflective Coriolanus identifies this personal transformation as a universal propensity in Nature. In a world of 'slippery turns', he muses, 'Friends now fast sworn, / Whose double bosoms seem to wear one heart ... break out / To bitterest enmity', while 'fellest foes ... by some chance, / Some trick not worth an egg, shall grow dear friends':

> So with me.
> My birthplace hate I, and my love's upon
> This enemy town.
>   (4.4.12–24)

Because the transformed hero is driven to act with the utmost brutality against one or more of those to whom he is bound by the closest ties, some critics nowadays – and radical ones in particular – are inclined to conclude that the nobility habitually ascribed to him is being exposed as superficial or in some sense inauthentic. Such a conclusion, however, is seriously mistaken and undoes the tragic intention and effect at a stroke, implying that the pity, wonder, and fear which the plays provoke in performance are symptoms of sentimental misapprehension.

Behind Shakespeare's delineation of the hero's moral fall lies a conviction that 'In men as in a rough-grown grove remain / Cave-keeping evils that obscurely sleep' (*Luc.*, 1249–50). One might regard this conviction as an essentialist evasion of historical contingency and social conditioning. In tune with the racist Iago, we might agree that the aphorism would at least fit the Moor of Venice, an 'erring barbarian' familiar with 'antres vast and deserts idle'. But there is quiet play in this tragedy on the relation between the words 'general' and 'particular', and it has the effect of hinting that 'the General' is a representative human being; such hints are reinforced by Iago's reminder that '[t]here's many a beast then in a populous city, / And many a civil monster' (4.1.61–2). When the mad Ophelia says, 'We know what we are, but we know not what we may be', she is recalling not only the baker's daughter who became an owl but also the refined prince of noble mind who killed her father and contemptuously lugged his guts into the neighbour room; and who himself had so aptly reminded her father that 'it was a brute part' (*Ham.*, 3.2.101) of the 'gentle Brutus' (*JC*, 2.1.278) that killed his friend Caesar in the Capitol. Misguidedly essentialist or not, the notion of cave-keeping evils in every human being was one which Shakespeare clearly took for granted.

The speed with which Othello's love and nobility are turned to hatred and baseness is sometimes taken as clear proof that both (if genuine at all) were uniquely fragile. But with Shakespeare speed is a common characteristic of the hero's transformation; it is a theatrical device emphasising both the extremity of the change and the vulnerable nature of all love and all nobility, indeed of all human worth. France observes in amazement that Lear's affection for his favourite daughter turns by way of 'the dragon . . . wrath' to black hatred in a 'trice of time' (*Lr.*, 1.1.122, 215); and concerning Coriolanus, suddenly 'grown from man to dragon', Sicinius asks: 'Is't possible that so short a time can alter the condition of a man?' (*Cor.*, 5.4.9–13).

5

Shakespearean tragedy is centrally concerned with the destruction of human greatness embodied in individuals endowed with 'sovereignty of nature' (*Cor.*, 4.7.35): men whom almost everyone instinctively calls 'noble'. What constitutes true nobility in action invariably proves problematic for the hero, especially when he becomes entangled in the ethical contradictions associated with the notion of 'honour'. Shakespeare habitually exposes to ironic critique a conception of nobility – and so of honour – which is based exclusively on individualist self-assertion and warlike valour; nobility so conceived is implicitly equated with potential barbarism, a denaturing of the self. The tragedies encode an ideal of true nobility which we have touched on already and which was entirely familiar to his audience. Its origins lie in the humanist notion of an educated aristocracy as delineated in Sir Thomas Elyot's *The Governor* (1531) and Baldassare Castiglione's *The Courtier* (1528); in the chivalric ideal of the knight – especially as interpreted by Chaucer in *The Knight's Tale* – as both valorous and compassionate; and in the classical ideal of the soldier-statesman, everywhere implicit as a standard of judgement in Plutarch's *Lives of the Noble Grecians and Romanes* (trans. North, 1579) and embodied in his characterisation of Pericles. The common factor in this long and mutating tradition is the assumption that although the nobility as a class are soldiers by profession, the complete nobleman is one who excels in the arts of both war and peace: he is skilful with sword and tongue and unites in his character the qualities we designate as 'masculine' and 'feminine'. Shakespeare articulates this ideal in both *1 Henry VI* – 'A braver soldier never couchèd lance; / A gentler heart did never sway in court' (3.6.20–21) – and *Richard II* – 'In war was never lion raged more fierce, / In peace was never gentle lamb more mild / Than was that young and princely gentleman' (2.1.174–6). Like Chaucer in *The Knight's Tale*, Shakespeare sometimes associates the dual nature of the aristocratic hero with the myth of Mars and Venus; and he does so because of that myth's well-known interpretation as an allegory of Nature's *concordia discors*. Like Chaucer, too, he likes to play on the social and behavioural meanings of the word 'gentle' as a reminder that a fiery spirit is only half of what is expected in a nobleman.

The villain-hero of *Richard III* is by his own admission a man only 'half made up', framed by Nature for 'Grim-visaged war' and not for love (1.1.9–21); the other tragic protagonists have passionate natures capable not only of heroic wrath and striving ambition but also of great love, and consequently of intense suffering: symptomatically, the first of them is a grieving father who 'hath more scars of sorrow in his heart / Than foeman's marks upon his battered shield' (*Tit.*, 4.1.125–6).[19] The hero's fall involves a self-betrayal or identity loss which constitutes a breakdown in the balance of a richly endowed nature where feeling is so powerful that it is never far from the point of destructive excess. It is this nature which gives rise to the notion that what makes the tragic protagonists great is also what destroys them; 'strengths by strengths do fail', says Aufidius, struggling to understand Caius Martius Coriolanus (*Cor.*, 4.7.55), the man who has the god of war and wrath inscribed in his name. Others may give these characters prudent advice on how to avoid impending disaster, but Romeo's answer to such advice is telling: 'Thou canst not speak of that thou dost not feel' (3.3.64).

Loosely speaking, then, anger and ambition (these comprehending pride, a sense of honour, and the desire for glory) and on the other hand love and grief, are the passions whose overflow brings disaster; and it should be stressed that the first pair are to be seen initially in as positive a light as the second. Following the Stoic philosophers of old, Elizabethan moralists defined anger as a brief madness; but the 'noble anger' which Lear invokes (2.2.450) is a traditional feature of the heroic type, being symptomatic of courage and a sense of both justice and personal worth. The concept of noble anger also points to the affinity between tragic and heroic literature: 'the wrath of Achilles' is the subject of Homer's *Iliad*, it drives the action of Seneca's *Troas* in the person of Achilles' avenging son Pyrrhus, and Pyrrhus is a character with whom Hamlet consciously identifies; indeed Reuben Brower has claimed that 'all tragic heroes in European literature are measured against Achilles'.[20] As for ambition, the dangers to society which its unbridled forms constituted was a familiar subject in Shakespeare's England; but equally commonplace was the notion that 'ambition [is] the soldier's virtue' (*Ant.*, 3.1.22–3; cf. *Oth.*, 3.3.355).

In these attitudes to passion we are confronted with a mindset, characteristic of the period and well fitted to tragedy, which greatly admires and greatly fears excess: where a soldier can be praised because '[h]is captain's heart . . . burst[s] the buckles on his breast' (*Ant.*, 1.1.6–8) and condemned because he 'cannot buckle his distempered cause / Within the belt of rule' (*Mac.*, 5.2.15–16); where lovers who defy society are indicted of blind folly and honoured as 'pure gold' because they show that love of its very nature transcends limit (*Rom.*, 2.1.175–7; 5.3.298). Othello's much quoted claim that he was vulnerable to Iago and his message of hatred because he loved not wisely but too well has been viewed with disdain by many critics. But if it merits disdain, so too does the claim of Timon, the great philanthropist whose boundless bounty undoes him and turns his love of his fellow-men into a raging hatred: 'unwisely, not ignobly, have I given' (2.2.171). Yet the compassionate exclamation which Timon's change inspires in his long-suffering steward precludes a cynical response to his claim: 'Poor honest lord, brought low by his own heart, / Undone by goodness!' (4.2.37–8).

The violent actions of Shakespeare's noble heroes can be linked generically to the monstrous crimes of ancient myth rendered familiar in the Renaissance through the tragedies of Seneca and the *Metamorphoses* of Ovid. They may therefore have seemed rather less astonishing to a contemporary than they do to a present-day audience. However, beginning with Titus, the noble Roman who kills his son and daughter, Shakespeare seems to invite the charge of implausibility by stressing the shocking nature of these violent deeds. Othello's suffocation of Desdemona in her bridal bed is hardly more terrible than the way Brutus – 'the noblest Roman of them all' – bathes his hands exultantly in the blood of the friend he has stabbed to death. And yet Shakespeare will always re-emphasise the fallen hero's nobility, his greatness of heart. Sometimes the contradiction located in such characters is expressed in boldly paradoxical terms: 'You have deserved nobly of your country, and you have not deserved nobly' (*Cor.*, 2.3.88–9; cf. *Ant.*, 5.1.30); but the more typical emphasis, implicit or explicit, and one which helps plausibility, is on the inherent frailty of all humans, including the finest: 'a noble nature / May catch a wrench' (*Tim.*, 2.2.204–5; cf. *Ant.*, 5.1.31–3).

Plausibility is obtained in other ways. First of all, there is the continuous reminder of an intrinsically unstable natural order in which things can rapidly 'decline' to their 'confounding contraries' (*Tim.*, 4.1.20). More obviously, the fatal act is often unpremeditated and rash, the product of an unbearable access of passion, or of temporary madness or something close to madness. Or the hero may be the victim of some profound error related to an idealising capacity which enables him in his own mind to harmonise the fatal act with his moral self-conception, so that what he does seems to him both just and necessary, even a ritual sacrifice performed for the good of the community. Or he has the pure misfortune of being faced with the one challenge that his nature and experience do not equip him to deal with.

He may also be the victim of one or more artful manipulators who know him better than he knows himself: close associates or seeming 'friends / Who can bring noblest minds to basest ends!' (*Tim.*, 4.3.465–6). The figure of the manipulator in Shakespeare's tragedies is descended by way of the morality Vice from the devil of Christian mythos, the tempter who deploys the arts of the orator and the actor in making evil seem good to his deluded victim (see p. 155).

The manipulator is granted heroic status in the devilish protagonist of *Richard III* ('the wonder at a capacity greater than one would expect is the feeling most often inspired by the heroic');[21] but his characteristic role is the secondary one of an *agent provocateur* who operates on the passions of the hero and also, it may be, on others whose susceptibility to his wiles confirms the hero's representative nature. The manipulator sets about changing the hero in full consciousness of what he or she is doing and may even observe the ongoing process with scientific detachment: 'Work on; my medicine works' (*Oth.*, 4.1.43; cf. *JC*, 1.2.308–10).

6

In Seneca's tragedies there is usually a companion figure who warns the protagonist against the dangers of succumbing to passion; the chorus too sometimes moralises on the Stoic ideal of emotional detachment and control. Some of the protagonists' victims, and in the case of Hercules, the protagonist himself, meet death with an equanimity which exemplifies the Stoic ideal of constancy in the face of the worst that Fortune or tyranny can offer. Partly because of Seneca, but partly too because it was deeply embedded in Christian thought and Renaissance culture, Stoicism impinges on the passionate world of Shakespearean tragedy in a number of ways. There are counsellor figures such as Friar Laurence, John of Gaunt, and Menenius, who plead for patience and restraint (Iago appropriates this role with demonic skill). And there is the figure of Horatio, 'more an antique Roman than a Dane' in his attitude to suicide, and in the impression he gives of being one who 'in suff'ring all . . . suffers nothing' (*Ham.*, 5.2.293; 3.2.64).

The hero's attempts at self-control are evidence of his pre-tragic self: Romeo as 'a virtuous and well-governed youth', Hamlet as 'the soldier's, scholar's eye, tongue, sword', Othello as the imperturbable leader in the thunder of battle. These attempts serve also to emphasise by contrast the explosive power of the emotions which have begun to rack him. He may oscillate between moments of Stoic calm and passionate rage and grief; or his rages may hover uncertainly between the kind of rational, heroic anger approved by the Stoics and blind, vengeful fury. Hamlet dwells repeatedly on the conflicting values of impassioned, 'honourable' action on the one hand and rational control and Stoic resignation on the other (critics disagree on whether this dialectic is resolved in the end or not). Blending Stoic and Christian virtue, Lear proclaims that he will 'be the pattern of all patience and say nothing' in response to the cruelty of his daughters; but he has to pass through madness before 'the great rage' subsides in him, and even then the calm is shortlived. The *Lear* world is one whose 'strange mutations' repeatedly shatter the armour of patience.

Shakespeare unquestionably admired much of the Stoic inheritance, but he exposed the inadequacy of its more extreme attitudes to emotion. Thus Brutus's Stoic *apatheia* makes it possible for him to suppress his natural tenderness and murder his friend. *Hamlet* hints at a profoundly subversive point bitterly made by the Duchess of Gloucester in *Richard II* when Gaunt tells her they must wait patiently for God to exact justice on Richard: 'Call it not patience, Gaunt, it is despair' (1.2.29). Anger and lust tear the nation and its two leading families apart in *King Lear*, yet the posture of Stoic detachment self-consciously adopted by the grievously wronged Edgar is quickly rendered irrelevant by a recognition that the human heart, with its capacity for both love and hate, pity and rage, is the source of all that is best as well as all that is worst in human nature; thus the detached Edgar in the end enters the lists (both literally and metaphorically) and demonstrates his fitness for rule by virtue of his just anger and his compassionate love. It is not Coriolanus' ability to subject his notorious wrath to the claims of reason that saves Rome and redeems (and destroys) him, but an access of that natural gentleness which his mother's extreme version of Roman culture precluded. The symbolic geography of *Antony and Cleopatra* emphasises a cultural clash between control and passion, Stoic and Epicurean. At one level, Rome and what it stands for triumphs over Egypt; but at another level the clash is resolved in a synthesis which proclaims the partiality of each set of values: that synthesis being the suicidal marriage of the Roman general and the Egyptian queen.

The combination of truthfulness and formal perfection with which the spectacle of tragic events is presented is one reason why we derive both pleasure and satisfaction from what should in theory depress us.[22] Another reason is the fact that most great tragedies, and Shakespeare's in particular, concur with the maxim that '[t]here is some soul of goodness in things evil, / Would men observingly distil it out' (*H5*, 4.1.4–5). The ending of *Antony and Cleopatra*, with its note of triumph and exultation, is an extreme example of this aspect of Shakespeare's tragic practice. Varying greatly in degree of importance from one play to another, the positive element manifests itself in several ways. Most obviously, there is the restoration of social order, with an emphasis on reunification. In *Romeo and Juliet* the feud that divides the city and destroys the lovers is visibly ended with the mutual embrace of their remorseful fathers. In *Hamlet*, the enemy of the state becomes its saviour; in *Lear*, Albany changes sides and helps instal the virtuous Edgar as king; in *Macbeth*, the alienated nobility are re-united with their Prince, who gives 'thanks to all at once, and to each one' (5.11.40). In *Timon*, Alcibiades makes peace with the Athenians whom both he and 'transformèd Timon' grew to hate, declaring, 'I will use the olive with my sword / Make war breed peace, make peace stint war, make each / Prescribe to other as each other's leech' (5.5.19, 87–9). In the major Roman tragedies, the enemy of the dead hero is magnanimous in victory and acknowledges his nobility; a kind of reconciliation.

More important altogether are the reunions and reconciliations achieved by the protagonists themselves. Like Antony and Cleopatra, Romeo and Juliet are bonded in death, triumphing over those forces within and without which threatened to divide them. Hamlet exchanges forgiveness with Laertes and dies at one with his mother; the repentant Lear and Gloucester are forgiven by their wronged children; Othello begs and receives forgiveness from his wronged friend, Cassio, and dies 'on a kiss' beside Desdemona; Coriolanus takes his mother's hand and so forgives and is forgiven by Rome. Timon, however, dies solitary and unforgiving, making

                    his everlasting mansion
          Upon the beachèd verge of the salt flood,
          Who once a day with his embossèd froth
          The turbulent surge shall cover.
                                    (5.2.100–103)

Yet Alcibiades suggests that Nature forgives Timon, and he signals for others to
do likewise when he looks at the dead hero: 'rich conceit / Taught thee to make
vast Neptune weep for aye / On thy low grave, on faults forgiven. Dead is /
Noble Timon' (5.5.82–5). Given the the intimacy of the Elizabethan theatre,
and the presuppositions and ideals of the time, it must have been easy for a
contemporary audience to become imaginatively involved in the reconciling
process, one which entails confirmation of the hero's nobility as well as
forgiveness of his rash and ignoble acts. Such magnanimity, of course, does not
come quite so easily to many (and especially to readers) in today's anti-aristocratic
and anti-heroic culture.

    The most important distillation from the experience of things evil is
understanding, or what in Aristotelian terminology is called 'recognition'. The
journey of Lear and Gloucester from blindness to vision foregrounds a spiritual
process which affects most of Shakespeare's tragic characters to some degree; it
includes even Macbeth, who realises that the golden round of kingship which
he so desperately desired cannot compare in value to love and friendship lasting
into ripe old age. Perhaps we should feel uneasy about Hamlet's insistence that
Rosencrantz and Guildenstern are not near his conscience, and his public
assertion (contradicting what he said in private to his mother) that it was not he
but his madness that killed Polonius. Is he in this respect somewhat like Brutus,
who dies failing to perceive that the killing of his friend for the crime that he
might commit was profoundly wrong? We may be on surer ground when we
note Hamlet's recognition (based on a new-found belief in Divine Providence)
that it is not for him to choose the time for justice; a recognition which ultimately
allows him to die at peace with himself. Othello's recognition of error and guilt
is so great that he refuses divine mercy and commits suicide in the conviction
that he merits the torments of Hell. Some have accused him, however, of essential
blindness at the end, noting his failure to see that even if Desdemona were
guilty of adultery it would still have been wicked to kill her. However valid in
itself, the point is of doubtful dramatic relevance; to argue thus is to introduce
a kind of mundane calculus which seems out of place in a tragedy of titanic
emotion. On the other hand, the failure of the tragic hero to achieve complete
recognition need not constitute a limitation in the play itself; the understanding
which matters is that which the playwright enables the audience to achieve. But
such understanding characteristically involves an awareness that there is no
univocal answer to some of the questions – moral, axiological, and metaphysical
– raised by the tragic action.

    By far the most positive aspect of Shakespearean tragedy is the final restoration
of the protagonists' nobility, shown by the manner in which they meet death.
The quality usually involved here is that of constancy, signifying truth to self
and one's values: a spiritual triumph over the forces of change. Exemplified in

the deaths of Senecan characters such as Hercules and Polyxena, and in that of the historical Cato (Brutus's father-in-law), constancy was the supreme virtue in Stoic and neo-Stoic thought. But religious persecution gave it a special significance in the sixteenth century, as both the Protestant and Catholic martyrologies of the time vividly indicate. A phrase-concept of great importance in the long tradition of the noble death is that of dying 'like oneself'; and 'like a man' as distinct from a beast, upright and unflinching, with the kind of self-conscious decorum imputed to the first Thane of Cawdor: 'Nothing in his life / Became him like the leaving it' (*JC*, 5.4.25; *Mac.*, 1.4.7–8; 5.11.8).

In its most extreme form, constancy involves suicide, signifying a calm refusal to submit to a superior force and live in misery, dishonour, or disgrace. Brutus and Cassius are obvious examples, but the cases of Romeo and Juliet and Antony and Cleopatra are more truly Shakespearean, since they locate personal identity in the human bond and emphasise the dual nature of the self. Hearing of Juliet's death, Romeo stoically defies the stars and decides to join her; his conduct here contrasts vividly with the adolescent and indeed bestial frenzy of his first reaction to bad news, and marks his attainment of manhood. And Juliet, having already overcome her terrors of isolation in the tomb in order to be true to Romeo, is no less 'manly' and decisive than Romeo in taking her life beside him. Hinted at here is an idea which is fully developed in the suicides of Antony and Cleopatra, each of whom learns from and imitates the other in death; suicide thus symbolises a union of opposites by means of which the full potential of the noble self is disclosed. Othello's hell is that he is eternally separated from Desdemona; yet his dying on a kiss carries the suggestion of an 'atonement' (see 4.1.230) coextensive with the reintegration of self achieved by acknowledging and punishing the erring barbarian that he had become.

The theatricality of all these suicides, especially Othello's, is part of the Stoic style and can be matched in Seneca by, for example, the spectacular deaths of Astyanax and Polyxena, the second of which actually takes place in an open theatre where 'every heart / Was struck with terror, wonderment, and pity'.[23] Claims that we should take the theatricality of Shakespeare's suicides as self-deceiving egotism ignore not only the Stoic tradition in pagan literature but, more importantly, the Christianised Stoicism exemplified in the political executions, martyrdoms, and martyrologies of the sixteenth century. As their accompanying woodcuts vividly indicate, the narratives of execution in John Foxe's *Book of Martyrs* are as theatrical in conception as anything in Seneca; so too was the carefully studied manner in which Mary Queen of Scots and many other persons of high rank met their end on the scaffold in Tudor England. It was an age which gave substance to the observation, 'More are men's ends marked than their lives before' (*R2*, 2.1.11).

7

But before the composed ending there is all that distress: 'Is there no pity sitting in the clouds / That sees into the bottom of my grief?', asks Juliet in despair (*Rom.*, 3.5.196–7). As early as *Titus Andronicus*, Shakespeare gave much attention to scenes where the protagonist cries out in anguish to human or divine witnesses of his misery, miniaturising thus the relationship between the play itself and the off-stage audience. Shakespeare conceives of his tragic characters as individuals to be remembered less for their errors and misdeeds than for the sufferings and griefs they endure in consequence. Prompted in this by Seneca's rhetorical bravura, but vastly surpassing it in dramatic intensity, Shakespeare's eloquence expends itself with astonishing bounty and ever increasing poignancy on the lament of the lacerated heart. Even Macbeth, the relentlessly clear-eyed murderer, utters cries of unassuageable pain which ensure compassion: 'Canst thou not minister to a mind diseased, / Pluck from the memory a rooted sorrow . . . ?' (5.3.42–3).

The causes of suffering in Shakespeare's tragedies are diffuse and involve large abstract forces as well as human error and criminal malice. His characters frequently invoke Fortune in such a way as to grant her the status of a mysterious supernatural being with a cruelly unpredictable personality. In addition, his plots are sometimes informed by a principle of ironic circularity which seems to testify to the presence of the capricious goddess and her famous wheel. Unlike the authors of the Fall of Princes narratives, however, Shakespeare usually intimates that the changes which are imputed to treacherous Fortune are of human origin, and more precisely that her inconstancy corresponds with that of mutable human nature. The case of Richard II is exemplary: his fall from power (symbolised by his voluntary descent to the base court) is preceded by a scene in which he repeatedly swings up and down between wild optimism and total despair. Accident – Richard's delayed return to England, all those mistimed encounters in *Romeo and Juliet*, Emilia's discovery of the handkerchief – may contribute to the advancement of the tragic plot, but it would not have the negative effect it does without the characters being what they are. In that sense, character is fate: one's own character interacting with that of others.

Fate, signifying a predetermined order of events, is less frequently invoked but can be powerfully imagined. In *Julius Caesar* and *Hamlet*, a sense of impending disaster is established by ominous occurrences which provoke fearful speculation in the dramatis personae. What is most notable about such speculation, however, is that it initiates a continuing process of inquiry and interpretation focused mainly on the uncertain significance of what certain individuals mean or intend. Even as Cassius intimates to Casca that disorders in the natural and the supernatural world prefigure what Caesar will do to Rome, thoughtful spectators will respond to his 'But if you would consider the true cause . . . Why all these things change from their ordinance . . . To monstrous quality' (1.3.62–8) by answering that he himself is in process of effecting such a change in Rome and Romans. In *Macbeth* the weird sisters who contrive the hero's downfall merely point him in the way he was already inclined to go (like the 'fatal' dagger); moreover, their treacherous double-talk matches the doubleness in his own and in all nature: 'Double, double, toil and trouble.'

And yet there is a very important sense in which circumstances conspire to produce a situation in which disaster seems inevitable. Hamlet is trapped in a situation where to do nothing is to encourage the spread of evil and to act is to become part of it: 'O cursèd spite / That ever I was born to set it right!'

(1.5.189–90. In *Othello*, chance contributes uncannily to the fulfilment of a doom adumbrated in a series of ominous or ironic observations at the start of the play; but the most cursed spite of all is that the trusting Othello should have as his confidant a man like Iago, without whom the tragedy is inconceivable. Hamlet offers what looks like Shakespeare's explanation for the fall of all the tragic heroes when he speaks of noble and gifted men who are born with some vicious mole of nature ('wherein they are not guilty') that brings ruin upon them; but more often it is arguably their good qualities which, in the given circumstances, prove fatal and become or engender defects. What Iago says of his plan to exploit the 'inclining Desdemona' is applicable also to his attack on the nobly trusting ('free and open') Othello: 'I [will] turn her virtue into pitch, / And out of her own goodness make the net / That shall enmesh them all' (1.3.391; 2.3.351–3). Friar Lawrence comes nearer than Hamlet to the causal centre of Shakespearean tragedy when he observes – while philosophising on the paradoxes of Nature – that 'virtue itself turns vice, being misapplied' (2.2.21).

In the pagan universe of *King Lear* the gods are continually invoked as participants in the tragedy. Their existence, however, is implicitly called in question by the fact that the good and bad events imputed to them are shown by the immediate dramatic context to be of human origin. Very significantly, the deity who is invoked most solemnly and characterised most fully is Nature, a figure whose generosity and ferocity, kindness and cruelty, accounts for the divisions and self-divisions which afflict Lear and his kingdom. The habit of finding causes for human misery outside the realm of Nature is shown here to be part of the confusion in which most of the characters live. Lear points in the right direction when he speaks to the warring elements and asks: 'Is there any cause in nature that makes these hard-hearts?' (3.6.35–6).

In Christian theology, Divine Providence signifies God's ordering of a world rendered imperfect by the Fall, a mode of government which uses all acts and happenings, both good and bad, for an ultimately just and benevolent purpose. In Shakespeare's tragedies and in his tragical histories with a Christian setting, Divine Providence is invoked with varying degrees of emphasis and conviction. At the end of *Romeo and Juliet* the Friar says that '[a] greater power than we can contradict' has thwarted his plan to use the marriage of the lovers as a means of reconciling the two families (5.3.153–4); presumably he would agree with the Prince, who adds that Heaven has, instead, used the deaths of the lovers both to punish the feuding families and to end their discords. But the Friar has shown himself to be a natural philosopher rather than a theologian, and a more satisfactory explanation for the tragedy and its outcome can be found in his disquisition on Nature's dialectical order, where medicines can prove poisonous and poisons medicinal.

Although saturated with doubt and uncertainty, *Hamlet* comes puzzlingly close to a firm providentialism. Horatio believes that 'Heaven will direct' his 'country's fate' (1.1.114; 1.4.68) and Hamlet in the last act begins to see the controlling hand of Providence in his rash and bloody deeds. There can be little doubt that many in Shakespeare's audience would have internalised the Hamlet-Horatio understanding of the tragedy (they have been told by the hero and his friend 'what the show means'); but we can be sure that others would have found it strange that after all Hamlet's sufferings and scruples Divine Providence has arranged for Denmark to be ruled by a violent opportunist with no respect for international law or human life. Moreover, the ghost is the most palpable sign of the supernatural realm; and not only is it entirely ambiguous ('from heaven or from hell'), it is driven by distinctly human passions and recruits Hamlet to its cause by invoking two conceptions of Nature, one associated with 'foul crimes', the other with filial love. Here, as in the incantations and 'natural magic' (3.2.243–8) of Lucianus, whose divinity is witchcraft's Hecate, the supernatural points us back to the unpredictable forces in nature; when light comes, Hamlet's erring spirit returns to its habitation 'in sea or fire, in earth or air' (1.1.134). So whatever significance is attached to Fortune, Fate, and the supernatural in the tragedies, the crucial fact is that they always operate in complete consistency with, and can easily be construed as projections of, the workings of Nature in the actions of men and women.

8

Despite its inherent thrust towards violent confusion, Nature is implicitly understood as an order; and that order is seen primarily in terms of Time. If it is possible to answer Bradley's question, 'What is the ultimate power in Shakespeare's tragic world?', the most reasonable answer would seem to lie here. In pre-modern cosmology, time is the measured movement of the elemental world and, like it, discloses a cyclic pattern of binary and quadruple opposites: day and night, spring and autumn, summer and winter. Accordingly, the confusion of night and day is a characteristic feature of Shakespeare's tragic world. Violent action being often nocturnal either in conception or in execution, night is conceived as a time of rest and peace violated and as a symptom of chaos: the imagery of *Julius Caesar*, *Othello*, and *Macbeth* involves the mythical identification of Night and Hell (Erebus) as the children of Chaos. More importantly, the deeds which generate the tragic action are untimely or mistimed in the sense that they are dilatory or (much more often) either rash or cunningly swift.

Tragic catastrophes, too, reveal the corrective action of time. It is corrective first of all in the sense that it is retributive: untimely acts, whether tardy or rash, are punished in kind. Richard II 'wasted time' and then took from Hereford and 'from Time / His charters and his customary rights'; and 'now doth time waste' him (2.1.196–7; 5.5.49). Cassius kills Caesar 'in the shell' (before his presumptive crime is committed) and then has to kill himself on his own birthday: 'Time is come round, / And where I did begin, there shall I end . . . Caesar thou art revenged' (2.1.34; 5.3.23–5, 44). There is a comparable sense of symmetrical justice in Macbeth's recognition, 'Time, thou anticipat'st my dread exploits' (4.1.160). Variously accented, the pattern of Time's justice can be detected in most of the tragedies. However, this is not to imply that there is neat over-all distribution of justice in most of the tragedies. The villains get their deserts, but it cannot be said that the tragic characters are always responsible for what befalls them, nor even that the issue of responsibility is a primary concern. It can be argued indeed that the disproportion in Shakespearean tragedy between culpable error (where there is any) and consequent suffering, and between the sufferings of the noble and the wicked, is so great as to preclude any idea of justice and rationality. But that is surely too simple, however much it might coincide with how we ourselves would interpret the same events. It would be more appropriate to say that Time – much like Bradley's undefined 'ultimate power' – acts retributively through a convulsive action which sweeps away all but the most fortunate and the most astute.

Time's action is corrective also in the sense that it is restorative, a force for renewal. The cyclic and dialectical order of Nature entails that the positive undertone in Shakespeare's tragic endings is a necessary and logical counterpart to the negative undertone in his comic endings. Nevertheless, the overall impression in the tragedies is of a world where Time is put disastrously out of joint with terrifying ease, and can only be set right again at huge cost. George Chapman's aphorism, *'The use of time is fate'*, is very apt in relation to Shakespearean tragedy, especially if we stress the ominous note in the phrasing.[24]

9

Over the centuries, Ben Jonson's claim that Shakespeare is not of an age but for all time has been continuously endorsed in different ways. Jonson, however, was not denying that Shakespeare addressed the specific concerns of his audience in ways they understood. Historically minded critics rightly remind us that his plays were inevitably shaped to a very considerable extent by the particular experiences and institutions of the age in which he lived. One of the many advantages in approaching the plays from the perspective of Tudor-Jacobean politics and ideology is that we begin to perceive just why tragedy flourished to such an extraordinary degree in the period; for at every level, it was an age characterised by conflict and change: intense, heroic, painful, bitter, and violent.

The collapse of Christianity into two hotly antagonistic sects had a profound effect on Tudor England. The nation was torn between Catholic and Protestant claims to religio-political supremacy, a division which fuelled three rebellions, three attempted invasions, and several assassination attempts on Elizabeth. Moreover, the religio-political division split families and friends, gave rise to cruel personal betrayals, resulted in numerous executions for treason, and left men like John Donne uneasy in conscience after their pragmatic shift from one faith to the other: 'O to vex me, contraries meet in one'.[25]

Interconnected with the Reformation was the decline of feudalism, the rise of authoritarian monarchy, and the waning power of the old aristocracy. It has been plausibly argued therefore that Shakespeare's tragedies reflect 'a tragic view of the decline of feudalism' and that his heroes 'are all living in a new world and are smashed by it'.[26] Insecure as well as authoritarian, and creating unity by coercion and persecution, the Tudor regime severely reduced the freedoms of all its subjects; it thus created an environment in which the inherited tragic themes of tyranny, injustice, revenge, and the outraged revolt of the alienated individual had special resonance.

If the Reformation brought about an intensification of religious faith for many, the spectacle of two theologies diabolising each other necessarily generated an overwhelming sense of religious doubt in the minds of others. Moreover, the 'wars of truth' extended into philosophy, political theory, and science, where Montaigne, Machiavelli, and Copernicus boldly attacked ancient convictions. Sir Thomas Browne was surely in tune with the time when in 1635 or thereabouts he recalled that the wisest thinkers 'prove at last, almost all Scepticks, and stand like Janus [the double-faced deity] in the field of knowledge'. Looking back on the period, he saw it as a time of violent and tragic disunity. And like Shakespeare, he appealed to the contrarious model of Nature as one way of making some sense of it all: 'this world is raised upon a mass of antipathies' and man himself is 'another world of contrarieties'.[27]

It is certainly true that we will never approach a full understanding of Shakespeare's tragedies if we ignore their historically specific filiations. The fact remains, however, that the greatness of these plays has been acknowledged for centuries by audiences and readers in diverse cultures who have relatively little knowledge of that kind. And they do so for the simple reason – I conclude by re-stating an old and battered but enduring truth – that Shakespeare not only engaged with but went through and beyond the contemporary to capture in brilliantly realised characters and deeply moving scenes some of the most fundamental aspects of human nature and experience: the strength and vulnerability, the goodness and the wickedness of men and women; the desolation and courage of the individual at war with society; the cruel injustices and the terrifying uncertainty of life itself.

Chapter 7

Coriolanus: an Essentialist Tragedy

.

1

The title of the present chapter will doubtless seem to many both provocative and naive. For in radical literary theory and criticism, 'essentialism' functions as an index to over two thousand years of philosophical and ideological error from which we in our generation have finally liberated ourselves.

In philosophical discourse, the term refers primarily to a metaphysical doctrine, dating back to Aristotle, which holds that certain entities have essences or properties without which they could not be what they are. In radical theory and criticism, the term is applied most often to the notion of human nature and personal identity as unchanging: history does not change human nature, society does not structure the human subject; thus study of the past becomes the contemplation of an eternal present in which culturally specific differences are largely ignored. Essentialism as so defined is not only anti-historical; it is also deeply conservative, an ideological stratagem for naturalising the dominant social order, smoothing over its contradictions, and inhibiting change. For critics who purport to be rigorously historical, but who at the same time wish to use the texts of the past to effect political change in the present, essentialism is understandably pernicious.

In the study of English Renaissance literature the seminal anti-essentialist influences would seem to have been Bertolt Brecht and Raymond Williams, and the main focus of interest has been on tragedy, chiefly Shakespearean. In this critical tradition, tragedy is not a body of plays about a single and permanent kind of fact. It is made up of varied historical experiences and is to be interpreted in the light of changing conventions and institutions rather than a universal and essentially unchanging human nature. The universalist theory of tragedy, with its insistence that suffering and evil originate in human nature as well as in social and political circumstances, is the product of liberalism's refusal to pursue a fully egalitarian programme. Shakespeare's tragedies, it is stressed, are social as well as individual; they are historically specific rather than universal, being the tragedies of men caught up in, and reflecting, the contradictions of a period poised between the death of feudalism and the rise of capitalism; a period on the verge of revolution.[1]

Refined and elaborated with the assistance of Foucault and Althusser, this Marxist narrative is most conspicuous perhaps in the work of Catherine Belsey and Jonathan Dollimore; but it is very apparent too in other less doctrinaire interpreters such as Annabel Patterson. Critics working in this tradition seek to elicit a powerfully anti-essentialist and historically contingent message from the

123

tragedies of Shakespeare and his contemporaries; and the conflicts and contradictions which affect the tragic characters are of interest to them only in so far as they can be shown to originate in the socio-economic conditions of the given historical period. The anti-essentialist emphasis of British cultural materialists such as Dollimore is shared by their American counterparts, the new historicists. It is so strong that Jean Howard, in her approving 1986 survey of both wings of the radical movement, asserts prescriptively that a genuinely new historical criticism of Renaissance literature must *start* with the assumption that man is not an essence but a historical construction.[2] It does not seem to matter whether the texts manifestly endorse that view or whether it will have to be extracted from them by aggressive reading 'against the grain'.

Although anti-essentialist critics are self-consciously committed to intellectual emancipation, they are arguably insular in their theoretical and methodological stance in this as in other areas. For not only are they determined to find what they are looking for; they also fail to acknowledge that major changes have taken place outside their own discursive field in attitudes to essentialism. No reference is ever made to Saul Kripke and Hilary Putnam, whose work in the 1970s and 1980s on semantic theory, metaphysics, and the philosophy of logic and science has effectively reinstated essentialism as a necessary and valuable hypothesis in Anglophone philosophy.[3] Nor is reference ever made to Scott Meikle, a Marxist philosopher who has paid due attention to the work of Kripke and Putnam. Meikle's book is arrestingly entitled *Essentialism in the Thought of Karl Marx* (London, 1985), and its powerfully argued claim is that the Aristotelian category of essence lies at the heart of Marx's theoretical and practical enterprise. Since Meikle is a British Marxist, it is especially noticeable that cultural materialists have not yet acknowledged his existence. But that is hardly surprising, since to take his findings on board might be to subvert their own project. One anti-essentialist who has shown some self-questioning is Diana Fuss; she concedes that there is a good deal of essentialism in constructionist thinking and that some constructionists have daringly begun to admit this. While insisting that she remains an anti-essentialist, Fuss seeks to preserve and utilise the category of essence and justifies this contradiction by reference to Derrida's stoical concession that we can never get beyond metaphysics.[4] Nowhere, however, does she refer to Kripke, Putnam, or Meikle; unlike Derrida, they would not help to sustain a dogmatic commitment to anti-essentialism.

To adjudicate authoritatively on the essentialist debate in relation to essence per se, or in relation to human nature, requires philosophical training for the first and for the second a polymathic grasp of anthropology, biology, history, and psychology; neither of which I possess. My conviction, however, is that in the time-span of recorded history human nature does reveal constant features; it also appears to me that we would never undertake study of the human past, or of other cultures, unless we believed we had enough in common with its inhabitants to allow us to interpret their actions and understand their distinctiveness. And as I have indicated already, it seems demonstrable to me that Shakespearean tragedy is informed throughout with an essentialist view of human and universal nature; so clearly informed that one can speak with reasonable confidence of conscious authorial intention. I find in these plays what Paul Avis has found in the historical philosophy of Machiavelli, Bodin, Hobbes, and even Guicciardini: essentialism (or uniformitarianism, as Avis terms it) together with a forward-looking awareness of cultural uniqueness. History, it is suggested, makes sense to us, and provides lessons for the present, because, as Machiavelli puts it, 'if the present is compared with the remote past, it is easily seen that', although customs vary, 'in all cities and in all peoples there are the same desires and the same passions as there always were'.[5] To be more precise, although Shakespeare creates a distinctive historical and cultural environment for each of his tragedies, he habitually interprets psychological, interpersonal, and socio-political conflict with reference to that familiar Empedoclean model of nature which I have already discussed here and elsewhere.

2

Coriolanus might seem to be a play which would resist universalist interpretation in the light of this model. A thoroughly political tragedy with no obvious metaphysical overtones, it is concerned with class conflict and the manipulation of power in a realistically conceived, historically specific society. It re-creates republican Rome at the precise point where the plebeians were in danger of losing their newly acquired constitutional rights. Furthermore, in dealing with the mutiny which provokes this crisis Shakespeare minimises the original complaint about usury, foregrounds the complaint about lack of corn, and in this way establishes a strong parallel with the English enclosure and corn riots of 1607 and earlier. And to underpin this connection with the social tensions and conflicts of his own time, he throws into the riotous first scene an impressively precise contemporary reference by alluding to the great frost of 1607/1608, when fires were lit on the frozen Thames. Thus in many critical accounts of the play the dramatic action loses its Roman specificity and becomes instead a metaphor for England's problems in the age of Shakespeare. So for Annabel Patterson 'the essence of the play' is its 'political theory', its 'radical critique of the [undemocratic] English system' in the light of the early Roman republic and its constitutional enshrinement of popular representation. Like Jonathan Dollimore (though less fiercely so), Patterson is dismissive of 'the universalist tradition of critical reading' which 'operates at the transcendental, transhistorical level' – a reading which sees *Coriolanus* as a play less about politics and class than about 'heroic individualism' set against 'a large picture of human nature'.[6]

So hostile is Dollimore to the essentialist notion of heroic individualism or innate virtue that he argues (in Foucaultian style) that Coriolanus' greatness is a mere name, an ideological effect of political powers antecedent to and independent of him: an argument which he seeks to support by reference not only to the text but also to the historical decline of the military and political power of the aristocracy in the seventeenth century.[7] By thus reducing the hero to a man of straw, Dollimore effectively denies the play its status as tragedy and its claim on our emotions. And this, as we have seen, is entirely typical. The Marxist rejection of individualism, its commitment to radical change and its intolerance of anything resembling acquiescence in defeat, together with the

Brechtian ban on empathy, combine to give radical criticism of Shakespeare its inbuilt, though always unacknowledged, hostility to tragedy as such. Because they foreground 'contradiction' more conspicuously than any other form of literature, the tragedies are studied with great interest. But they are never really studied as tragedies: never as plays whose generic context is every bit as informing as their socio-political context. Radical critics have eagerly appropriated Mikhail Bakhtin's theory of the subversive carnivalesque, but they have noticeably ignored his declaration that 'Poetics should really begin with genre.'[8]

3

It cannot be denied that *Coriolanus* is a profoundly political play with fascinating Jacobean resonances; but current insinuations that it is no more than that create an imbalance which is just as extreme as the alleged imbalance created by purely ahistorical, formalist readings of the text. In addition to its historical particularity, both Roman and Jacobean, the play has an essentialist, transhistorical core which is manifestly not the imposition of a reactionary, liberal-humanist criticism. Like all his tragedies, it shows Shakespeare's intention of holding the mirror up to nature – as he understands it – while in the process of dramatising the brief chronicle of a particular time.

We might begin by noting that although Shakespeare links conflict in republican Rome with conflict in Jacobean England, that linkage belongs to a process of comparison and generalisation which is operative within the historical setting of the Roman action itself. It is frequently claimed that the roots of the tragedy lie specifically in the militarism of the Roman nobility; in that respect, however, Rome and Corioli, Coriolanus and Aufidius, are just the same. The envious, glory-hunting Aufidius is simply a less successful and more brutal version of his Roman rival; the Romans defeat the Volscians, but it is the Volscians who begin hostilities, and for no apparent reason (in Plutarch, Rome is the aggressor); and when Coriolanus joins them he is 'godded' for his martial prowess every bit as much as he had been at Rome. As Shakespeare well knew, Mars, father of Romulus, was Rome's official patron; but the most pointed expression of respect for that deity is uttered by a Volscian (5.6.100).[9] Militarism as such is under scrutiny: but militarism seen as a cultural reification of what Fulke Greville in his *Treatie of Warres* called 'the humour radicall / Of violence':[10] that is, the universal instinct for strife and conflict, an instinct which is no less prevalent among politicians and soldiers-turned-politicians (for all of whom words can be swords) than it is among soldiers. In short, the contradictions and conflicts which afflict the Rome of Coriolanus are ultimately located within the Empedoclean model of nature.

In view of the fact that the play conspicuously lacks metaphysical overtones and a feeling for circumambient nature, this claim might seem initially implausible. However, the model is vividly present in the oppositional design which affects every aspect of form in the tragedy.[11] The key to the play's mode lies in Menenius' comment on the news that Coriolanus has befriended his deadly enemy: 'he and Aufidius can no more / Atone than violentest contrariety'

(4.6.73–4). The most significant manifestations of contrarious thinking are to be found in the ubiquitous references to one or more of the four qualities, elements, and humours. That most historically contingent allusion to coals of fire on ice (1.1.172) – probably a reference to the great frost of 1607/8, when it was reported that pans of fire were lit on the Thames – is universalised within a network of antithetical motifs involving the hot and the cold, fire and water. There are about thirty fire images in the play, most of them associated directly or indirectly with Coriolanus: with his 'soaring insolence', his notoriously choleric temperament, and his apocalyptic desire to burn Rome and its musty inhabitants (exactly as 'martial' Tamburlaine burned Babylon). But the fire image is invariably conjoined with its opposite, and this imagistic antithesis is central to the play's imaginative exploration of the inner and outer conflicts which are focused on the principal character. The fire-water antithesis is the focal point for a whole constellation of interconnected polarities: hate and love; war and peace; rage and pity (tears); valour(honour) and mercy; 'surly nature' and 'gracious nature' (2.3.185, 193); patrician and plebeian; pride and humility; male and female.

The universal implications of the fire–water symbolism are greatly enhanced by its implicit association with Mars and Venus: the two planets whose conjunction was said to cause a suspension of the baneful influences of Mars in the sublunary world; the two divinities from whose union was born the goddess Harmonia. The Mars–Venus myth yielded two well-known interpretations in the Renaissance, one negative, the other positive. In the negative interpretation Harmonia is ignored and the myth illustrates the debasing effects of female power on the man of action. In the positive interpretation, Harmonia is remembered and the myth becomes an allegory of the concordant discord, the reconciliation of love and strife, which sustains the macrocosm and the microcosm; it is further associated with the aristocratic ideal of masculine aggression tempered by feminine tenderness, valour married to gentleness and compassion. Both interpretations are implicated in *Coriolanus* (as they had been in *Tamburlaine the Great*, *Othello*, and *Antony and Cleopatra*).[12]

There are several heavily accented references to Mars, but of course the most obvious allusion lies in the hero's name: Martius, meaning Mars-like or martial. The importance of this name is made apparent in various ways. The protagonist is called Martius twice as many times as he is called Coriolanus. In Shakespeare's prefixes and stage directions, he begins and ends as Martius. Although the correct order of his full name is 'Caius Martius Coriolanus', on three occasions Shakespeare (to the dismay of classically trained editors) disregards this order and puts 'Martius' before 'Caius'. Moreover 'Martius' is the hero's family and not his individual name, and yet Shakespeare uses it both for intimate and for public occasions.[13] All the phenomena and qualities traditionally associated with both the mythological and the astrological Mars (he 'struck / Corioles like a planet' [2.2.113–14]) are fed into Martius' characterisation: fire, blood, noise, smoke, ruined cities, weeping widows, grim and frowning expression, red eyes, muscular arm, smoking sword. His own death too is triggered by a furious reaction to the claim of Aufidius – who earlier exclaimed, 'O Martius, Martius . . . thou Mars' (4.5.102, 119) – that he is no longer worthy to name that god.

He himself has no doubt that the essential Coriolanus is defined by his martial name. But just as in time (during the age of the Caesars) Rome would be dedicated to Venus (mother of Aeneas) as well as to Mars, so too Martius is to realise an identity which – symbolically speaking – involves the goddess who tempered the war god's fury and persuaded him to lay aside his arms. No explicit reference is made to Venus (no more than there had been in *Othello*); but given the particular role played by women in Martius' life, none was necessary. Although she is his mother, Volumnia's attempt to persuade him to be hypocritically mild and gentle with the indignant plebeians and tribunes, and so avert calamity, evokes the negative version of the myth, with its characteristic emphasis on grotesque transformation: the attempt, he believes, is an invitation to teach himself 'a most inherent baseness' and to turn his trumpet-like 'throat of war' into a eunuch's piping voice (3.2.111–23). Her successsful attempt to persuade him not to burn Rome corresponds with the other version of the myth. However, she herself is in no sense an authentic Venus-figure, but rather an aggressive female playing the peaceful role with politic skill. It is the gentle and almost silent Virgilia, as well as the gracious Valeria, whose presence validates the event as a triumph for the female principle and the spirit of Venus. The credit for this victory is collective, and it suggests divinity: 'Ladies, you deserve / To have a temple built you. All the swords / In Italy . . . could not have made this peace' (5.3.206–9).

4

The concept of concordant discord postulates a bond of opposites harmoniously conjoined and clearly distinguished; a unified duality or complex oneness; an at-onement which acknowledges and reconciles difference. But the overall character of this play is one which projects disjunctive singularity, violent conflict, change from one opposite into the other, and, more important, a total confusion of the opposites, regression to a state of psychic and social chaos. Martius' pride, crystallised in the famous boast, 'Alone I did it', is the expression of a conviction that he needs no one: neither assistance nor praise. This singularity is coextensive with the spirit of opposition, personified in him from the start. In the first scene he brutally shatters Menenius' attempt to mediate between the plebeians and the patricians. He earnestly seeks the plebeians 'hate . . . and leaves nothing undone that may fully discover him their opposite' (2.2.20). Even when hostilities have ceased and his great enemy has retired to Antium he longs for yet another self-defining confrontation: 'I wish I had a cause to seek him there / To oppose his hatred fully' (3.1.19–20). The oppositional spirit which animates him is reflected throughout the play in the antithetical principle which informs sentence structure, imagery, and the design and sequencing of scenes. What emerges in consequence is a harsh, tense, rigid world of unmediated extremes and polarised absolutes. It finds appropriate expression in the sudden explosion of verbal and physical violence which concludes the play.

Martius' pride is also bound up with a sense of his own constancy and a corresponding contempt for 'the mutable' (3.1.65) plebeians: 'With every minute you change your mind, / And call him noble that was your hate, / Him vile that was your garland' (1.1.181–3). This contempt is ironically misplaced, since an incapacity for flexible change is the initiating cause of his own downfall: he commands 'peace / Even with the same austerity and garb / As he controlled war' (4.7.43–5). Moreover, Rome's chief defender will become its chief enemy, an extremity of change which is defined in the archetypal terms of love and hate: 'my birthplace hate I, and my love's / Upon this enemy town' (4.4.23–4). Menenius, who sees himself as father to Martius, describes himself as 'a humorous patrician . . . hasty and tinderlike upon too trivial motion' (2.1.46–50). 'Humorous' means over-susceptible to the flow of the bodily humours, and so changeable. And it must be taken as an oblique reference to Menenius' 'son', the man whose choleric, intemperate nature makes a mockery of the 'constant temper' (5.2.92) which he frequently boasts of. It is important none the less that Menenius should describe himself as humorous; as in all Shakespeare's Roman plays, we are given to understand that the patricians are just as mutable as the people whose fickleness they despise, and more insidiously and dangerously so. Menenius can be ferociously rude to the tribunes one moment and exquisitely gracious to Roman ladies the next (2.1.1–100). The unbending, forthright Volumnia becomes a cynical advocate of hypocrisy in Act 3; and in Act 5 she engages in a coolly calculated piece of impassioned acting which she must know will result in the death of her son if it succeeds.

More dangerous than the head-on conflict of extreme opposites, or the sudden transformation of one opposite into the other, is the state of confusion; this is the complete antithesis of that true 'integrity' which Martius so admires (3.1.158), but does not understand. The tragic context in Shakespeare invariably reminds us that the word 'confusion' means not only the indiscriminate mixing of things unlike, and the uncertainty which that promotes, but also cataclysm, chaos. It is chaos which Martius has in mind when he says: 'my soul aches / To know, when two authorities are up, / Neither supreme, how soon confusion / May enter 'twixt the gap of both, and take / The one by th' other' (3.1.107–11). He assumes that the way to maintain the state's integrity is simply to eliminate from its political procedures one of the mutually confounding pair. In this assumption he is profoundly wrong, since all integration in the given model of nature is the product not of isolated singleness but of unified and distinguished duality; Rome will not remain Rome unless the plebeians and the patricians can function together in some kind of partnership and accept their mutual dependence. The violent physical conflict provoked by Martius in 3.1 between members of the two classes (a hot explosion of choler spreading from himself to the 'incensed' commoners [lines 30, 62, 82–3, 309]) brings Rome very close to the condition of chaos which he himself predicted. The ominous image for 'Chaos . . . come again' in Shakespearean tragedy is usually a great storm, with the four elements violently at war with each other. But in *Antony and Cleopatra* it is a flood, the submergence or liquefaction of all solid shapes in the overflowing waters of the Nile. And in Act 3 of *Coriolanus* it is that of a city disintegrating in flames. The ominous motif is heavily accented by quasi-choric expressions of panic and dismay; and, of course, it anticipates the great fire which becomes a very literal threat in Act 5:

What is about to be? I am out of breath.
Confusion's near, I cannot speak.
                              (3.1.187–8)

    Fie, fie, fie!
This is the way to kindle, not to quench.
To unbuild the city and lay flat.
                              (lines 194–6)

That is the way to lay the city flat,
To bring the roof to the foundation,
And bury all which yet distinctly ranges
In heaps and piles of ruin.
                              (lines 202–5)

The chaos which threatens to obliterate all distinctions in Rome emanates from the nobility's attitude to war. The play embodies a critique both of Roman-Volscian militarism and of a Renaissance aristocratic code which tended to identify honour and nobility exclusively with martial endeavour. But like *Macbeth* it carries an implicit recognition that the peace of every civilised community depends on the courage of its soldiers, that violence is inescapable, and that the best we can do is to contain it. Containment implies limit and limit distinction: the bond of opposites functions as both. But limit and distinction are precisely what the Roman nobility and its representative hero have lost.[14] Martius loves war so much that he hates those of his fellow Romans who do not, and he even develops a kind of love for his greatest enemy: 'were I anything but what I am, / I would wish me only he' (1.1.230–31). The values of peace (love and compassion) and war (valour) are invariably seen by Shakespeare as female and male, so that here they are entwined in a confusing relationship which is figured in powerfully gendered terms: bloody violence eclipses and appropriates both maternal and nuptial love.[15] Volumnia has so completely internalised the Roman identification of nobility with martial valour that she has suppressed in herself all traces of tenderness and pity and become, like Lady Macbeth, a female man. Instead of transmitting the milk of human kindness to her son through nurturing love, she has instilled in him a conviction that violence is lovely and to be loved: she tells him he sucked his valiantness from her (3.2.129), and assures his tender-hearted wife that 'The breasts of, Hecuba / When she did suckle Hector look'd not lovelier / Than Hector's forehead when it spit forth blood / At Grecian sword contemning' (1.3.40–43). This assurance prefigures a homoerotic displacement of conjugal love in the intense emotional relationships that develop between husbands who share a passion for war. Martius embraces Cominius 'in heart / As merry as when' his 'nuptial day was done / And tapers burn'd to bedward' (1.6.30–32). Being an enemy turned friend, Aufidius magnifies this kind of confusion when he embraces Martius to the exact same bridal tune: 'more dances my rapt heart / Than when I first my wedded mistress saw / Bestride my threshold' (4.5.117–19). Since it is in this passionate speech that he addresses Martius as 'Mars', it may be that we are to see in the reconciliation of these two mighty opposites yet another strange perversion of the Mars–Venus myth. That myth, it will be recalled, was a common motif in epithalamia and masques celebrating aristocratic marriages.

5

This intensely focused vision of conflict, transformation, and confusion in nature's oppositional order constitutes the predominant impression of the play. But there is also adumbrated a psycho-social norm of opposites conjoined in a relationship of harmonious contrariety, unified duality, organic wholeness; this is the standpoint from which both the patricians and the tribunes of the people are found wanting; it is the 'single privileged discourse' which Catherine Belsey maintains is not to be found in this play.[16] There is the example set by Cominius of a Roman soldiership which mediates between the extremes of cowardice and foolhardiness and exhibits at the same time a warm and effective partnership between patrician and plebeian (1.6.1–9). There is Martius' reference to 'friends . . . whose double bosoms seems to wear one heart' (4.4.14). And of course there is Menenius' image of the state as an organic body in which all parts serve the whole. It is true that he not only misapplies the familiar analogy (identifying the patricians rather than the hungry plebeians with the belly); he also deploys it in a fundamentally dishonest manner, using it to support the fiction that he and his fellow patricians are loving fathers to the plebeians (as the name 'patrician' [Latin *pater*, father] suggests). In addition, his use of the organic metaphor largely accords with the use to which it was put in Tudor propaganda, laying more emphasis on the hierarchical than on the interdependent relationship of the body's members. Nevertheless, by addressing the people as 'incorporate friends' who 'mutually participate' with the patricians in the functioning of the body politic (1.1.101, 129), he calls up an interpretation of the analogy which stressed mutuality and shared aims, was familiar in the Middle Ages, and was still alive in the sixteenth century.[17] More important perhaps in relation to Shakespeare's conception of the play as heroic tragedy is the enthusiastic welcome extended to Coriolanus when he returns from Corioli as Rome's triumphant defender. Men and women, old and young, plebeians and patricians, '[w]ith variable complexions, all agreeing' (the phrase is richly suggestive, being an allusion to the doctrine of the humours in the human microcosm) spontaneously combine here to provide the play with its only manifestation of complete social harmony. This spectacle of society at one with itself and its heroic defender is bitterly resented by the two tribunes; they determine to undo it by playing on the people's 'ancient malice' to Martius and on his own choleric complexion (2.1.210–55). In the words of Menenius, they have completely mastered 'the map' of his 'microcosm' (line 62) – a term not used elsewhere in Shakespeare, and very pertinent to the argument here.

Among the play's intimations of harmonious contrariety – with opposites conjoined *and* distinguished – in the personal as distinct from the social sphere is the character of Virgilia as presented in 1.3. Grieving while her husband is at war, and horrified by Volumnia's enthusiastic talk of blood and wounds, she can too easily be taken not just as Volumnia's defining opposite but as a feeble creature in herself. That, however, is to ignore the second half of the scene, which is pointedly devoted to her courteous but firm refusal to bend to the combined exhortations of Volumnia and Valeria to 'turn' her 'solemness out of door' and join them in a cheery social round.[18]

6

Apart from distinguishing between a time for 'mirth' (1.3.104, 109) and a time for gravity, Virgilia here combines love and sympathy with strength. Just so, her husband would have to combine valour with love and compassion if he were to realise to the full Shakespeare's ideal of heroic manhood. His mother's incisive comment, 'You might have been enough the man you are, / With striving less to be so' (3.2.19–20), points to a restless and intense striving for self-realisation.[19] Although in this quest Martius consciously seeks to become another Mars, strife incarnate, there are none the less clear hints that he has a 'doubled spirit' (2.2.116), capable of both tears and fire. His mother, who has successfully thwarted such a development, calls attention to it when he returns in triumph from Corioli and she addresses him as 'my gentle Martius' (2.1.171; cf. 3.2.59). No doubt she means 'honourable', 'noble', 'well-born', but the other sense of the word 'gentle' forces itself on our attention, so that the phrase registers instantly as a perfect oxymoron. However, that there is a gentle Martius still waiting for full expression there can be no doubt. We perceive this immediately after the oxymoron is uttered when the man of thunderous voice turns from his mother to greet the weeping Virgilia. If he rebukes her silent tears, he does so tenderly and with obvious appreciation of what they signify: 'My gracious silence, hail! . . . Ah, my dear, such eyes . . .' (2.1.174–6).[20] There is the same tenderness, again in stark contrast to the immediately preceding scenes, when he comforts his sorrowing family and friends before departing for exile. In view of these revelations, it seems wrong to attach a negative significance to the incident at Corioli when, in his exhaustion, he forgets the name of the Volscian prisoner whom he wants to repay for a past kindness. He admits that during the battle his own kindness was quickly displaced by rage: 'He cried to me . . . but then Aufidius was within my view, / And wrath o'erwhelm'd my pity' (1.9.81–5). What is important is not that he forgets the man's name after the fighting, and so is unable to secure his release, but that his pity returns in the midst of his exhaustion. The fact too that the anonymous Volscian was a 'poor' man (lines 81, 84) and not, as in Plutarch, a 'wealthie man',[21] was surely intended to give the incident a positive significance.

The attempts of Cominius, of Menenius, and finally of the women to persuade Martius not to destroy Rome are all premised on the existence of this other side to his nature. The tribunes too are aware of it: 'You know the very road into his kindness, / And cannot lose your way', says Brutus to Menenius (5.1.59–60). Of course Menenius does lose his way, as did Cominius. Their failure to move Martius ('his injury / The gaoler to his pity' [lines 64–5]) is carefully designed to establish his change of heart as a triumph for feminine qualities and values: *Venus victrix*.[22] Martius has now become, like Mars, an implacable god of choler and fire; but the emphasis is on fire. The plan to burn Rome, of which there is no suggestion whatever in Plutarch, is of immense symbolic value in the great dialectic of contraries. What deserves special attention at this juncture, however, is that Martius' fiery wrath, and the whole idea of burning Rome, are imaginatively associated with that bodily organ where one would also look for signs of tenderness and pity – the eye: 'I tell you, he doth sit in gold, his eye / Red as 'twould burn Rome' (5.1. 63–4).

This point has considerable bearing on the role played by Virgilia in Martius' final surrender to – or reconciliation with – the other side of his nature. Her role in this, I would argue, is more important than his mother's. As usual, Virgilia says little, but her tearful reticence is eloquent; much more eloquent than Volumnia's muscular rhetoric. Seeing Virgilia in tears (it is she who leads the supplicant procession), and before he speaks to his mother or she to him, Martius finds that the whole edifice of his obstinate fury and hatred has begun to dissolve: 'What [are] . . . those doves' eyes / Which can make gods forsworn? I melt, and am not / Of stronger earth than others' (5.3.27–9). He tries to renew his obstinacy, but instead embraces her in 'a kiss long as my exile, / Sweet as my revenge'. Most tellingly, too, he addresses her as 'best of my flesh' (lines 42–5). Why is it then that he retreats from this almost silent resolution of revenge into love and of contrariety into oneness? Why is the process of resistance and capitulation renewed, and at such length? My answer is that his *mother* now begins to speak, and that she *speaks*. By her discourse as well as her presence she instantly conjures up the hard self-image she has created for him, her first words being: 'Thou art my warrior'. How else can he respond now but with a show of stubborn, military resistance, as to a threatening opposite? – 'Do not bid me dismiss my soldiers, or capitulate . . . Desire not / T'allay my rages and revenges with / Your colder reasons' (lines 62, 81–6). And so Volumnia must launch into her 90 lines of persuasion. He listens in silence, unresponsive, and reacts only at the half-way stage when his wife and son add a few words. And it is not their words, but their countenances, their eyes, that move him; he rises to leave, feeling that he will surrender if they remain in sight: 'Not of a woman's tenderness to be, / Requires nor child nor woman's face to see' (lines 129–30). To prevent him leaving, Volumnia renews her verbal attack, even though she sensed at the outset that she 'should be silent and not speak' (line 94). She succeeds in delaying his departure, but her strenuous appeal to his regard for reputation leaves him unmoved. Angrily, she perceives he is not listening, not even looking at her; that it is Virgilia he sees and who moves him: 'Why dost not speak? . . . Daughter, speak you: / He cares not for your weeping. Speak thou, boy' (lines 153–6). Wife and son, however, like father, remain silent; so Volumnia continues, this time in a vein of querulous self-pity: 'Thou hast never in thy life / Show'd thy dear mother any courtesy' (lines 160–61); whereupon he moves once more as if to leave. Volumnia now makes an inspired change of tactics; instead of speech, she assaults Martius with the spectacle of three women and a boy all kneeling before him in petitionary silence: 'I am husht until our city be afire, / And then I'll speak a little' (lines 181–2). On stage there should be a tense, protracted silence after Volumnia renounces speech and before Martius moves. His surrender is formally to her, but spiritually it is to the silent, tearful grace of his wife, best of his flesh. He holds his mother '*by the hand silent*', and his 'eyes sweat compassion' (line 183, SD; line 196).

Because he knows that his change of heart will almost certainly cost him his life, and because he goes back alone to face the Volscians, Martius here achieves heroic integrity, a union of (hot) valour and (moist) pity; his tragedy being that he reaches such a consummation only through death. He has renounced the ethic defined by Edmund for the benefit of the captain who was asked to hang Cordelia: 'To be tender-minded / Does not become a sword'. Aufidius contemptuously condemns him from just such a standpoint, but the crudity of his phrasing emphasises the rightness of what Martius has done: 'At a few drops of women's rheum, which are / As cheap as lies, he sold the blood and labour / Of our great action' (5.6.45–7); 'he whin'd and roar'd away your victory' (line 98). It is suggested too that were it not for the malice of Aufidius, Martius might have achieved a much larger reconciliation of opposites, with peace not only between Rome and the Volscians but also between himself and the commoners. When he marches back as peacemaker to the Volscians, he does so, according to Shakespeare's stage direction, '*the Commoners being with him*' (SD, line 70). And as one of the conspirators bitterly remarks, in an idiom reminiscent of the old Martius, 'their base throats [they] tear with / Giving him glory' (lines 53–4).

Many have claimed that at the end Martius reverts to his old simple self, as if he has learned nothing. He is still so enslaved to the martial code of personal honour, and so uncontrollable in his responses, that a mere taunt from Aufidius – 'Name not the god [Mars], thou boy of tears!' (line 100) – provokes the furious, boastful outburst which triggers his murder:

> *Cor.* Measureless liar, thou hast made my heart
> Too great for what contains it. 'Boy!' O slave!
> Pardon me, lords, 'tis the first time that ever
> I was forc'd to scold. Your judgements, my grave lords,
> Must give this cur the lie; and his own notion,
> Who wears my stripes impress'd upon him, that
> Must bear my beating to his grave, shall join
> To thrust the lie unto him.
> *First Lord.* Peace, both, and hear me speak.
> *Cor.* Cut me to pieces, Volsces, men and lads,
> Stain all your edges on me. Boy! False hound!
> If you have writ your annals true, 'tis there,
> That like an eagle in a dove-cote, I
> Flutter'd your Volscians in Corioles.
> Alone I did it. Boy!
>
>   (lines 103–16)

But it is impossible to hear this in the theatre without a sense of exhilaration,[23] and without sensing too that this is a noble anger and a noble pride, different in kind from all the other outbursts we have heard before. For here is a solitary hero defying his inevitable fate, to be administered by a treacherous enemy who assuredly will not 'do it alone'. More important, here is a blaze of anger provoked by a repetitive, sneering claim that tears and responsiveness to tears are unbecoming in a soldier. What better way could there have been for Martius to die? Even the Volscian senators implicitly endorse what he has achieved when they say to Aufidius: 'Thou hast done a deed whereat valour will weep.' And so too – in the play's last great emotional reversal – does Aufidius himself: 'My rage is gone, / And I am struck with sorrow' (lines 132, 146–7). Valour and tears, rage and pity: such are this hero's epitaph and legacy. It has to be admitted that Martius is the least attractive and the most obviously flawed of all Shakespeare's tragic heroes: 'He hath faults, with surplus, to tire in repetition' (1.1.44–5). Yet his faults are never seen in dissociation from his virtues ('You have deserved nobly of your country, and you have not deserved nobly' (2.3.87–8), and in the contrarious discourse which shapes the play that necessarily points to the possibility of a resolved contradiction, a 'harmonious contrarietie'.[24]

7

The essential Coriolanus can best be defined in anatomical terms: not in terms of the body, nor even the eye (important though that symbol is), but in terms of the heart. As in *King Lear*,[25] the heart, from which emanates pity and rage, functions both as the symbolic centre of the play's contrarious world and as a reminder that intensity of feeling, greatness of heart, *magnanimitas*, is a necessary condition for heroic stature.[26] Coriolanus seems to believe that the heart is synonymous with the self: 'No more of this, it does offend my heart', he exclaims (2.1.167). From the martial standpoint of both the Roman and the Volscian nobility, the heart is simply the source of courage, anger, and manliness. So Volumnia tells Martius, 'I mock at death / With as big a heart as thou . . . Thy valiantness was mine' (3.2.127–9). Menenius claims that Martius is too noble for this world because 'His heart's his mouth . . . being angry, [he] does forget that ever / He heard the name of death' (3.1.253–8; cf. 3.3.23–30). And Aufidius tells Martius that 'men of heart' blushed to see him weep (5.6.99). In this perspective, the heart is perceived as hard and impenetrable. Just as Volumnia was used to load her son 'With precepts that would make invincible / The heart that conn'd them' (4.1.10–11), so Martius urges his men to put their shields before their 'hearts and fight / With hearts more proof than shields' (1.4.24–5). But the military imagery reluctantly concedes that the heart is not naturally invulnerable; it has to be protected. Thus the very first reference to the heart (made by Martius in the opening scene) contains a proleptic irony of great significance. When he angrily warns Menenius that the concession of power to the plebeians will 'break the heart of generosity' (line 210), he means it will 'give the final blow to the nobility' (Johnson). But there is a play on the word 'generosity' which implies that nobility is generosity in the sense of magnanimity, emotional vulnerability, compassion; the phrase thus prefigures the transformation which constitutes both the fall and the fulfilment of 'gentle Martius'. Very neatly, the beginning of that transformation is marked in the last act when Martius asks Aufidius to observe how firmly he has rejected Menenius' appeal for mercy: 'This last old man, / Whom with crack'd heart I sent to Rome, / Lov'd me above the measure of a father' (5.3.8–10). Syntactic ambiguity indicates here that two cracked hearts were involved in that stiffly painful scene and that the heart of Martius will not be proof against the combined appeals of wife, mother, and child. No reference is made to the heart in the immensely moving scene which follows, and none is needed. But Shakespeare carefully defines the death of Martius as the death of a great heart, an explosion of soldierly, heart-felt rage against soldierly contempt for tears and compassion: 'Measureless liar, thou hast made my heart / Too great for what contains it' (5.6.103–4). Like his Shakespearean predecessors, Martius is both heroic and tragic because his feelings – his anger, his hate, and finally his love – are 'above the measure', 'measureless'.[27]

Even *Coriolanus* then allows us to conclude that the attempt to wrench Shakespearean tragedy free from a universalist discourse is textually and historically unsound, and distracts attention from much of its conscious, controlled complexity. Each tragic world in Shakespeare is culturally distinctive but at the same time it is grounded on a construction of reality which his contemporaries considered to have a timeless validity. That construction of reality, moreover, cannot be dismissed as an ideological stratagem for naturalising an undemocratic social order and eliding its contradictions. It may be seen at worst as an attempt to moderate the extremes and blunt the hard edges of a hierarchical order, but equally it may be seen (simply) as a resounding vote for reciprocity, whatever the social system. Since it is a symbolic derivative of male–female relations and basic human passions, it accounts in no small degree for the perennial power, operative across diverse cultures, of these tragedies. Being based too on the notion of an unstable unity and a fundamental contrariety, it can never be said to simplify; on the contrary, it is endlessly productive of contradiction, ambiguity, and paradox. Indeed it may be in part responsible for the intriguing fact that radical critics of Shakespeare are so often undecided individually or divided collectively on whether he is a radical dramatist whose plays question and subvert the major socio-political values of his time, or a patriarchal conservative whose plays produce disorder and subversion only to contain it.

Chapter 8

The Discourse of Prayer in *The Tempest*

My language! Heavens!
        (1.2.431)

You taught me language, and my profit on't
Is I know how to curse. The red plague rid you
For learning me your language!
                (1.2.365–7)[1]

1

Few critics today would attach special significance to Ferdinand's mildly pious little exclamation. For many, however, Caliban's outburst is highly significant, and its meaning more or less fixed. They see it as the most important utterance in a play whose dominant discourse seeks to euphemise colonialist oppression, yet fails to suppress contradiction. The protest of reality itself, the curse produces a moment of absolute moral victory for the enslaved native of the island and is so potent in its devastating justness that it casts a shadow over the final scene, determining in effect our overall conception of the play.

In some of the more persuasive colonialist interpretations, Caliban's curse on his language teacher is taken as proof that language functions in the play in exact accord with the alleged pronouncement in 1492 of the Spanish bishop and grammarian Antonio de Nebrija: 'Language is the perfect instrument of empire.'[2] Such readings, however, do not consider the play's many other allusions to language and how they might strengthen or weaken the colonialist interpretation of Caliban's curse. These allusions function as part of a specific discourse, the language of prayer; it is to this context, I believe, that Caliban's curse (like Ferdinand's pious exclamation) belongs, and from which we must derive its significance. The discourse of prayer, it must be said, is fairly conspicuous in all the romances: it is interinvolved with their providentialist ideology, their special fondness for the numinous, and an idealist mode of characterisation which habitually associates noble characters (the heroines especially) with sainthood and divinity. But although important in this context, the discourse of prayer as used in *Pericles*, *Cymbeline*, and *The Winter's Tale* differs considerably from its role in *The Tempest*, where it is distinguished by its paradoxical and dialectical character and its central involvement in the play's meanings. In fact a more illuminating comparison for *The Tempest* would be with the contribution made by the discourse of prayer to the dramatic character and thematic bias of *King Lear*.[3]

Through analysis of the way in which prayer functions in *The Tempest* I hope to challenge not only the claim that language functions on the island as a colonialist tool but also the notion of an essentially egoistic and tyrannical Prospero and a finally unreconciled Caliban; I would also hope to show that instead of legitimising an intrinsically oppressive hierarchical order, the play, while not dispensing with the hierarchical model of society, advances a levelling, horizontal ethic of interdependence and reciprocity. Although my method is primarily one of close reading, it will entail reference to the way in which the text encodes certain aspects of early modern culture hitherto ignored by critics, and is in that sense firmly historicist. Nevertheless, I shall be implicitly endorsing humanist conceptions of *The Tempest* as a work which is intentionally and effectively of transhistorical as well as contemporary significance. Moreover, although I would not deny that it is deeply engaged with problems of power, authority, and subjectification, my extratextual move will not be towards political but rather towards religious, affective, and rhetorical aspects of Tudor and Jacobean culture. Since politics and religion were so intimately related in the period, this distinction might seem problematic, but I do not accept the assumption that religion should be understood solely in terms of power.

2

I shall begin by noting that the root context of Caliban's curse is a conceptual antithesis that runs throughout *The Tempest*, an antithesis in which the other term is blessing. Curse and blessing are intimately related and unstable opposites, since each is a form of prayer, and since in religious and popular thought what begins as a curse often becomes a blessing, and vice versa. Blessing and curse, however, are not the only forms of prayer in *The Tempest*: there is petitionary prayer and the prayer of worship or adoration. Prayerful and prayerlike forms of expression were classified as figures of speech in rhetorical tradition. In the 1593 edition of Henry Peacham's *The Garden of Eloquence*, 'the most extensive and accurate treatment of the figures in English', the curse (*ara* or *imprecatio*), the blessing (*eulogia* or *benedictio*), and the petitionary prayer (*obtestatio*) are grouped among the so-called 'Figures of Exclamation', those 'commonly used to utter vehement affections in vehement formes'.[4] A figure in the same group closely related to *ara*, and one to which Prospero is often inclined, is *cataplexis* or *comminatio*, in which the speaker 'denounceth a threatening against some person, people, cities, common wealth or country, declaring the certaintie or likelihood of plagues, or punishments to fall upon them for their wickedness' (Peacham gives a biblical example).[5] And a figure closely related to *eulogia* is *paenismus*, where the speaker expresses joy that some good has been obtained or some evil avoided: not necessarily a prayer, but yet an utterance where the speaker might feel, or seem to feel, that he or she is blessed, that something providential has occurred (the paean was originally a thanksgiving chant for deliverance addressed to Apollo or Artemis). Peacham's example is from the

Virgin Mary's 'Magnificat', where Mary rejoices beyond a common joy on hearing that she is to be the mother of the Redeemer: 'From henceforth all generations shall call me blessed' (Luke 1: 47–8).[6]

In Shakespeare's language of prayer, it is undoubtedly the curse that modern audiences and readers will remember best. Both formal and informal, calculated and impulsive, curses abound in the histories and tragedies. Shakespeare's curses are the language of fury, hatred, helplessness, and despair wrought to its uttermost. But the language of prayer continuously if less audibly highlights contrary aspects of human feeling and experience. It is used in expressions of love, kindness, and gratitude, in outbursts of joy and wonder, and in countless eloquent pleadings for mercy, forgiveness, and compassion. Although his plays are essentially secular, Shakespeare drew upon the language of prayer and religion as a storehouse of emotion and symbol to which his audience was readily responsive, using it as a mode of intensified expression for the feelings and values which were of greatest concern to him. The religious symbology of Petrarchan tradition no doubt contributed to this habit of fusing secular and religious expression. It came easily, however, in a culture where 'God buy you' (that is, 'God redeem you') was a common variant for 'God be with you', and neither had yet been contracted to 'goodbye'.[7]

Of special significance in *The Tempest* (as in *Lear*) is the parental blessing and its opposite, the parental curse. The parent's blessing, for which the child customarily knelt, was a familiar and cherished ritual in the Tudor and Stuart period, one which extended into the adulthood of both son and daughter. Richard Whytforde, an early Tudor authority on child-rearing, advised that 'chylder [should] use and accustome theme selfe dayly to aske theyr fathers and mothers blessynges'; and he explained that 'the blessyng of the parents doth fyrme and make stable the possession and the kynred of the childe'.[8] Recalling how he was brought up to reverence his father, Roger North wrote in the later seventeenth century that 'the constant reward of blessing, which was observed as sacred, was a *petit regale* in his closet'.[9] Thus in the most emotionally charged moments in the romances, a daughter or son kneels and a parent blesses (*Per.*, 21.200; *Cym.*, 5.6.266–9; *WT*, 5.3.120–24; *Tmp.*, 5.1.180–84). In *Cymbeline* too the brothers Arviragus and Guiderius beg their 'father' Belarius's blessing before going to war, feeling that without it they will perish in battle; and at the end Belarius restores them to their true father thus: 'The benediction of these covering heavens / Fall on their head like dew' (4.4.44–50; 5.6.351–3).

But the parental curse was deemed no less powerful than the blessing; indeed it seems to have been regarded with special dread and awe: 'the curse of the parents doth eradicate and . . . utterly destroy' the possessions and the kindred of the children, asserted Whytforde (sig. D5v). Such a curse was thought to have blighted the House of Percy in the seventeenth century. In 1628 the ninth Earl of Northumberland's eldest son married the granddaughter of Robert Cecil. Northumberland was bitterly opposed to this union, for Cecil had been largely responsible for his 16 years in the Tower of London. But there were no children to the marriage and superstitious gossip long afterward maintained that this was due to a curse laid by the angry Earl on his son's union. The childlessness of his beautiful daughter Lucy, who married an untitled favourite of James I despite his strenuous opposition, was similarly ascribed to the paternal curse.[10] The tragedy of King Lear and his daughters is comparable, beginning as it does with the bride-to-be departing from her father's kingdom 'stripped' of his 'benediction' and 'dowered' with his 'curse' (1.1.203, 265; Q 17.44), and moving swiftly to another terrible crisis in which he puts the curse of barrenness on her sister. As we shall see, too, the possibility of a father's curse initially shadows the impending union of Ferdinand and Miranda in *The Tempest*.

3

The most offensive curse in *The Tempest*, however, is arguably neither Prospero's nor Caliban's. In the opening scene, the word 'plague' in the boatswain's outburst, 'A plague upon this howling' (that is, the cries of the courtiers) (1.1.35) is followed in the Folio by a long dash; this must have replaced a blasphemous oath or string of oaths which was heard on stage.[11] For the boatswain is immediately condemned as a 'blasphemous, incharitable dog', an 'insolent noisemaker' (lines 39–43); and when he reappears in the last scene in a dumbstruck condition he is greeted ironically as a loud-mouthed blasphemer chastened by experience: 'Now, blasphemy, / That swear'st grace o'erboard: not an oath on shore? / Hast thou no mouth by land?' (5.1.221–3). But the boatswain's outburst was forgivable, since he was being obstructed and distracted by the passengers in his attempts to keep the chain of command between the master and the men ('I pray now, keep below', he had said politely enough to the courtiers [1.1.10]); and it is clear at the end that he is well-intentioned, dutiful, and beyond serious reproach. Although blasphemous, his execrations are comparable to Prospero's 'cataplectic' outbursts against the rebelliousness of Caliban, Ariel, and Ferdinand. But it should be observed, too, that in this opening scene the boatswain's blasphemies are eclipsed by the desperate pieties of others: 'All lost! To prayers, to prayers!', shout the Mariners; Gonzalo cries, 'The King and Prince at prayers! Let's assist them, / For our case is as theirs'; and Gonzalo brings the scene to an end, as Prospero will end the play, with an echo of the Lord's Prayer: 'The wills above be done' (lines 49–52, 63). From the start, the discourse of prayer embodies a sense of the interdependence of human beings as well as of their common dependence on powers they cannot control. It conspires thus with the emblematic nature of the opening scene to reinforce the universal implication of the play: the imperiled ship, with its fearful and fractious passengers, recalls not only the ship of state, any state, but also 'human nature' which, says Bacon in his essay 'Of Adversity', 'saileth in the frail bark of the flesh thorough the waves of the world'.[12]

The long and complex second scene includes Caliban's first curses and a wide range of prayers, together with references to unsolicited blessings or graces. Miranda, one of the play's two main voices of charitable compassion, pleads on the voyagers' behalf with Prospero, the surrogate deity who commands the storm. Her prayers are answered because she is addressing someone in whom 'the very virtue of compassion' (line 27) outweighs the desire for vengeance: 'Tell your piteous heart / There's no harm done' (lines 14–15). Echoing the

Rheims translation of the Bible and its account of St Paul's miraculous voyage from Palestine to Rome, Ariel reports that everyone on board, like everyone on Paul's ship, has survived shipwreck and landed on the island with 'not a hair perished' (line 219; Acts 27: 34). At the end of the scene, however, Prospero plays the implacable god in response to Miranda's triple appeal for pity on Ferdinand's behalf: 'Speak not you for him' (line 463; also lines 478, 504). The reason for his harshness, however, is that he has a blessing in store for Miranda; that reason is buried in his cryptic but noticeably emphatic if not impassioned response to her question as to why he raised the storm: 'I have done nothing but in care of thee, / Of thee, my dear one, thee my daughter' (lines 16–18). (I shall return to this important explanation later.)

However, like any powerful ruler, white magician, or saint, Prospero is no deity but a dependent mortal; and he knows it. As told in this second scene, his own story of survival duplicates the experience of the first scene. He was, he tells Miranda, 'blessedly' helped hither 'by Providence divine' (lines 63, 160). And Providence operated first through Gonzalo, who 'out of his charity' (line 163) supplied him with the material necessities for the journey as well as his books; and secondly through Miranda herself, who was to her despairing father what the comforting angel was to the storm-tossed Paul: 'O, a cherubin / Thou wast that did preserve me. Thou didst smile, / Infus'd with a fortitude from heaven, / When I have deck'd the sea with drops full salt . . . which raised in me an undergoing stomach, to bear up / Against what should ensue' (lines 152–8).

Also in the second scene are Ariel's angry protest and Prospero's cataplectic responses. It might reasonably be said that Prospero's outbursts at this point are hardly distinguishable from Caliban's. His angry words, however, are not curses in the true sense but threats. And although they undoubtedly suggest furious severity and a harsh, inflammable nature, there are mitigating circumstances here which too often are ignored. In the first place, Prospero is working desperately against time when his two servants erupt rebelliously (see lines 36–7, 179–89). More important, perhaps, is the way in which Ariel, being reminded that Prospero freed him from an eternity of pain, acknowledges his own ingratitude, begs 'pardon' for his outburst (line 297), and promises to complete his tasks. Caliban, who also stands accused of ingratitude (lines 347–50), will require more than threats before he will ask for pardon and grace; but he will; as will others, his irascible master included.

The second scene also contains the lovers' expressions of mutual wonder and worship. It has long been observed that in Ferdinand's first words to Miranda there is an echo of Aeneas' address to Venus in Book I of the *Aeneid* ('*o dea certe!*').[13] But it was commonplace in Greek romance and its medieval and Renaissance derivatives for the hero to mistake the heroine for a supernatural being (goddess, angel, or fairy) at first encounter.[14] Moreover, this familiar motif (and the Virgilian echo) is assimilated here to a complex system of religious metaphor. Each lover is divine to the other, the divine symbolising humanity in its ideal form. To Miranda, who carries wonder and admiration in her name, Ferdinand is 'a thing divine' (line 421). To him she is 'Most sure, the goddess / On whom these airs attend', and he prays to her for 'some good instruction' on how he should conduct himself on the island: 'Vouchsafe my prayer' (lines 424–8). Worship is thus the play's metaphor for love and admiration; it is what makes service acceptable, even desirable. So it is relevant also to Caliban, who figures as Ferdinand's antithesis in one of two juxtaposed, semi-emblematic scenes: the truculent logman who curses his master ('All the infections that the sun sucks up / From bogs, fens, flats, on Prosper fall' [2.2.1–2]) is contrasted with the 'patient log-man' who blesses and feels blessed by his mistress in his menial task: 'I do beseech you – / Chiefly that I might set it in my prayers – / What is your name?' (3.1.34–6, 67). Caliban once loved and is still in awe of his master; but such now is his hatred of Prospero that he loses what judgement he has, accepts Stephano as master, and kneels in idolatrous admiration of a gross fool, his man in the moon: 'I do adore thee' (line 139), 'I prithee, be my god' (line 148), 'I'll swear myself thy subject' (line 151). No more maledictions then for the time being: 'while thou liv'st, keep a good tongue in thy head' is his new master's injunction (3.2.113).[15]

Also antithetical to Caliban is 'Holy Gonzalo', as Prospero calls him (5.1.62). Throughout the long scene where he is ridiculed by Antonio for being 'spendthrift . . . of his tongue' (2.1.25), he is motivated in almost everything he says (including his notorious utopian fantasy) by a compassionate desire to distract his master from despairing thoughts about his son's possible death (compare with Miranda's role as the smiling cherubin who saved her father from despair).[16] Correspondingly, Gonzalo criticises Sebastian for feeding Alonso's gloom by suggesting that he is responsible for his son's death: 'My lord Sebastian, / The truth you speak of doth lack some gentleness / And time to speak it in. You rub the sore / When you should bring the plaster' (lines 141–4). It becomes apparent at this point that speech is being thematised in the play. Thus Antonio's attempt to seduce Sebastian into a usurpation plot focuses attention on a courtly perversion of speech's archetypal, rhetorical function. 'He's a spirit of persuasion, only / Professes to persuade the King . . . his son's alive', comments Antonio sarcastically on Gonzalo's benevolent chatter, precisely when he himself is trying to talk Sebastian into murder (lines 240–41).[17] Set thus against Antonio's evil persuasions, the naive-sounding speech of garrulous Gonzalo is rendered doubly positive by its prayerful dimension. His abrupt waking from the sleep shared by himself and Alonso saves both of them from death; and his first words on waking, almost as if the exclamatory words themselves had wakened him, are: 'Now good angels / Preserve the King!' (lines 311–12). His last words in the scene are a prayer for the missing son designed to lift the father's still sinking spirits: 'Heavens keep him from these beasts! / For he is sure i' th' island' (line 329).[18] Implicit here is a recognition, conspicuous in *King Lear* (where Shakespeare plays on the synonmity of 'blessing', 'benediction', and 'benison'), that to bless is to speak well (*bene dicere*).

4

In the mysterious spiritual economy of the island, the fate of the King and his missing son is wholly dependent on Prospero's prayer for his daughter. Prospero watches unobserved the blossoming relationship between Miranda and

Ferdinand that he appeared to oppose and exclaims: 'Heavens rain grace / On that which breeds between 'em' (3.1.75–6). With this prayer, I would suggest, we begin to see much of what the play is centrally about: a father's blessing for a daughter who is herself a blessing. This claim might seem as large as it is novel; but consider Prospero's name in relation to the following affinities (italics mine). Sebastian comments sardonically on the marriage of Alonso's daughter in Tunis: ''Twas a sweet marriage, and we *prosper* well in our return' (2.1.77) – meaning that it was a bitter marriage and that they are cursed on the return voyage; for he adds accusingly: 'you would not *bless* our Europe with your daughter' (line 130). Then in Prospero's wedding masque Juno says to Ceres: 'Go with me / To *bless* this twain, that they may *prosperous* be, / And honoured in their issue' (4.1.103–5). Reflected here is the fact that in Shakespeare's time the word 'prosper' (and its derivatives) was so commonly attached to the idea of blessing as to be almost synonymous with it. To pray for someone's well-being – to bless that person – was to ask that he or she would prosper; and to be blessed by heaven or the fairies was to be prospered by them (like the Latin *prosperare*, 'to prosper' meant both to flourish and to cause to flourish). This near synonymity of the two concepts and terms is commonplace in the Old Testament, where it probably originates; but numerous examples of it can be found in the Shakespeare canon too: 'God and St George . . . prosper our colours in this dangerous fight!' (*1H6*, 4.2.55–6); 'bless it [the marriage] to all fair prosperity' (*MND*, 4.1.89); 'The Lord bless you; God prosper your affairs' (*2H4*, 3.2.289); 'leave we him to his events, with a prayer they may prove prosperous' (*MM*, 4.1.496–7); 'Kind gods, forgive me that, and prosper him' (*Lr.*, 3.7.90); 'Fairies and gods prosper it with thee . . . O you mighty gods . . . If Edgar live, O bless him!' (*Lr.*, 4.5.29–40).[19] *OED* provides pertinent extracanonical instances in Nashe's 'God cherrist and prosperd them with all the blessings he could' (1593) and Cromwell's 'a people so prospered, and blessed' (1651). And since it is close in spirit to the paradoxical temper of *The Tempest*, this from Bacon's *Essays* should be noted: 'Prosperity is the blessing of the Old Testament; adversity is the blessing of the New; which carrieth the greater benediction, and the clearer revelation of God's favour.'[20] What I am suggesting, then, is that the name of Prospero, a name historically associated with the dukedom of Milan, but which here on four occasions becomes 'Prosper', is so deployed by Shakespeare as to signify blessing. Above all, it signifies the blessing of marriage and children. And towards the end it seems also to suggest another kind of blessing, one which is auxiliary to the first. Prospero's last-act promise of 'calm seas, auspicious gales' and 'expeditious' sail (5.1.317–19) evokes the conventional description of favourable winds and trouble-free voyages as 'prosperous' (*Err.*, 1.1.40; *AWW*, 3.3.7; *WT*, 5.1.160).

This identification of 'the name of Prosper' (3.3.99) with the idea of blessing suggests that Caliban's much discussed name may have been affected by the play's discourse of prayer and its antithetical and ultimately paradoxical principle. In the most thorough examination to date of the various theories which have been advanced to account for this name, Alden T. Vaughan and Virginia Mason Vaughan have cast doubt on the 'cannibal' etymology. They have found the 'carib'/'Caribana' etymology quite persuasive, and more persuasive still the claim of Albert Kluyver (made in 1895) that the name derives from the gipsy word for 'black' – *cauliban* or *kaliban* (they note that the gipsy language flourished in sixteenth-century England).[21] I too find Kluyver's theory persuasive, not only because of the structural identity of the name and the adjective but also because Prospero calls Caliban a 'thing of darkness' and a 'devil' (we might recall Lear's execration, 'Darkness and devils!' [1.4.230]). But I would suggest too that the name has another, closely related meaning which is unfolded to us on the principle of *in vino veritas*. Act 2, scene 1 ends with Gonzalo's prayer for his master's son; 2.2 opens with Caliban's fit of cursing against *his* master and ends with his drunken, word-playful song: ''Ban, 'ban, Cacaliban / Has a new master' (lines 183–4). We are alerted thus to the fact that cursing is part of Caliban's name: pertinent here are Edgar's reference to Bedlam beggars 'roaring . . . sometime with lunatic bans, sometime with prayers' (*Lr.*, 2.2.177–82), and York's response to Joan's curses: 'Fell banning hag, enchantress, hold thy tongue' (*1H6*, 5.4.13). Caliban also prefixes the word 'ban' with an appropriate echo of the Greek word for 'bad' or 'evil' ('*kakos*'). A common enough prefix in English, it occurs elsewhere in Shakespeare only in relation to the much cursed 'cacodemon' of *Richard III* (1.3.144), another character who is deformed both physically and spiritually.[22]

5

Even their names then indicate that Prospero and Caliban are involved in a dialectic of blessing and curse; and at the heart of this relationship is the fate of Miranda. Looking into the dark backward and abysm of time, Prospero tells Miranda that her presence on their dangerous voyage turned foul play and trouble into a blessing. But her future on the island can hardly seem auspicious to him; he can only assume that after his death her fate will be rape and motherhood to a brood of little Calibans (1.2.349–53). Hence the shipwreck and his cryptic but earnest explanation that it was all done '*in care of thee, / Of thee, my dear one, thee, my daughter*'. By his 'prescience' (line 181), Prospero saw who was on the passing ship; saw that the voyage home and the future for Miranda would be prosperous only if a genuine peace were established between himself and his old enemy; and saw too that the best way to such a peace would be to unite the two kingdoms through marriage. Everything he does on the island once he has secured the safe landing of the shipwrecked voyagers – separating the mariners and servants from the royal party, isolating Ferdinand from the rest of that party and engineering his 'fair encounter' with Miranda, bringing Alonso through despair and remorse to say, 'I . . . do entreat thou pardon me my wrongs' (5.1.120–21): all this falls into place as being subordinate and auxiliary to the plan for Miranda's salvation. Thus it is surely as incorrect to say that 'Miranda's marriage . . . is designed by Prospero as a way of satisfying himself', 'a means of preserving his authority',[23] as it is to claim that the storm was part of a 'revenge plan' abandoned only in a 'fifth-act conversion' inspired by Ariel (at 5.1.16–30).[24]

Perhaps the most important aspect of Prospero's plan is his tacit acknowledgement that the first prerequisite for a blessed marriage is mutual attraction and choice;

he knows he cannot enforce this, and he clearly sees himself blessed when it happens spontaneously as his 'soul prompts it' (1.2.423, 444, 453). Another and complementary prerequisite which he has in mind, which he considers to be necessary to society as a whole, and which he articulates very explicitly, is restraint, the willed curtailment of freedom, something he himself has to practise when he has his enemies in his power and could well become the tyrant Caliban holds him to be. Without evidence of restraint, he believes, Ferdinand's attraction to Miranda will not be a love based on respect and 'worship' ('With my body I thee worship'), but rather tyrannous, Calibanesque lust. Hence his insistence that if Ferdinand seeks to consummate his union before 'All sanctimonious ceremonies' and 'full and holy rite' are ministered, it will be cursed with sterility and conflict: 'No sweet aspersion shall the heavens let fall / To make this contract grow; but barren hate, / Sour-eyed disdain, and discord . . . with weeds so loathly' (4.1.15–21).

Given Ferdinand's solemn assurance that his passion is under control, almost all the emphasis in the betrothal masque and its aftermath is on blessing. In the 'Solempnizacion of Matrimonye' as established in the Elizabethan Prayer Book, the following blessings (borrowed from the Psalms) are conferred upon the wedded couple:

> Blessed are they that feare the Lorde, and walke in his waies.
> For thou shalt eate the labour of thy handes, O wel is the, and happy shalt
> thou be.
> Thy wife shalbe as the fruitfull vine upon the walles of thy house.
> Thy children like the Oliue braunches rounde about thy table.
> . . . thou shalt see . . . prosperitie, al thy life long:
> Yea . . . thou shalt see thy childre's children, and peace.
> Then shall the earthe bryng furthe her encrease, and God . . . shal geue us
> his blessyng.[25]

Prospero's wedding masque translates these blessings into a classical idiom complicated with suggestions of an English climate and landscape (4.1.60–66, 128–38) in a Mediterranean world. Passing Cyprus en route, Iris arrives to inform Ceres, goddess of earth's plenty, that she has been called 'some donation freely to estate / On the blessed lovers' (lines 85–6). Juno, goddess of marriage, tells Ceres, 'Go with me to bless this twain, that they may prosperous be', and sings:

> Honour, riches, marriage-blessing,
> Long continuance, and increasing,
> Hourly joys be still upon you!
> Juno sings her blessings on you.

Her companion sings of 'Earth's increase' and 'vines with clust'ring bunches bowing', and ends her song: 'Ceres' blessing so is on you' (lines 103–17).[26]

In the last scene, Alonso and Gonzalo add their voices to the prosperous marriage theme and, implicitly, to the ancillary theme of the prosperous voyage. Believing Ferdinand is dead, and hearing Prospero has lost a daughter, Alonso exclaims: 'O heavens, that they were living both in Naples, / The King and Queen there!' (lines 151–2). His discovery that this despairing prayer is to be answered gives an ecstatic quality to the blessings uttered by himself and Gonzalo, adding *paenismus* to *benedictio*:

GONZALO   Look down you gods,
And on this couple drop a blessed crown;
For it is you that have chalked forth the way
Which brought us hither.
ALONSO   I say 'amen', Gonzalo.
GONZALO   Was Milan thrust from Milan that his issue
Should become kings of Naples? O rejoice
Beyond a common joy! And set it down
With gold on lasting pillars: in one voyage
Did Claribel her husband find at Tunis,
And Ferdinand her brother found a wife
Where he himself was lost; Prospero his dukedom
In a poor isle; and all of us ourselves,
When no man was his own.

(lines 204–16)

Gonzalo here reinforces a paradoxical idea already made explicit in the first exchange between the reunited Ferdinand and Alonso: 'Though the seas threaten, they are merciful, / I have cursed them without cause', said the son; to which the father responded antiphonally: 'Now all the blessings of a glad father compass thee about!' (lines 181–3). The same paradox was operative earlier when Alonso's 'great guilt', provoked by the tempest which followed the vanishing banquet, prompted him to think that he was cursed forever by Prospero when in fact he had been subjected to an experience designed by Prospero to lead him through 'heart sorrow' to 'a clear life ensuing'. Asked by Gonzalo – 'I' th' name of something holy' – why he stood in a 'strange stare', Alonso replied (with an acute sense of the sacred and its different languages):

O, it is monstrous, monstrous!
Methought the billows spoke and told me of it,
The winds did sing it to me, and the thunder,
That deep and dreadful organ-pipe, pronounced
The name of Prosper. It did bass my trespass.
Therefore my son i' th' ooze is bedded, and
I'll seek him deeper than e'er plummet sounded,
And with him there lie mudded.

(3.3.93–102)

Symmetrically, the notion of a curse transformed to a blessing first appeared in Prospero's account of his own and his child's exposure to the elements in their terrible voyage; it is manifestly basic to the meaning of the play.[27]

And yet even the blessing celebrated at the end is qualified by Shakespeare's inescapably dialectical sense and by the pressure of the scene's ceremonial and literary intertexts. The contingent nature of the lovers' happiness is acknowledged within the masque by reference to the myth of Proserpina and Pluto ('dusky Dis') and without through its abrupt termination by the 'thing of darkness' and his plot (4.1.89; 5.1.278). This recalls the Prayer Book's marriage ceremony, where the central blessings are followed by reminders of Satan and the Fall in prayers, shared between minister and congregation, for the Lord to 'deliuer us from euil' and 'euermore defende' the wedded pair 'From the face of their enemie'; it recalls too the warning motif of epithalamic tradition enumerating the perils that threaten the marriage being celebrated.[28] Furthermore, Prospero confesses that the blessed marriage of his daughter is a 'dear loss' which he can only endure – convert to another resolved paradox – by praying to Patience for her 'soft grace' and 'sovereign aid' (5.1.144–50).

Prospero's concluding speech ('my ending is despair / Unless I be relieved by prayer') extends the discourse of prayer into the life of the audience. An epilogue's conventional appeal for a gracious response blends artfully with a variation on the Lord's Prayer, a humble acknowledgement that Prospero is dependent on sinful others for pardon and prosperous winds if he is not to remain unredeemed, accursed, imprisoned. Prospero has said that he must acknowledge Caliban as his own (lines 278–9); and indeed there is a curious parallelism between the two at the end. Caliban admits that he was an ass to worship a dull fool and decides to 'seek for grace' and 'pardon' from his master (lines 279, 298–301); Prospero buries the book which he once prized above his kingdom (1.2.168), reduces himself to a common player, and prays to common mortals like ourselves. Caliban's curses, we may conclude, are as integral to the dialectical structure and the discourse of prayer in the play to which they belong as are the cataplectic threats of Prosper and the execrations of Lear, the dragon king who kneels for pardon. They are part of a structure of thought which insists on human limitation and interdependence and on the consequent need for self-restraint, self-knowledge, repentance, forgiveness, generosity, and cooperation: 'Let's assist them, / For our case is as theirs!'

6

There is, then, an abundance of textual evidence in *The Tempest* to suggest the presence of a playwright fully in control of his material and to question the essentially negative accounts of Prospero and his actions which political critique so often abstracts from the play by means of strategic quotation and deconstructive allegations of textual self-contradiction. Some perhaps might claim that the discourse of prayer, elegant and artful though it may be, is simply 'further' evidence of an attempt to euphemise colonial domination of the island. But this argument, I believe, would be hard to sustain. Comparably with its deployment in *Lear* and in the other romances, the language of prayer in *The Tempest* is overwhelmingly focused on the travellers' consciousness of their creatural weakness and dependence, and on their desire to overcome misfortune – shipwreck on an island that none of the nobility wants to colonise: 'Some heavenly power guide us / Out of this fearful country!' (5.1.107–8). Because it contains undoubted echoes of the New World in its richly allusive, symbolic, and universalising design, and because it is clearly concerned with government and control (as well as self-control), one can easily understand why the play has been appropriated as a colonialist allegory, especially by inhabitants of the Caribbean islands. But I would contend that the conception of Prospero as colonist loses much of it persuasiveness – has to be located near the periphery of the play's range of semantic possibilities – when we perceive that his every word, prayer, and act is designed to effect the escape of his daughter and himself from a place they never chose to inhabit.[29]

This is not to say, however, that my own and the colonialist reading of *The Tempest* are mutually exclusive; that one must see the play from the point of view of either Prospero or Caliban. I have already alluded to the harshness in Prospero's exercise of power. I would have to concede further that his punitive treatment of Caliban has a distinctly vindictive and personal edge to it, and that Caliban's position after the attempted rape differs not at all from that accorded by their colonial masters to the Amerindians and the Irish in the seventeenth century. It should be remembered, however, that Prospero's harshness extends to his own kind, that it varies from the seemingly involuntary to the carefully calculated, and that it is never without reasonable or benevolent intent. Caliban is gleefully unrepentant about the attempted rape and clearly signals that he would try again if he had his freedom; Ariel is being held to his side of a bargain at a time of desperate need; Ferdinand is being tested in self-control and in his respect for Miranda; Prospero's enemies are subjected to corrective punishments designed to bring them through suffering to self-knowledge and a change of heart; and all these intents, as I have argued, are part of an overall plan for Miranda's happiness in a world elsewhere.

Moreover, Shakespeare's characterisation of Prospero suggests that he was more tough-minded than many of his critics in his willingness to acknowledge that even the most enlightened and generally beneficent exercise of power has its dark side, and that its coercive and punitive aspects are unlikely to be welcomed by those who experience them. The historical critic must acknowledge too that in the context of attitudes to law and authority in Shakespeare's England, when the absence of a police force and a standing army meant that punishments had to be compellingly deterrent, Prospero's treatment of Caliban would not have seemed needlessly cruel. Elizabeth's advisers often lamented her excessive mildness and clemency; yet this is the woman who, after the pathetically half-hearted and bloodless rising in the North in 1569, angrily demanded – and got – the heads of seven hundred of 'the common sort' who followed the rebellious Catholic earls. There is no evidence that her reformed subjects faulted this colossal barbarity.

7

Uncovering a major discourse in *The Tempest* hitherto unnoticed by commentators, challenging thereby the claim that the play is dominated by a discourse of colonialism to which Caliban's curse is a decisive clue, and redefining the nature of Prospero's governing intention, the interpretation offered here has methodological implications which deserve final emphasis. By ignoring the imaginative and delicately controlled patterns of image, symbol, motif, and diction which give the attentive eye and ear such pleasure, radical criticism also ignores the complex structures of meaning which they embody and which are apt to challenge the fitness of certain interpretive paradigms to particular texts. Disdain for the New-Critical practice of close reading (of the text as a whole) does not promote reliable interpretive procedures. Of course the unduly selective use of textual evidence in support of pre-formed interpretive paradigms – the avoidance of negative or disconfirming evidence – is by no means new in literary criticism (and it remains for readers to decide whether such a tendency is apparent in any part of this book). But where there is a strong ideological commitment, whether socio-political or religious, behind a critical practice, and in particular where criticism is being used with the explicit or implicit intention of effecting social change, there is an almost inevitable bias in the direction of undue selectivity. Precisely exemplified in colonialist readings of Caliban's curse, such a bias should be questioned no less vigorously than was the same bias in the Christian allegorists of yesteryear.[30]

Chapter 9

Marlowe Plus and Minus 'Theory': the Case of *Doctor Faustus*

'View it well'
(*Faustus*, 1.38)

1

By far the most influential play during the English Renaissance was *The Spanish Tragedy*, written (*c*.1585–90) by Thomas Kyd, the unfortunate playwright who was imprisoned, tortured, and professionally ruined as a consequence of having shared lodgings with Christopher Marlowe. One of the most remarkable features of this tragedy is its overt theatricality: its consciousness of itself as drama; its presentation of dramatic entertainments as part of the plot; its continuous use of metaphors that emphasise the resemblance between life and the stage, action and acting, intrigue and plot. There is no theatricality of this kind in Marlowe's *Tamburlaine the Great*. But due in some measure no doubt to the enormous popularity of Kyd's play, the ludic conception is conspicuous in Marlowe's later work: in *Edward II* and, most notably, in *The Jew of Malta* and *Doctor Faustus*.

It was not until the 1960s and after that critics began to pay close attention to the self-consciously theatrical element in Renaissance drama (Shakespeare and the Jacobeans, rather than Marlowe, first attracted attention). They did so to a very large extent because it echoed certain leading preoccupations in the intellectual life of the period. These preoccupations derived from sociological role theory and, later, from poststructuralist and Marxist theories of the self or 'subject'. (Their prevalence in France and the United States during this period owed much to the general sense of disillusion and scepticism generated by the Algerian and Vietnam wars and to a related awareness of the extent to which the individual is at the mercy of the state and its mystifying ideologies.) Role theory suggested that the self is a bundle of roles and that identity is socially bestowed. It encouraged the systematic analysis of social behavior and social structures on the model of drama, in which all action and all roles are prescribed. Role theory thus undermined the commonsense notion of the continuity of the self; it also presented a radical challenge to the humanist emphasis on the ability of men and women freely to shape – in some measure – their own lives and selves.

Postructuralist and Marxist theorising on the nature of 'the subject' quickly assimilated role theory, and for obvious reasons. Marxism insists that human consciousness is determined by social being and not vice versa, and in a sense deconstruction is all about play. The latter's attack on the idea of the unified and stable self followed inevitably from its rejection of structures and of determinate meaning in language: the floating, playful signifier, the endless play of *difference* (where the meaning of every word is dependent on the meaning of another and another and so on), and the notion of perceived reality as mere text, combined to produce the conception of the floating, playful, textualized self (hence Eagleton's floating, self-less Macbeth).

It is easy enough to detect this complex of ideas at work in recent interpretations of the play element in *Doctor Faustus*. Stephen Greenblatt's is not the most extensive but it is certainly the most influential. Like all Marlowe's heroes, Greenblatt explains, Faustus struggles to fashion an identity for himself, but in vain; his self is constructed by the dominant culture against which he rebels, but the 'theatrical energy' and the 'histrionic extremism' that characterise his self-fashioning acts distinguish him from everyone else in the society to which he belongs. This frenetic endeavour to create an identity is expressive, too, of a loss of all belief in transcendent reality, a metaphysical despair that suggests that 'all objects of desire are fictions, theatrical illusions shaped by human subjects'. Thus, like Marlowe's other heroes, Faustus courageously copes with consciousness of the void that awaits him by means of a destructive delight in role-playing, by entire absorption in the game at hand: 'This is play on the brink of the abyss, absolute play.'[1] Greenblatt's study thus encompasses in its interpretive frame of reference not only the socially constructed, multiple self projected by social anthropology, Marxism, and poststructuralism but also the joyous epistemological nihilism of Jacques Derrida and his forebear Friedrich Nietzsche. One recalls in particular Derrida's approval (in 'Structure, Sign and Play in the Discourse of the Human Sciences') of 'the Nietzschean *affirmation*, that is, the joyous affirmation of the play of a world of signs without fault, without truth, and without origin'.[2]

Simon Shepherd builds on Greenblatt's ideas but has his own, characteristically Marxist stance. He, too, finds in the play element of this tragedy a concern with the social construction of the self; even the comic action, when Faustus appears to have his leg pulled off ('I am undone!'), exposes the myth of the unitary subject and shows how 'identity is made and readily unmade'.[3] Marlowe's dramatisation of show and spectacle, with an onstage audience watched by an offstage one, is a proto-Brechtian device that intensifies a prevailing deconstruction of meaning; this in turn contradicts the attempts of religious figures in the drama to impose a coherent pattern of behaviour on Faustus, a character 'moved by the *endless* inter*play* of desire and dissatisfaction' (98; my italics). Shepherd's emphasis, however, is more political than psycho-sociological or philosophical. What the play element in the tragedy primarily signifies for him is 'delight as repression, pleasure as deception' (101), a political phenomenon of allegedly substantial importance in Elizabethan society. Just as the devils distract Faustus from thoughts of repentance by means of play and illusion, just as Faustus himself uses magical illusion to silence a critical knight and charm a group of clowns into a state of comical dumbness, so the Elizabethan ruling class used theatre to help the people forget the real conditions of their lives, to silence scepticism, and to 'manipulate . . . exploit and silence' the lower class (103). Marlowe, Shepherd implies, wryly concedes that what he and his fellow playwrights are really doing is distributing opium to the masses.

Roger Sales builds respectfully on both Greenblatt and Shepherd in what is undoubtedly the most thoroughgoing account of the theatrical element in the play: role-theory determinism, deconstructive epistemological nihilism, and a Marxist vision of Elizabethan society as a system of repression are all in evidence.[4] Marlowe's plays are historically contextualised in a society where public life is conceived of as a 'Theatre of Hell': a world of espionage, conspiracy, treason trials, staged public punishments and executions (the latter being seen through the lens of that key poststructuralist text, Michel Foucault's *Discipline and Punish*, especially its chapter on 'The Spectacle of the Scaffold'). In poststructuralist fashion, Sales sees Marlowe's historical setting not as context but as text – dramatic text, however. Everything in this society, he explains, was dramatised. His view of the Elizabethan political play-text allows him to see Faustus and the Elizabethan playwright as mirror images of each other. Like the playwright, Faustus is a kind of vagrant or masterless man (a type viewed by the Elizabethan authorities as a dangerous source of social instability). Like the playwright, he is socially marginalised, the grove in which he conjures being comparable to the public theatres located in the Liberties or outskirts of London (cf. Mullaney on Shakespeare and 'the place of the stage', pp. 15–17 above). Just as the Elizabethan playwright is rescued from his politically vulnerable, masterless condition by royal or aristocratic patronage, so Faustus is given employment and a place in society by Lucifer, whose concerns and tactics are those of a Renaissance prince (141–4). Like any such prince, Lucifer legally binds his subject to him in order to prevent him from rebelling and allows him little in return. As Faustus's performances show, all theatricality does is to fill empty spaces. Despite his early fantasies of imperial conquest, Faustus remains 'dependent upon patronage' (153). He is a mere entertainer, playing at best to coterie audiences and producing shows that do nothing to change the world (152–3). Finally, he is reduced from playwright to actor, being 'condemned to play the part that has been written for him in the theatre of Hell. He must deliver his dying speech from the scaffold and then meet his executioners' (158).

These kindred approaches to the theatricality of *Doctor Faustus* are representative of current critical trends, but I believe them to be profoundly misleading; they blind us not only to the play's central meanings but also to its great subtlety of verbal, symbolic, and theatrical expression. Perhaps the most striking aspect of Greenblatt's elegant commentary is its distance from the text. Although he coins memorable phrases on the hero's theatricality, never once does he quote, or even allude to, any of the numerous passages in the text where theatrical performance or theatrical metaphor is involved. Thus his use of the role metaphor is not determined and controlled by the text; rather, it is brought to the text and freely applied. His remarks on desperate role-playing and energetic theatricality refer to *Tamburlaine* as well as *Doctor Faustus*, even though there are no staged plays and no theatrical metaphors in *Tamburlaine*: as in Sales's book, sociological role theory, with its notorious tendency to kidnap all human behaviour indiscriminately, takes precedence over the texts and blurs the distinctive significances and formal qualities of each. As if to present his method as rigorously historical, he begins his chapter on Marlowe with a lengthy quotation from a contemporary document exemplifying Elizabethan colonialist endeavours. Not untypically, however, he seriously if not wilfully misinterprets this text (see p. 171, n. 10 below); and he makes no attempt whatever to locate the theatricality of *Doctor Faustus* in the theological discourse or the dramatic tradition to which it belongs, as a genuinely historical approach would require. This lack of both textual and contextual constraint means in effect that instead of the interpretive frame serving to illuminate the text, the text serves rather to give body to the ideas on which the frame is based. For those familiar with Marlowe, Greenblatt's striking phrases point much less obviously in the direction of *Doctor Faustus* than in that of Nietzsche, Foucault, Derrida, and social theorists such as Clifford Geertz and Irving Goffman.

The interpretations offered by Shepherd and Sales reflect the difficulty of extracting a primarily political interpretation from a primarily religious text. Emulating in this the practice of Greenblatt, they respond to the problem in much the same way as did those grave men in the Middle Ages and the Renaissance who felt it necessary to find moral edification in the erotic, mythological tales of Ovid: they allegorise the text. But there is no hint in Marlowe's play that it should be construed allegorically; the political allegory is arbitrarily imposed on it. Unlike Greenblatt, however, both Shepherd and Sales do make forays into the text; yet when they do so, the interpretations they draw tend to fit only the immediate context and to produce contradiction when pursued in relation to the rest of the text. As with Faustus himself, whose biblical quotes in the opening scene are fatally abbreviated, selective quotation brings short-term benefits only. For example, since Faustian illusion makes public fools of the Emperor and a knight, it doesn't make sense to see a specifically working-class victimisation in its fooling of the clowns. Indeed, the whole argument that play should be seen as an instrument used by a cynical ruling class to keep the rest of the people in a state of political passivity is invalidated by the fact that the Emperor is the most enthusiastic and most grateful, as well as one of the most deluded, admirers of Faustus's art. (The enthusiasm of the English aristocracy for dramatic entertainments of all kinds corresponds with the Emperor's enthusiasm and further weakens the play-as-political-repression argument.) In Sales's interpretation, too, explicit identification of the devils with the Elizabethan ruling class problematises the significance of God, the Good Angel, and the Old Man, all of whom oppose Faustus's addiction to play and illusion, and all of whom, in a politically subversive allegory, would be expected to represent the dominant order. How can they be accommodated to the political argument? Where do they fit in? The question is ignored.

2

In what follows, I shall attempt to offer a reading of theatricality in *Doctor Faustus* that is consistent with the play as a whole and that is inductively drawn from both the play's verbal and nonverbal language and its own discursive and dramatic contexts. A helpful starting point for such a reading will be an account of the relationship between the terms 'lusion', 'illusion', and 'delusion'. Whereas the word *ludic* is a fairly familiar newcomer to our language, the word *lusion* has long since come and gone. Most Latinists like Marlowe would have known what it meant, but it was included in a dictionary of hard words in the mid-seventeenth century, where it was defined as 'a playing, game, or pastime' (see *OED*). It is worth recording here because it serves to draw attention to a basic affinity between the ideas of play, illusion, and delusion that is fundamental to *Doctor Faustus* and its cultural matrix: all three of the associated words derive from the Latin *ludere* (to play) and *ludus* (play, drama). The verb *illude* (now obsolete) and the noun *illusion* in its first and now obsolete sense have a meaning that is also very relevant here: 'mockery, derision, making sport of'. (Pertinent to this context – where Faustus defects to pagan divinities and pleasures and would 'play Diana', goddess of witchcraft – *OED* cites 'it illudes, or mockes the worshippers of these Idols', and 'illudyd by the goddesse . . . Dyan'.) Since *illude* also signifies tricking, imposing upon, deceiving with false hopes, deceiving the bodily or the mental eye by false prospects (*OED*), it also comes very close to the word *delude*, which means to play with someone to his injury or frustration, to befool the mind or judgement, or (a sense now obsolete) to mock, deride, or laugh at.

The ideas of play, game, acting, and mocking laughter were all associated with the devil almost from the beginnings of Christian thought down to the sixteenth century. Even in early Latin treatises on the spiritual life the words *ludere*, *illudere*, and *deludere* are constantly used as synonymous terms for the devil's attempt to ensnare the soul. The relationship between the soul and its enemy is seen both as a gladiatorial contest and a theatrical or illusionary event where the victor triumphantly derides the deluded victim or the unmasked attackers.[5] This identification of evil in serious discourse with game, contest, and theatrical play might seem paradoxical. The explanation for the paradox lies mainly in the fierce hostility of the church fathers to the pagan *spectacula* (plays, games, and gladiatorial contests). Associated as they were with the cults of the old gods, these spectacles were condemned as part of Satan's endeavour to win the faithful back into idolatry. In their attacks on pagan spectacle, the church fathers deployed Plato's well-known arguments against drama and rhetoric for their own purposes and, in the process, gave to the Christian myth of the devil its characteristic features. By a reverse process, the diabolical tempter and accuser of biblical tradition became a creature of boundless, disordered energy, and also a theatrical and oratorical artist who ensnares his victims by means of beguiling shows, cunning impersonations, and persuasive speech. This model of the demonic evil is commonplace in the religious literature and folklore of the Middle Ages. It lies behind the sportive, histrionic, and smooth-tongued Vice of the morality plays and through him exercised a great influence on Renaissance drama. However, since traditional demonology was still very much alive in the sixteenth century, as the witchcraft mania testifies, the conception of evil as sportive and histrionic would probably have affected the dramatists' representation of temptation, corruption, and villainy anyhow.

Other aspects of the devil myth are of relevance to the student of *Doctor Faustus*. Particularly important is the affinity between the demon, the magician, and the actor. All three were condemned in antitheatrical discourse as masters of illusion and transformation bent on glamourizing the immoral and making evil seem good. Significant, too, is the fact that in Puritan diatribes against the stage in the sixteenth and seventeenth centuries, all the old arguments that the church fathers had mobilised against the 'diabolical' art of drama were reproduced and given fresh currency.[6] The playwrights therefore would have been fully acquainted with the ideological basis of the anti-theatrical movement. The chief means they employed to counter anti-theatrical propaganda was to accept and dramatise the theological identification of play with treacherous change and mere evil, and in so doing to distinguish implicitly between play that deludes for wicked purposes and play that works in the service of truth and morality by unmasking theatrical vice and villainy.[7] All the defenses of the drama failed, of course. The Kings party was defeated, the Puritans had their way, and the playhouses were closed in 1642 for about 18 years.

3

In the Elizabethan conception of drama, much emphasis was placed on the element of show and spectacle: what attracts the eye. This fact is very pertinent to *Doctor Faustus*, a play that dramatises ocular experience to a unique degree. We are continually made conscious of the eye, of what it beholds, likes, and dislikes; how it reacts and affects the mind; how it is attracted, fascinated, repelled, manipulated, and misused. Anyone responsive to Marlowe's numerous biblical allusions and alert to this ocular emphasis is likely to be reminded of two well-known passages referring to the dangers associated with the eye, passages well established in the discourse that is most relevant to *Doctor Faustus*. One of these passages is the description in the Book of Genesis of the forbidden fruit as 'good for meat, and . . . pleasant to the eyes', and the serpent's assurance that if it is eaten 'your eyes shall be opened, and ye shal be as gods' (Gen. 3: 5–6; Geneva version). It is impossible not to recall this passage when, for example, Lucifer offers to entertain Faustus with a pageant of the Seven Deadly Sins. A delighted Faustus exclaims, 'That sight will be as pleasing unto me, as Paradise was to Adam', and Lucifer sharply tells him to forget about Paradise and 'mark this show; talk of the devil and nothing else'; and Faustus, having seen the show, declares, 'O this feeds my soul' (5.277–80, 336).[8]

The other passage occurs in the short First Epistle of John (one of the two biblical texts quoted, truncated, and misinterpreted by Faustus in his opening soliloquy). Addressing young men, John tells them not to 'love the worlde, neither the things that are in the worlde. If any man love the worlde, the love of the Father is not in him. For all that is in the worlde (as *the lust of the flesh, the lust of the eyes, and the pride of life*) is not of the Father, but is of the worlde. And the worlde passeth away, and the lustes thereof' (1 John 2: 15; emphasis added). Taken up and quoted by a multitude of Christian moralists and preachers, the key phrase here in relation to Faustus – mockingly described by Mephastophilis as a 'fond worldling' embroiled in 'a world of idle fantasies' (B.103) – is, of course, the parenthetical trinity.

From the beginning of the play to the end, Faustus's enslavement by the devils is intimately associated with his love of what is pleasant to the eye and his corresponding hatred or fear of what is not. His visual problems are primarily in his response to two things, books and shows. In the first scene he takes up Justinian's book of universal law and dismisses it as offering no more than 'external trash' (1.36). He then takes up 'Jerome's Bible' and adjures himself, in a phrase that is to become a refrain in the play, to 'view it well' (1.38). But he does not view it well; seeing, selecting, and quoting only what is 'hard' in the epistles of Paul and John, fitting them to a grimly deterministic theology which justifies his rebellion, he dismisses the Bible in its entirety as 'unpleasant, harsh, contemptible, and vile' (1.41, 110).[9] Conversely, he is 'ravished' by the enchanting arabesques – 'lines, circles, schemes, letters and characters' – of the necromantic book that he presently scrutinises, and so judges its subject to be 'heavenly' (1.50–51, 110).

In his first scene with Mephastophilis, Faustus's weakness and fallibilty are again shown in ocular form. He insists that he must not be attended by an 'ugly' familiar; he infers from the fact that Mephastophilis makes an appearance on being conjured that he has power over him; and he sees only what he wants to see, denying the existence of Hell to a suffering devil who stands before him in person. But it is in his second encounter with Mephastophilis, when the deed is signed, that his capacity for deception and self-deception is most conspicuously associated with seeing and not seeing; here the book (both the book of truth and the book of fantasies) and the show are jointly foregrounded. Faustus is initially moved toward the fatal deed by the Evil Angel's claim that thoughts of contrition, prayer, and repentance are 'illusions, fruits of lunacy / That make men foolish that do trust them most' (5.18–19). The ironic inversion is obvious enough, and it provides an excellent pointer to the significance of what follows. Preparing to sign his covenant with Lucifer (his anti-Bible), Faustus says, 'View here the blood that trickles from mine arm'. When it mysteriously stops flowing, he refuses to read the omen correctly and instead blasphemously quotes Christ's last words on the cross (*'Consummatum est'*). When a second and more explicit omen appears (*'Homo fuge'* ['Fly, O man']: probably another biblical echo), Faustus responds with a biblical quotation, which in its original context stresses God's inescapable presence ('Whither should I fly?'). He tries to tell himself that his 'senses are deceived', and then admits, 'I see it plain, here in this place is writ, / *Homo fuge*!'[10] Although Faustus asserts that he will not fly, Mephastophilis senses Faustus's instability and promptly produces his first theatrical distraction. The reverse of Jerome's Bible and its remembered phrases, this is superficially delightful (dancing devils 'giving crowns and rich apparel') and essentially meaningless: 'What means this show?' asks Faustus, and Mephastophilus replies: 'Nothing Faustus, but to delight thy mind withal, / And show thee what magic can perform' (5.57–85).

In the signing of the deed, which follows the show, Mephastophilis promises to 'perform' and 'effect all promises' made to Faustus, and the context is such that the word *perform*, in the sense of 'to do' or 'to act', becomes and remains thereafter a key pun: 'the miracles that magic will perform' (1.136) have no more substance than what 'your eyes [that is, the audience] . . . see performed' on stage (chor. 3.16–17). It is no accident that the phrase 'form and substance' appears in the first sentence of the deed, or that Mephastophilis promises in the deed to appear to Faustus in what 'form or shape soever he please' (5.96, 103). Faustus is now trapped in the world of delusive, ever-changing, and insubstantial appearances.

The second part of the deed scene reinforces these ideas. Faustus's desire for a wife is answered with a comic-horrific show, a devil 'dressed like a woman, with fireworks' (satiric image of a nagging wife?), followed reassuringly by the promise of a 'bright' and 'beautiful' courtesan: 'She whom thine eye shall like, thy heart shall have' (5.152–5). This promise is immediately succeeded by another distraction, the gift of a magical book whose 'lines' and 'circles' will bring wealth and power if only he will 'peruse it thoroughly' (5.155–7; B text says 'peruse it well' [Greg, 553], thus recalling the original look at Jerome's Bible more exactly). The same pattern is repeated after Faustus's sudden movement of regret and prayer later in the scene: first a terrifying show to soften him up, then a delightful one to distract him, then the gift of a fantastic book. When he prays to Christ, a menacing Lucifer appears ('O what art thou that lookst so terrible?'), frightens him into a renewed expression of allegiance, produces the show of the Seven Deadly Sins mentioned above ('We are come from hell to show thee some pastime' [5.261, 274]), and promises to let Faustus 'see hell, and return', since 'in hell is all manner of delight'. Faustus clearly does not see that he is being 'illuded' by this grim ironist, but no offstage audience could miss the mocking effect. Before parting, however, Lucifer gives him the book that is to be his passport into the world of shifting and illusory appearances: 'In meantime, take this book, peruse it thoroughly, and thou shalt turn thyself into what shape thou wilt' (5.339–42).

Like the witch of popular lore, Faustus becomes a devil-propelled aeronaut. But his global travels are represented as part of the devil's continuing attempt to secure his allegiance by gratifying the lust of his eye. Upon reaching Rome, Faustus recalls 'with delight' that he has seen 'buildings fair and gorgeous to the eye' in France, Germany, and other parts of Italy, but now he 'longs to see the monuments / And situation of bright-resplendent Rome' (7.2, 10, 45–46). (On the pre-Rome travels, the B text has: 'There did we view the kingdoms of the world, / And what might please mine eye, I there beheld' [B.72].) At the same time, Faustus is to be allowed to play mocking tricks on the pope and his cardinals by making them the victims of optical illusion. (He does not see that their situation mirrors his own.) In the B text, Faustus and his familiar conceive of this trickery in theatrical terms: 'Then in this show let me an actor be, / That this proud pope may Faustus' cunning see . . . any villainy thou canst devise . . . I'll perform it Faustus' (B.72–3). Moreover, they subject two of the cardinals to a hoax whereby they are severely punished by the pope – promised 'hellish misery' – in consequence of being struck by Mephastophilis 'with sloth, and drowsy idleness' as they 'turn their superstitious books' (B.74, 78). The pope's angry question, 'Wherefore would you have me view that book?' (B.77), varies the refrain that goes back to the beginning of Faustus's fall from grace ('Jerome's Bible, Faustus, view it well'), and the import of his words is visually reinforced by the stage direction 'Enter the Cardinals with a book'. Since critics have never commented on this highly significant complex of images and ideas, one can hardly accuse the longer B text of labouring the point.

Faustus's largely amiable exploits in German courts are prepared for in a formal speech (chorus 3) whose rhetorical structure (using the figure of symploche, where the end repeats the beginning) carefully suggests that everything he does involves the visual and the theatrical. The speech begins, 'When Faustus had with pleasure ta'en the view / Of rarest things', and ends, 'What there he did in trial of his art / I leave untold: your eyes shall see performed' (lines 1–2, 17–18; cf. B: 'Thou shalt see / This Conjurer performe such rare exploits' [Greg, 1213–14]). Faustus's first visit is to the German Emperor, in whom we at last meet someone of importance who shares Faustus's lust of the eye. (Robin the clown's desire to 'make all the maidens in our parish dance at my pleasure stark naked before me . . . so I shall see more than ere I felt' [6.3–5] is an obvious low-life version of the same.) The Emperor asks Faustus, 'Let me see some proof of thy skill, that mine eyes may be witnesses to confirm what mine eares have reported.' Thereafter the Emperor's relation to Faustus bears an ironic resemblance to that between Faustus and Mephastophilis, both as we saw it at the start and as we shall see it later in the Helen scene. Appealing specifically to Faustus's necromantic powers, the Emperor asks to see his ancestor 'Alexander the Great, chief spectacle of the world's pre-eminence', together with 'his beauteous paramour' (9.68, 24–33). Faustus replies that he will do all that 'by art and power of my spirit I am able to perform'. Conscientiously, however, he explains that he cannot 'present before your eyes the true substantial bodies' of the deceased, but only 'such spirits as can lively resemble them' (9.39–48). Yet such is the verisimilitude of the spectacle that the awed Emperor takes illusion for reality: 'Sure, these are no spirits, but the true substantial bodies of those two deceased princes' (9.66–7).

Again, the B text characteristically amplifies and reinforces this central theme, with much emphasis on spectacle. The simple show required by the A text's stage direction, 'Enter Mephastophilis, with Alexander and his Paramour', is developed into an elaborate pageant of love and conquest introduced by music and a fanfare of trumpets. Alexander is *seen* conquering his enemy and *seen* embracing and crowning his paramour in a dumb show that could be said, in its context, to epitomise the lust of the eyes, the lust of the flesh, and the pride of life. So deluded, too, is the Emperor by the show's verisimilitude – 'so ravished / With sight of this renowned emperor' – that he moves to embrace the two spirits and has to be restrained by Faustus, who exclaims, 'My gracious lord, you do forget yourself: / These are but shadows, not substantial' (B.85–6): words that could be spoken in such a way as to suggest a certain melancholy self-awareness, but that could equally be delivered in a manner that stresses, with piercing dramatic irony, the extent of Faustus's blindness and folly. There is certainly a sharp, ironic pointer to Faustus's folly in trading his soul for illusions and trivia when the emperor delightedly catches sight of the mole or wart that 'this fair lady, whilst she lived on earth, / Had on her neck'. Exclaims the Emperor,

'Faustus, I see it plain! / And in this sight thou better pleasest me, / Than if I gained another monarchy' (B.85).

The Emperor is given an illusionary bonus in Faustus's feat of imitating Diana, patroness of witches, by putting horns on the knight who expresses scepticism about his magical powers. The A text doesn't cue this incident into the visual-theatrical frame of reference, but the B text does. Says Faustus to Benvolio/ Actaeon, 'And I'll play Diana and send you horns presently', and the Emperor exclaims, 'O wondrous sight!' (B.85). The B text provides similar cuing, with additional emphasis on the extravagant valuation of illusory delights, in the scene where Faustus displays his powers for the benefit of the Duke and Duchess of Vanholt: 'Thanks, master doctor, for these pleasant sights; nor know I how sufficiently to recompense your great deserts in erecting that enchanted castle in the air; the sight whereof so delighted me, as nothing in the world could please me more' (B.95).

The ocular-theatrical theme climaxes in the two appearances of a devil in the form of Helen of Troy, 'the pride of Nature's works' (12.22). Faustus conjures up the first vision in response to his friends' request 'to see that peerless dame of Greece' (12.5). In the A text, the First Scholar praises Faustus for 'this glorious deed' (an ironic allusion to the fatal 'deed of gift'), and in the B text, for 'this blessed sight'; in both texts he expresses the hope that Faustus will be 'happy and blest ... evermore' for accomplishing it (the dramatic irony is equally effective either way). Moreover, in the speech of the Old Man in B that follows the departure of the scholars, Faustus is given a warning about mistaking demonic illusion for heavenly reality that pointedly harks back to his crucial inference that whereas divinity is 'harsh, contemptible and vile', magic is ravishing, heavenly. Warning Faustus that magic is likely to 'charm thy soul to hell' and banish him 'from the sight of heaven', the Old Man adds, 'It may be this my exhortation / Seems harsh and all unpleasant; let it not, / For, gentle son, I speak it not in wrath ... but in tender love, / And pity' (B.101). The Old Man might be Jerome himself, interpreting correctly the epistles of Paul and John, selective quotation from which had signalled the end for Faustus – his 'tumble in confusion' (to quote the triumphant Bad Angel).

The second appearance of 'heavenly Hellen' (the old spelling incises the hero's confusion) is specifically designed to 'glut' Faustus's sexual longings and to help him forget spiritual realities (12.73–8). It is prefaced by Mephastophilis's lines neatly twinning the ocular and theatrical motifs: 'Faustus, this, or what else thou shalt desire, / Shall be performed in twinkling of an eye' (12.80–81). The scholars had innocently recalled that Helen's 'heavenly beauty' cost the Trojans defeat in a ten-year war with the 'angry Greeks'. Now, in Faustus's ecstatic address (12.81–100), the destructive and hellish implications of the vision are intimated through ironically inappropriate figures of speech: lyric conceit ('Her lips suck forth my soul'), mythological allusion ('Brighter art thou than flaming Jupiter / When he appeared to hapless Semele'), and hyperbole ('Was this the face that ... burnt the topless towers of Ilium?'). In Faustus's imagination, too, the illusory image is transformed into the heroine of a new drama. Like the Emperor, Faustus is so enchanted for the moment by his vision of a pagan past that he would enter it himself, would 'an actor be' in 'blind

Homer[s]' (5.202) fictions. Indeed, he would make them present and future realities where acting is action:

> I will be Paris and for love of thee,
> Instead of Troy shall Wittenberg be sacked,
> And I will combat with weak Menelaus,
> And wear thy colours on my plumed crest:
> Yea, I will wound Achilles in the heel,
> And then return to Helen for a kiss . . .
> And none but thou shalt be my paramour.
>   (12.88–93, 100)

Among the various ironies embedded in Faustus's great final soliloquy (13.59–115), where he seeks unavailingly to escape from inexorable reality, are echoes of his fondness for pleasant sights and his dislike of what seems ugly and unpleasant. The daylight, which he calls for as an escape from what darkness brings, is conceived by him as the opening of 'fair Nature's eye'. He can 'see, see where Christ's blood streams in the firmament', but, like daylight, it eludes him. Instead, he can 'see where God . . . bends his ireful brows'. He bids the earth to 'gape' and hide him from God's wrath, but God's grim look still follows him – 'My God, my God, look not so fierce on me! – and 'ugly hell gape[s]' to receive him in its maw. His last complete sentence is, 'I'll burn my books!': he does not mean (as many have suggested) all his books, all learning, which would not make sense, but rather the necromantic books whose 'lines, circles, schemes, letters, and characters' bewitched his eye and mind.

The B text impressively reinforces the lusion-illusion-delusion complex in the last scene by means of staging, props, and action, as well as language. The scene opens with the demonic trinity entering to 'view' and 'mark' how Faustus 'doth demean himself' in his last desperate moments: he is the miserable protagonist of their play. They are probably located above in the gallery, and their attitude toward their 'fond worling' is one of mocking contempt: 'How should he be, but in desperate lunacy . . . his labouring brain / Begets a world of idle fantasies, / To overreach the devil. But all in vain' (B.102–4). The trinity watches silently as Faustus acts out with his servant a better version of their relationship with him. Faustus asks Wagner if he has 'perused' his will, and a grateful Wagner (who presumably holds the document) replies, 'I do yield / My life and lasting service for your love.' They are silent, too, as Faustus explains to the scholars that he has willed his soul to Lucifer and Mephastophilis. When the scholars depart, urging prayer, Mephastophilis enters to ban such thoughts: 'Despair, think only upon hell; / For that must be thy mansion, there to dwell' (B.105). There could be acute demonic mockery in this sentence, linking up Mephastophilis's accusation of 'desperate lunacy', with Faustus's love of 'divine astrology', and with his playing the part of Diana (Luna, the Moon), goddess of witchcraft. For as Elizabethans with minimal knowledge of astrology could have recalled, *mansion* means not only a 'dwelling place' but also 'one of the twenty-eight divisions of the ecliptic occupied by the moon on successive days' (see *OED*, which cites Hawes, 1509, 'Dyane . . . entered the Crab, her propre mancyon'). Elizabethans would also have recalled their belief that 'lunacy' is a form of temporary madness caused by changes of the moon.

There is certainly ironic mockery in what follows, conjoined with a triumphant claim to ocular trickery. The puns here on *passage* (cf. Bad Angel's 'Go forward, Faustus, in that famous art'), on *Dam'd*, and on *I*, and the use of the key verb *view*, are all most pertinent:

> (Faustus)
> O thou bewitching fiend, 'twas thy temptation
> Hath robbed me of eternal happiness.
> (Mephastophilis)
> I do confess it Faustus, and rejoice!
> 'Twas I, that when thou wer't i' the way to heaven
> Dam'd up thy passage; when thou took'st the book
> To view the Scripture, then I turned the leaves
> And led thine eye.
> What weep'st thou? 'Tis too late, despair, farewell.
> Fools that will laugh on earth, must weep in hell.
>   (B.105)

After this, the Good Angel and the Bad Angel enter to show, as well as to describe, the consequences of Faustus's having 'loved the world' instead of 'sweet divinity' (B.104–7). A throne, symbolising the 'resplendent glory' in heaven that could have been his, descends to the accompaniment of music. Then, 'Hell is discovered', according to a stage direction. Presumably, a trapdoor is opened, with smoke issuing forth, in sharp visual contrast to the ascending throne, and the Bad Angel gleefully enumerates the horrors to be seen below. Noticeable here is the use (as in chorus 3) of the figure symploche to frame the idea of hell pains as punishment for the eye's lust. Noticeable, too, is Faustus's agonised appreciation of that idea:

> (Bad Angel)
> Now Faustus, let thine eyes with horror stare
> Into that vast perpetual torture-house.
> There are the Furies tossing damned souls,
> On burning forks; there, bodies boil in lead.
> There are live quarters broiling on the coals,
> That ne'er can die! This ever-burning chair
> Is for o'er tortured souls to rest then in.
> These, that are fed with sops of flaming fire,
> Were gluttons, and loved only delicates,
> And laughed to see the poor starve at their gates.
> But yet these are nothing. Thou shalt see
> Ten thousand tortures that more horrid be.
> (Faustus)
> O, I have seen enough to torture me.
>   (B.106)

4

The fantasies to which Faustus falls victim can be reduced to two delusions, the more important of which is the belief that magic will make him godlike. For him, the essence of divinity is power. He dismisses the lawful sciences and professions as being fit only for 'servile' and 'base' creatures (1.36, 109) and chooses magic because it will make him like Jove, 'lord and commander' not only of the natural elements but also of demons and men (1.77). Faustus expects to have 'servile spirits' who will enable him to eclipse all rivals in the political world, just as he has done unaided in the intellectual. Thus he will 'reign sole king' of the German provinces (1.94) and the Emperor will become his deputy or viceroy (4.111).

Faustus's initial attitude toward Mephastophilis is imperious; he requires Mephastophilis to be 'always obedient to my will' and 'do whatever Faustus shall command' (3.31, 99). Although at first Mephastophilis explains (to no effect) that he can 'perform' no more than Lucifer 'commands' (3.43), at their next meeting (before signing the deed) he tells Faustus what he wants to hear: 'I will be thy slave and wait on thee' (5.46). After the signing, their relationship changes completely: Mephastophilis refuses to grant the request for a wife and to tell him who made the world. Faustus's consequent threat to repent is instantly answered by the terrifying appearance of Lucifer himself, commanding Faustus (in the B text) to act like 'an obedient servant' (Greg, 667), which he promptly does. Faustus's expectation of command over earthly leaders is similarly unfulfilled. Such honour as he wins is that due only to a great 'performer'. Indeed, his relations with the great are essentially servile; any show or trick they ask for he provides with humble eagerness. This extreme contrast between promise and performance, to which there is nothing comparable in the source narrative (*The Damnable Life and Deserved Death of Doctor John Faustus*), is underlined clearly enough in the A text (9.12–16), but the B text appreciatively strengthens the emphasis. The magician meekly declares there that 'poor Faustus to his utmost power' will 'love and serve the German emperor' and will 'lay his life' at the 'holy feet' of Bruno, the Emperor's candidate for the papacy; indeed, he is seen to 'kneel and kiss the emperor's hand' when taking his leave of him (B.84, 87). His claim that 'the emperor shall not live but by my leave' and his contempt for base servility (1.30–36) reverberate in the memory with extraordinary force at this point.

Faustus's divine command, then, like Mephastophilis's humble obedience, is mere show and pastime, something that comes and goes in the twinkling of an eye. The other great delusion of which Faustus is the ironic victim is the belief that his rebellious adherence to Lucifer is heroic. He sets himself up at the start as a model of 'manly fortitude' in dismissing thoughts of Hell (3.86); Mephastophilis later encourages him in this self-conception: 'Then stab thine arm courageously . . . be thou as great as Lucifer' (5.49–52). As always in Marlowe's plays, however, the key term for heroic quality is not manliness or courage but resolution, signifying strength of will, the ability to keep one's word and unswervingly follow one's chosen course of action. Thus, Cornelius warns Faustus at the start that 'the miracles that magic will perform' will materialise only if 'learned Faustus will be resolute' (1.133).

The touch of bombast, however; in Faustus's response to this warning ('As resolute am I in this / As thou to live, therefore object it not'), and the way he has to prompt himself when the moment of conjuration arrives ('Then fear not Faustus, but be resolute, / And try the uttermost magic can perform' [3.14–15]), suggest that this resolution has no firm basis in his character, but is really a role assumed to meet the demands of a 'desperate enterprise' (1.81). This suggestion is confirmed by the B text, where 'desperate resolution' is precisely what brings about the humiliating downfall of the sceptical knight Benvolio, one of Faustus's ironic counterparts:

> If you will aid me in this enterprise,
> Then draw your weapons, and be resolute:
> If not, depart: here will Benvolio die
> But Faustus' death shall quit my infamy.
>   (B.87)

The parallel is nicely secured by Benvolio's use of the assertive *will* and *shall*. Characteristic of the resolute style ('For *will* and *shall* best fitteth Tamburlaine', declared Marlowe's personification of the resolute type), these words are heard again at their most impressive in the speech where Faustus projects himself into the role of Homeric hero: 'Here will I dwell . . . I will be Paris . . . Instead of Troy shall Wittenberg be sacked . . . I will wound Achilles . . . none but thou shalt be my paramour.'

Integral to Faustus's conception of himself as a resolute individualist is the belief that he will uncover truths hidden from the rest of humankind. He assumes that at his command, servile spirits will 'resolve' all enigmas and mysteries for him. Marlowe's use of the word *resolve* in this sense simultaneously implies the sense of heroic determination. Faustus imagines, and then performs, the part of an imperious interrogator determined to get at the truth of things:

> How I am glutted with conceit of this!
> Shall I make spirits fetch me what I please,
> Resolve me of all ambiguities,
> Perform what desperate enterprise I will?
>   (1.78–81)
>
> . . . meet me in my study at midnight,
> And then resolve me of thy master's mind.
>   (3.100–101)
>
> Well, resolve me in this question.
>   (5.237)

But Mephastophilis and Lucifer resolve nothing of importance, and offer Faustus little more than 'freshmen's suppositions' and diverting shows that mean 'nothing' (5.85, 231).

Instead of resolution, what we quickly begin to perceive in Faustus is a radical instability. When he says to Mephastophilis, 'I will renounce this magic, and repent' (5.187), the determined 'will' indicates just where his resolution should be exercised. But Faustus, unable to resist the demonic voices of despair, fails the test. In doing so, however, he protects his heroic self-image by inverting the sense of 'resolution', suggesting that to retreat is to advance: 'Now go not backward: no Faustus, be resolute, / Why waverest thou?' (5.6–7), and 'Why should I die then, or basely despair? / I am resolved! Faustus shall ne'er repent' (5.207–8). The emptiness of this heroic self-image is painfully exposed in the penultimate scene when his terrified surrender to Mephastophilis's threats to dismember him (provoked by his thoughts of repentance) is sharply contrasted with the defiance of the Old Man to the same threats. The contrast is given additional force by the Old Man's entry in the middle of the Helen speech precisely when Faustus is declaring that he 'will . . . combat with weak Menelaus' and 'wound Achilles in the heel' (12.88–92). Singularly unheroic, too, is Faustus's spiteful request that the Old Man be tormented for urging him to repent and so exposing him to Mephastophilis's wrath (the Old Man is unmoved by the threat because, as Mephastophilis concedes, and Faustus fails to grasp, he can harm the body but not the soul). Most pointed of all, however, is the manner of Faustus's death, carried screaming to Hell by the demon whom he once lectured on the need for manly fortitude in enduring Hell's torments.

Faustus's confused understanding of himself and his desperate enterprise is finely underscored by Marlowe's ironic recognition that in one of its senses the word *resolution* is synonymous with its antonym. It signifies not only fixity and persistence but also disintegration, the breaking up of something into its component parts. Marlowe begins to hint at this contradiction in the scene where Faustus formally binds himself to Hell. Urging himself to 'be resolute', Faustus declares that the love of Belzebub is 'fixed' in him, and then signs the pact (5.6,12); at the same time, Mephastophilis fetches fire to 'dissolve' the ominously congealed blood and is soon admitting that 'when all the world dissolves . . . every creature shall be purified' and 'all places shall be hell that is not heaven' (5.124–7). Combined with the image of congealed and melted blood (echoing perhaps his 'waxen' and 'melting' Icarian wings [chor. 1.21–2]), the diction here suggests that the resolute Faustus is now one with the spirit of change and dissolution. This idea is presently embodied in one of the play's most important verbal and nonverbal symbols: henceforth, all Faustus's resolves to repent will be instantly undone by the devils' threats to tear him to pieces. (In the B text this symbol – as anticipated in the comic scenes – acquires a grimly literal status at the end when Faustus's body is discovered 'all torn asunder' by the devils whom he served [B.108].) The final irony, however, is not that Faustus's desperate resolution has trapped him in the terrors of violent physical dissolution; it is that he dies longing for the dissolution of his soul, bitterly acknowledging that only the souls of dying beasts are 'soon dissolved in elements' (13.106).

5

Faustus's engagement with play, then, should not be interpreted as the effort of a gifted individual to realise his true potential and construct an identity in defiance of a society that arbitrarily resists self-fulfillment and determines identity. Like all authoritarian and stratified societies, Elizabethan society did function to a considerable extent in that manner. It does not follow, however, that *Doctor Faustus* necessarily reflects such a process. According to the texts as we have them, it is not society with its repressive engines and ideologies that resists Faustus, but reality. Faustus's role-playing is simply an attempt to deny or escape from what he is, both as a human being and as an individual. He seeks to deny what he is as a human being because omnipotence and omniscience are not human attributes, and he seeks to deny his individual identity because in Christian belief that is a function of the soul.

The critic determined to impose a materialist reading on the text seizes on the comic scene in which Faustus's apparent loss of his leg prompts the cry 'Alas, I am undone' and construes this as subverting the idea of an essential self. An opposite meaning, however, is to be inferred from the motif of the torn body: as the Old Man, Mephastophilis, and finally Faustus himself all declare, the body may be torn, but the self remains with the soul. We may not like this version of the Faust myth and may feel that the myth could be made to mirror our deepest concerns more comprehensively. In that case, however, we should leave *Doctor Faustus* as it is, with all its subtleties intact, and do what countless imaginative writers have done: write our own version of the myth. The most appropriate comment on the theatricality of the protagonist in Marlowe's play is provided by the protagonist himself: 'My gracious lord, you do forget yourself: these are but shadows, not substantial things.'[11]

Notes

1   Taking Stock: Radical Criticism of Shakespeare

1   John Drakakis, in *Alternative Shakespeares*, vol. 2, ed. Terence Hawkes (London: Routledge, 1997), 241–2.
2   'Radical Shakespeareans' is the term applied by Drakakis to the contributors to *Alternative Shakespeares*, 2: 239.
3   *Alternative Shakespeares*, 2: 13.
4   'The Humanist Tradition in Eighteenth-Century England – and Today', *New Literary History*, 3 (1971), 167; cf. Roland Barthes, 'Literature is Constitutively Reactionary', *Critical Essays* (1964), trans. Richard Howard (Evanston, Ill.: Northwestern University Press, 1972).
5   'Notes towards a Radical Culture', in *The New Left*, ed. Priscilla Long (Boston: Porter Sargent, 1969), 426.
6   *Literary Theory: an Introduction* (Oxford: Blackwell, 1983), 81, 202.
7   *William Shakespeare* (Oxford: Blackwell: 1986), 1–2.
8   'The Golden Age of Criticism', *London Review of Books*, 9 (12) (25 June 1987), 15–18.
9   *A Theory of Literary Production* (1966), trans. Geoffrey Wall (London: Routledge, 1978), 136–55.
10   *The Political Unconscious: Narrative as a Socially Symbolic Act* (London: Methuen, 1981), 56.
11   Christopher Norris, 'Poststructuralist Shakespeare', in *Alternative Shakespeares*, ed. John Drakakis (London and New York: Routledge, 1985), 64.
12   *The Independent on Sunday*, 3.1.1993; cf. Sinfield, 'Give an Account of Shakespeare and Education', in *Political Shakespeare*, ed. Jonathan Dollimore and Alan Sinfield (Manchester: Manchester University Press, 1985), 142.
13   *Faultlines: Cultural Materialism and the Politics of Dissident Reading* (Oxford: Clarendon Press, 1992), 240.
14   'The Cultural Materialist Attack on Artistic Unity, and the Problem of Ideological Criticism', in *Ideological Approaches to Shakespeare*, ed. Robert P. Merrix and Nicholas Ranson (Lewiston/Queenston/Lampeter: Edwin Mellen Press, 1992), 39–56.
15   See, for example, Pierre Macherey, *A Theory of Literary Production*, 155: 'The order which it [the literary work] professes is merely an imagined order, projected on to disorder, the fictive resolution of ideological conflicts, a resolution so precarious that it is obvious in the very letter of the text where incoherence and incompleteness burst forth . . . The disorder that permeates the work is related to the disorder of the ideology (which cannot be organised as a system).'
16   'History and Ideology: the Instance of *Henry V*', in *Alternative Shakespeares*, ed. Drakakis, 215.
17   Catherine Belsey, *Critical Practice* (London: Methuen, 1980), 129.
18   *Alternative Shakespeares*, 2: 2.

19 'Postructuralist Shakespeare', 49–66.
20 *Alternative Shakespeares*, 2: 10.
21 Drakakis, Introduction, *Alternative Shakespeares*, 3–4; Norris, 'Postructuralist Shakespeare', 49–66 (he is developing an observation of Derrida's on 'nationalism and universalism' – 'Living on: Border Lines', in *Deconstruction and Criticism*, ed. Harold Bloom *et al.* [London: Routledge, 1979], 94); Sinfield, 'Royal Shakespeare: Theatre and the Making of Ideology', in *Political Shakespeare*, ed. Dollimore and Sinfield, 171.
22 *Shakespeare Criticism: a Selection*, ed. D. Nicol Smith (London: Oxford University Press, 1949), 80.
23 Ibid., 27.
24 'Literature, History, Politics', in *Modern Criticism and Theory: a Reader*, ed. David Lodge (London and New York: Longman, 1988), 403.
25 Derrida dissolves the author, says A.D. Nuttall, but every page of his own work is 'clamorously eloquent of its author's identity' – *A New Mimesis: Shakespeare and the Representation of Reality* (London and New York: Methuen, 1983), 37.
26 'Bardolatry: or, The Cultural Materialist's Guide to Stratford-on-Avon', in *The Shakespeare Myth*, ed. Graham Holderness (Manchester: Manchester University Press, 1988), 20–21.
27 *Shakespearean Negotiations* (Oxford: Clarendon Press, 1988; repr. 1997), 6–7.
28 *Reading Shakespeare Historically* (London and New York: Routledge, 1996), 17.
29 *Shakespeare* (New York and London: Harvester Wheatsheaf, 1989), 72.
30 *Alternative Shakespeares*, 2: 4–5.
31 *Critical Practice*, 58.
32 *Shakespeare Criticism*, ed. Nicol Smith, 3, 16.
33 *Shakespearean Negotiations*, 95.
34 Brian Vickers, *Appropriating Shakespeare: Contemporary Quarrels* (New Haven, Conn. and London: Yale University Press, 1993), 150–51. This book is indispensable for anyone challenging either radical theory as such or radical criticism of Shakespeare. Another study of the same kind, but of less ambitious scope, is A.D. Nuttall's pioneering *A New Mimesis: Shakespeare and the Representation of Reality* (note 25). Jonathan Bate has some fine observations on Shakespeare's distinctive use of his sources in *The Genius of Shakespeare* (London and Basingstoke: Picador, 1997), 132–53.
35 *Shakespeare Criticism*, ed. Nicol Smith, 18 (Dryden quote), 14 (Cavendish quote).
36 'Upon Master Shakespeare, the Deceased Author, and his Poems'; reprinted in Shakespeare's *Complete Works*, ed. Stanley Wells and Gary Taylor (Oxford: Clarendon Press, 1988), xlvii.
37 Sonnet 84.
38 *Shakespeare* (Oxford: Blackwell, 1986), 2–3. Malcom Evans's *Signifying Nothing: Truths True Contents in Shakespeare's Text* (Brighton: Harvester, 1986), 113–23, offers a longer version of the same argument.
39 *The Subject of Tragedy: Identity and Difference in Renaissance Drama* (London and New York: Methuen, 1985), 33–4, 36, 49.
40 Sonnet 53.
41 *Roman Drama*, ed. Samuel Lieberman (New York: Bantam Books, 1964), 355.
42 *Philoctetes*, lines 902–3, 951–2, trans. Richard C. Jebb, *The Tragedies of Sophocles* (Cambridge: Cambridge University Press, 1905), 356, 358.
43 'Professing the Renaissance: the Poetics and Politics of Culture', in *The New Historicism*, ed. H. Aram Veeser (New York and London: Routledge, 1989), 21. See also Belsey, *The Subject of Tragedy*, 8.

44 See John Gray, *Liberalism* (Milton Keynes: Open University Press, 1986); Alan Bullock, *The Humanist Tradition in the West* (London and New York: Thames and Hudson, 1985); Graham Good, *Humanism Betrayed* (Montreal: McGill-Queens University Press, 2001).

45 *Renaissance Self-Fashioning: From More to Shakespeare* (Chicago and London: University of Chicago Press, 1980), 254–7. In 'After the New Historicism', *Alternative Shakespeares*, 2: 30–31, Steven Mullaney rejects Frank Lentricchia's imputation to Foucault (and so to Greenblatt and new historicism) of the bleakly deterministic notion that opposition to power is futile. He quotes Foucault's assertion in *The History of Sexuality* that 'where there is power there is resistance' and that resistance is not of necessity betrayed (30–31). However, as J.Q. Merquior points out (*Foucault* [London: Fontana, 2nd edn, 1991], 114–15), despite these occasional suggestions that power is not omnipotent, Foucault's texts abound in totalist expressions and phrases which render inescapable the idea of omnipotent domination: 'general tactics of subjection', 'generalized carceral system', 'carceral continuum', 'carceral texture of society', 'society of surveillance'; and in such assertions as: 'our schools and hospitals and factories are essentially mirrors of the prison, our lives are everywhere normalized from cradle to tomb'.

46 See below, p. 90.

47 See pp. 37, and 117 below; also my *Shakespeare's Tudor History: a Study of 'Henry IV Parts 1 and 2'* (Aldershot and Burlington, Vt.: Ashgate, 2001), 133–4.

48 Dollimore and Sinfield, *Political Shakespeare*, viii. The element of political determinism (the denial of agency) in new historicism has often been cited as distinguishing it from cultural materialism. This distinction has been played down by Dollimore, who remarks that Greenblatt's very desire to disclose the ideological process of containing subversion is 'itself oppositional and motivated by the knowledge that . . . it did not, and still does not, have to be so' – 'Shakespeare, Cultural Materialism and New Historicism', in *Political Shakespeare*, 15. Montrose too believes that all forms of what he calls 'the new socio-historical criticism' have the same goal of 'contesting the regime of power and knowledge that at once sustains and contains us' ('The Poetics and Politics of Culture', in *The New Historicism*, ed. Veeser, 31).

49 *Vorwärts* (1844).

50 'Foucault's Legacy: a New Historicism?', in *The New Historicism*, ed. Veeser, 237.

51 Dollimore and Sinfield, *Political Shakespeare*, vii.

52 For defence of the major New Critics against the familiar charge of ahistoricism, see René Wellek, *A History of Modern Criticism 1750–1950*, 6: *American Criticism* (London: Cape, 1986), 148–9.

53 *Newton's Sleep: Two Cultures and Two Kingdoms* (Basingstoke: Macmillan, 1985), 111, 125.

54 See my *Shakespeare's Tudor History*, 17–25.

55 See p. 52.

56 In *The Dematerialisation of Karl Marx: Literature and Marxist Theory* (Harlow, Essex and New York: Longman, 1994), Leonard Jackson, for example, argues cogently that cultural materialism is a form of idealism which has dematerialised Marx's theory of art.

57 Edward Pechter, 'The New Historicism and its Discontents: Politicizing Renaissance Drama', *PMLA*, 102 (1987), 293–4; Richard Levin, 'Negative Evidence', *SP*, 92 (1995), 394–5, and 'The Historical and Political Turn in Literary Studies', *REAL. Yearbook of Research in English and American Studies*, 11 (1995), 426–7.

58   *Modern Criticism and Theory*, ed. Lodge, 401, 409. In 'History and Ideology; the
     Instance of *Henry V*', Dollimore and Sinfield supply us with unproblematised
     historical facts and claim to get behind the mystifying strategies of the play to 'real
     historical conflict' (*Alternative Shakespeares*, 215–16, 219, 224–5).
59   *Alternative Shakespeares*, 2: 15.
60   *Alternative Shakespeares*, 25 (Introduction).
61   Alan Sinfield, 'Shakespeare and Education', in *Political Shakespeare*, 150, and 'Royal
     Shakespeare', in *Political Shakespeare*, 178; Graham Holderness, 'Radical
     Potentiality and Institutional Closure', in *Political Shakespeare*, 183.
62   *Reading Shakespeare Historically* (London and New York: Routledge 1996), 171.
63   Levin, 'The Historical and Political Turn in Literary Studies', 428.
64   Pre-publication comment printed on the cover.
65   See the extract from Twine in Appendix A of the Arden *Pericles*, ed. F.D. Hoeniger
     (London: Methuen, 1963), 164–71.
66   Philip Edwards (ed.), *Pericles* (London: Penguin Books, 1976), 20.
67   Hoeniger (ed.), *Pericles*, xiv; Ernest Schanzer (ed.), *Pericles* (New York and London:
     New American Library, 1965), 156. The Apollonius story is told in book VIII of the
     Confessio Amantis (John Gower, *The English Works*, ed. G.C. Macaulay, EETS 81,
     London: Kegan Paul, 1900, vol. 2).
68   Doreen Delvecchio and Antony Hammond, editors of the New Cambridge edition
     of the play (1998) challenge this view, but their impartial summary of the arguments
     in favour of it actually undermines the persuasiveness of their position; and the
     unique text given in the quarto is so corrupt that the extent of Shakespeare's
     responsibility for the rest of the play as it has come down to us is a very vexed
     question.
69   T.W. Craik (ed.), *King Henry V*, The Arden Shakespeare (London and New York:
     Routledge, 1995), 225.
70   Raphael Holinshed, *Chronicles of England, Scotland, and Ireland* (1587), 6 vols
     (London: Johnson, 1808), 3: 113–19, 120, 123.
71   *PMLA*, 111 (1996), 22.

2   Testing New Historicism

1   Oxford: Clarendon Press, 1988. References throughout are to this version of the
    essay and are given in the text.
2   Ernest William Talbert, *The Problem of Order: Elizabethan Commonplaces and an
    Example of Shakespeare's Art* (Chapel Hill: University of North Carolina Press,
    1962), 3, 191, 197–9. See also note 23 below.
3   Like Greenblatt's, my references are to the text of Harriot in *The Roanoke Voyages
    1584–1590*, ed. David Beers Quinn (London: Hakluyt Society, 1955), vol. 1. The
    text of Harman to which I refer is from *The Elizabethan Underworld*, ed. A.V. Judges
    (London: Routledge, 1930).
4   Greenblatt's misrepresentation of Machiavelli has also been noted by Brian Vickers,
    Appropriating Shakespeare: Contemporary Critical Quarrels (New Haven, Conn.
    and London: Yale University Press, 1993), 249–50.
5   Machiavelli, *The Discourses*, ed. Bernard Crick (Harmondsworth: Penguin Books,
    1970), 141 (disc. 2).
6   *The Prince*, Everyman edn, trans. W.K. Marriott (London: Dent; New York: Dutton,
    1952), 28 (ch. 6).
7   *The Discourses*, 142.

8   Compare Vickers, *Appropriating Shakespeare*, 252, and B.J. Sokol, 'The Problem
    of Assessing Thomas Harriot's *A briefe and true report* of his Discoveries in North
    America', *Annals of Science*, 51 (1994), 1–16. Both critics contend that Greenblatt
    does scant justice to the open-minded, scholarly Harriot.

9   Greenblatt may have felt licensed to make this claim because of a footnote in
    Quinn's edition of the *Roanoke Voyages* (1: 389, n. 4). Discussing John Aubrey's
    1684 letter on Harriot, Quinn says that Harriot possibly compiled a glossary. (We
    do know, of course, that Harriot devised a phonetic orthography for recording
    the Algonquian languages, being a remarkable linguist as well as a brilliant
    scientist.)

10 Greenblatt's practice of tailoring the evidence to fit the argument is particularly
    obvious (for any one who checks his source, in this case Hakluyt's *Principal
    Navigations*) at the beginning of his chapter on Marlowe in *Renaissance Self-
    Fashioning: From More to Shakespeare* (Chicago and London: University of Chicago
    Press, 1980), 193–4. Here he records how an English merchant, John Sarracoll,
    burned a Sierra Leonean village to the ground and gives it as an example of 'casual
    and unexplained violence' which (by implication) epitomises 'the relentless power-
    hunger of Tudor absolutism' as well as the conduct of its energetic merchants and
    adventurers. He says too that it was atypical only in the sense that 'it lacks the
    bloodbath that usually climaxes these incidents' (the natives having fled before
    Sarracoll and his men landed). In fact, however, the action of the Englishmen was
    neither casual nor unexplained; nor did it have the racist dimension which Greenblatt
    imputes to it. The English had been attacked by the Africans, who were in alliance
    against them with England's colonialist rivals, the Portuguese. As Paul A.S. Harvey
    points out, these facts do not excuse the violence, but they do place the event in the
    context of inter-European warfare and rivalry in which local peoples, who welcomed
    trade with the Portuguese, played their own part ('Reading Greenblatt', *Studies in
    Language and Culture*, 20 (1994), 258–9). For another example of Greenblatt's
    'rather loose use of history', see John Lee, 'The Man Who Mistook his Hat: Stephen
    Greenblatt, New Historicism, and the Uses of History', *EIC*, 45 (1995), 285–300.
    Lee notes that 'Greenblatt's moments of forgetfulness are not fortuitous'; he
    '*deliberately* suppresses' parts of his chosen piece of history and 'manipulates others'
    so as to ensure a neat fit with his argument.

11 Robert Greene, *A Disputation Between a He-Cony-Catcher and a She-Cony-Catcher*
    (1592), in *The Elizabethan Underworld*, 225, 265.

12 *A Manifest Detection of the most vile and detestable use of Dice-play* (1552), in
    The Elizabethan Underworld, 38.

13 On these documents and passports, and the problem of forgery, see A.L. Beier,
    Masterless Men: the Vagrant Problem in England 1560–1640 (London: Methuen,
    1985), 79, 142–4, 154.

14 My texts for the Henry plays are *Henry IV, Part 1*, ed. David Bevington (Oxford
    and New York: Oxford University Press, 1987); *Henry IV, Part Two*, ed René Weis
    (Oxford and New York: Oxford University Press, 1997); *King Henry V*, ed.
    T.W. Craik (London and New York: Routledge, 1995).

15 Vickers, *Appropriating Shakespeare*, 262–3, pertinently notes Greenblatt's failure
    (surprising in view of his respect for Bakhtin) to acknowledge the 'carnival' nature
    of Hal's conduct in the tavern.

16 Sir Thomas Elyot, *The Book Named the Governor*, ed. S.E. Lehmberg (London:
    Dent; New York: Dutton, 1962), 172–83 (3: 6–7). Cf. Cicero, *The Offices* (London:
    Dent; New York: Dutton, 1937), 8 ('to stand to one's words in all promises and
    bargains; which we call justice'), 152–63 (1.5; 3.24–32).

17   For Shakespeare's engagement with the issue of truth, treachery, and
     Machiavellianism in the histories, see my 'Swearing and Forswearing in Shakespeare's
     Histories: the Playwright as Contra-Machiavel', *RES*, 51 (2000), 208–29, and
     Shakespeare's Tudor History: a Study of 'Henry IV Parts 1 and 2' (Aldershot and
     Burlington, Vt.: Ashgate, 2001), 34–48, 93–140.
18   John Foxe, *The Ecclesiasticall Historie* (1583), 137, 1493, 1577, 1592, 1888.
19   *Chronicles of England, Scotland, and Ireland* (1587), 6 vols (London: Johnson,
     1808), 3: 101.
20   *Chronicles*, 3: 72.
21   Brook Thomas, *The New Historicism and other Old-Fashioned Topics* (Princeton,
     NJ: Princeton University Press, 1991), 44.
22   Holinshed, *Chronicles*, 4: 93, 137. Holinshed says the loss of Calais precipitated
     the illness from which Mary died (121). He fervently endorses her hope that the lost
     territory will one day be recovered in a victory that will erase the military and
     political 'dishonor' that has 'blotted' the realm of England (89, 103, 117).
23   J.B. Black, *The Reign of Elizabeth* (Oxford: Clarendon Press, 1959), 35.
24   William Empson, 'Falstaff and Mr. Dover Wilson', *Kenyon Review* (1953); reprinted
     in *'Henry IV Parts 1 & 2': A Selection of Critical Essays*, ed. G.K. Hunter (London:
     Macmillan, 1970), 153. On Tillyard, see A.P. Rossiter's 1951 Stratford lecture,
     'Ambivalence: the Dialectic of the Histories', first published in 1954 and later in his
     Angel with Horns: Fifteen Lectures on Shakespeare (London: Longman, 1961),
     40–64.
25   The problem of evidence seems to nag ineffectually at Greenblatt from time to time.
     At the beginning of *Renaissance Self-Fashioning* he justifies drawing large cultural
     generalisations from 'a small number' of texts, first by emphasising the 'resonance'
     and 'centrality' of his chosen texts and lives (evasive terms which beg the question),
     and then by caricaturing the methods of traditional scholarship: 'we cannot rest
     content with statistical tables, nor are we patient enough to tell over a thousand
     stories, each with its slight variants . . . after a thousand, there would be another
     thousand, then another, and it is not at all clear that we would be closer to the
     understanding we seek' (5–6). In the *Othello* chapter in the same book he gives only
     one example of the Europeans' Iago-ish ability to insinuate themselves into the
     natives' structures of thought and practice and turn those structures to their own
     advantage – but he assures us (in a favourite phrase) that this ability is apparent
     'again and again' in the colonial narratives (227). In *Learning to Curse: Essays in
     Early Modern Culture* (New York and London: Routledge, 1990), he admits that
     'there is virtually no evidence of the practice [of 'intense paternal observation of the
     young'] in medieval England'. This concession is calculated to win credence for the
     ensuing claim that 'for the seventeenth century . . . there is quite impressive evidence.
     For example . . .' (86) And that is it: one example. Like Foucault's, his exemplary
     'stories' are always apt or impressively told, but they are not evidence as normally
     understood.
26   *Postcultural Theory: Critical Theory after the Marxist Paradigm* (Basingstoke:
     Macmillan, 1993), 29.

3   War and Peace in *Henry V*

 1   Cf. Annabel Patterson, *Shakespeare and the Popular Voice* (Oxford: Blackwell,
     1989), 72; Graham Bradshaw, *Misrepresentations: Shakespeare and the Materialists*
     (Ithaca and London: Cornell University Press, 1993), 46.

2   The dissenter is Norman Rabkin: see his *Shakespeare and the Problem of Meaning* (Chicago and London: University of Chicago Press, 1981), 33–62.

3   One of the most impressive versions of the two-Henrys interpretation antedates the New-Critical readings by several decades: see Stopford Brooke, *Ten More Plays of Shakespeare* (London: Constable, 1913), 294–313.

4   *Chronicles of England, Scotland, and Ireland* (1587), 6 vols (London: Johnson, 1808), 3: 81–2. (Subsequent references to this volume of Holinshed are given in the text.) Writing in 1599, the lawyer R. Crompton also saw the killing of the prisoners as terrible but justified: 'for otherwise the king having lost diverse valiant Captaines and souldiers in this battell, and being also but a small number in comparison of the French kings army, and in a strange countrey, where he could not supply his neede upon sudden, it might have bene much daungerous to have againe joyned with the enemy, and kept his prisoners alive, as in our Chronicles largely appeareth' (*The Mansion of Magnanimitie*, sig. 92v.)

5   Edward P. Cheyney, *The Dawn of a New Era: 1250–1453* (1936), 165; Maurice Kean, *The Laws of War in the Late Middle Ages* (Aldershot: Gregg Revivals, 1983), 123; Theodor Meron, *Henry's Wars and Shakespeare's Laws: Perspectives on the Law of War in the Later Middle Ages* (Oxford: Clarendon Press, 1993), 118–19. However, by contemporary standards Henry V's treatment of the inhabitants of France during his wars was exceptionally humane and was so acknowledged by the French themselves. See Holinshed, *Chronicles*, 3: 77; Charles Oman, *The History of the Art of War in the Middle Ages*, 2nd edn, 2 vols (London: Methuen, 1924), 2: 387; Meron, *Henry's War and Shakespeare's Laws*, 116–17.

6   Froissart describes with stark realism the singular brutality with which the Black Prince, enraged by the treachery of its bishops and burghers, sacked the city of Limoges. But he celebrates the Prince's magnanimity, courtesy, and courage and hails him as 'the chief flower of all chivalry', 'the flower of chivalry of England' , and records that when he died even the French king and his nobles and prelates 'did obsequy reverently' in Paris for him. When he says that the Prince 'was always courageous and cruel as a lion' is he being ambivalent or offering what we might term 'realistic praise'? – *The Chronicles of Froissart*, trans. Lord Berners, ed. G.C. Macaulay (London and New York: Macmillan, 1895), 201 (ch. 283), 181 (ch. 239), 205 (ch. 314), 129 (ch. 164).

7   *The Works of Geoffrey Chaucer*, ed. F.N. Robinson, 2nd edn (London and Oxford: Oxford University Press, 1957), I (A)1978, 2013–16 (*The Knight's Tale*).

8   *Gerusalemme Liberata*, XIX, 30 (my translation).

9   Ed. L.A. Beaurline (Cambridge: Cambridge University Press, 1990).

10 Ed. Giorgio Melchiori, The New Cambridge Shakespeare (Cambridge: Cambridge University Press, 1998). Melchiori shows that the collaborating authors of this play, '[f]rom an initial plot based on Holinshed, devised a play-book comprising, reordering, and manipulating the ample material provided by Froissart' (25).

11 In a strenuously new-historicist reading, Larry S. Champion ignores the French endorsements of Edward's claim and purports to find behind the play's overtly heroic presentation a consistently ironic and subversive vision of sordid political treachery and brutal monarchic authority. See his '"Answere to this perillous time": Ideological Ambivalence in *The Raigne of King Edward III* and the English Chronicle Plays', *ES*, 69 (1998), 117–29.

12 Bale, *A brefe Chronycle concernynge the Examinacyon and death of the blessed martyr of Christ, Sir Johan Oldecastle the lorde Cobham* (1544); Foxe, *Actes and Monuments* (1563), 261–77.

13 In Holinshed's account of the reign of Henry V, the first problem which confronts the new regime is that of Oldcastle and his Lollard followers [62–4]); next comes the question of France.

14 In support of his impressively agile interpretation of Henry as a character whose negative features are as important as his positive ones, Graham Bradshaw claims that the bishops' praise of the King as a lover of the Church and as a miraculously reformed individual is insincere and rendered wholly 'unbelievable' by the fact that he 'wants to "strip" the Church to fill his "Coffers"' (*Misrepresentations*, 48). But Canterbury makes it quite clear that the Church's problem originates with 'th' exhibitors against us' in Parliament and not with the King (1.1.1,74). See also note 15 below.

15 Since Henry's father had on two occasions refused to support Parliament's demand ('the importunate petitions of the commons') that church lands should be confiscated to pay for military expenses incurred by the laity and the Crown, and accepted instead the tithe offered by Canterbury on behalf of the Church (Holinshed, *Chronicles*, 3: 30–32, 48–9, and cf. *Henry V*, 1.1.2–5), Shakespeare probably did not perceive anything especially cunning in the prelate's conduct or naive in the King's response. Holinshed seems to regard Canterbury's intervention as typical and predictable: in his view, all pre-reformation Canterburys were the same on such matters as church property and theological reform.

16 Gloss on 1.1.86 in the Arden edition, ed. T.W. Craik (London and New York: Routledge, 1995). All citations here are from this edition.

17 Modern historians agree that Salic law's alleged ban on succession through the female line was largely concocted in the fourteenth century as a retrospective justification for the Valois succession. See J. Potter, 'The Development and Significance of the Salic Law of the French', *EHR*, 52 (1937), 235–53. The English claim to the French throne must have been recognised by everyone in Shakespeare's time as a completely lost cause, but its justice was still asserted. John Stubbs lamented that because of the Salic law 'we [are] never the neere possession of our old right in France whych we so much desired' (*The Discoverie of a Gaping Gulf* [1579], sig. C7v). In *The View of France*, written in 1597 but published in 1604, Robert Dallington inveighed against the French who 'would needes make the world beleeve that it [Salic law] is of great antiquitie, whereof they very wrongfully tromped the heires of *Edward* the third, of their enjoying the Crowne of *France*, which to them is rightly descended by his Mother, and whose claime is still good, were the English sword well whetted to cut the Labels of the Law' (sig. E3r).

18 *1 Henry VI*, ed. Wells and Taylor, *The Complete Works* (Oxford: Clarendon Press, 1988), 2.5.61–92.

19 With two other English Catholics, Edward Squire received money from Spain to kill the Queen and Essex. Both attempts failed miserably; he was caught and interrogated by members of Council throughout October and November 1598, and is said to have died repentant. The conspiracy coincided with renewed Spanish preparations for an invasion of England. It seems to have made a strong impression. 'We see that the lives of anointed Princes are daily sought', wrote Raleigh to Cecil. And Charles Paget wrote to his friend Thomas Barnes: 'A conspiracy has been discovered against the Queen, and I am sorry to see that men will forget their duties in such an abominable manner, which makes me think the Devil is among them; but God overthrows their devices.' See *Calendar of State Papers, Domestic, 1598–1601*, 106–9, 112, 118, 120. (Cf. Henry's claim that the devil which seduced Scroop 'hath got the voice in hell for excellence', and Scroop's confession, 'Our purposes God justly hath discovered' [2.2.111–13, 151]).

20 Ed. *Henry V* (Oxford: Oxford University Press, 1984), 300. Cf. Craik (ed.), *Henry V*, note on 4.1.299–302. Echoing Stephen Greenblatt, Cedric Watts loads his case against the penitent Henry by equating him with the fratricidal Claudius. See John Sutherland and Cedric Watts, *Henry V, War Criminal?* (Oxford: Oxford University Press, 2000), 22.

21 Ed. René Weis (Oxford and New York: Oxford University Press, 1997).

22 See Anne Curry, *The Hundred Years War* (Basingstoke: Macmillan, 1993), 94. Holinshed says that because of the two factions and the king's mental feebleness 'the kingdome was maruelliouslie brought in decaie' (*Chronicles*, 3: 50).

23 See G.A. Hayes-McCoy, 'The Tudor Conquest (1534–1603)' and Aidan Clarke, 'The Colonisation of Ulster (1603–60)', in *The Course of Irish History*, ed. T.W. Moody and F.X. Martin, revised edn (Cork and Dublin: Mercier Press, 1994), 174, 189.

24 *Calendar of State Papers, Domestic Series, 1595–97*, 170–72, 178–80, 182, 198, 201–2, 207, 211–13, 256–8, 303–5, 322, 326; *CSPD 1598–1601*, 1–2, 28, 47, 51, 81, 109, 121–5; *CSPD 1601–1603*, 151. See also n. 19 above. One of the reasons for Essex's failure in Ireland in 1599 was the fact that the Privy Council was distracted by fears of a Spanish invasion of England, which dominated its thinking about shipping and prevented it from supplying him with the ships needed for his intended landing in the north of Ireland. See Wallace T. MacCaffrey, *Elizabeth I: War and Politics 1588–1603* (Princeton, NJ: Princeton University Press, 1992), 419, 438.

25 Robin Headlam-Wells, *Shakespeare on Masculinity* (Cambridge: Cambridge University Press, 2000), 1–18. Headlam-Wells argues that Shakespeare implicitly opposes a peace-loving to a violent, militaristic form of heroism (one identified with Orpheus, the other with Hercules). In my view, however, Shakespeare's ideal of heroism or nobility is a *union* of military and civic virtue, valour and 'human kindness', 'sword' and 'tongue'. See above, p. 57, and my chapter on the tragedies.

26 'On our side the hope of treaty was not suffered to die, but the other side sought to entertain us with words till the enterprize of Ireland was ready, of which we knew nothing' – *CSPD, 1601–1603*, 6 February 1602). See also MacCaffrey, *Elizabeth I*, 230–32.

27 J.E. Neale, *Queen Elizabeth* (London: Jonathan Cape, 1934), 384.

28 Before setting sail from Southampton, Henry wrote to Charles, saying: 'right noble prince our cosyn and aduersary, sometymes the noble realmes of England & Fraunce were united, which nowe, be separated and deuided, and ... then they were accustomed to be exalted through the universal worlde' (Hall, *Chronicle* [1548]; repr. 1809, 61).

29 See my *English Renaissance Tragedy* (Basingstoke: Macmillan, 1986; repr. with alterations, 1988), 55–81, 93–9.

30 For example, J.H. Walter (ed.), *Henry V* (London: Methuen, 1954), Introd., xii–xxxi; Peter G. Phialas, 'Shakespeare's *Henry V* and the Second Tetralogy', *SP*, 72 (1965), 155–75; Gary Taylor (ed.), *Henry V*, Introd., 27–74; T.W. Craik (ed.), *King Henry V*, Introd., 32–80; Brian Vickers, *Appropriating Shakespeare: Contemporary Quarrels* (New Haven, Conn. and London: Yale University Press, 265–7.

31 *The Arte of English Poesie* (1589), ed. G.D. Willcock and A. Walker (Cambridge: Cambridge University Press, 1936), 174.

32 *Tamburlaine the Great Parts I and II*, ed. John D. Jump (London: Arnold, 1967), 1: 2.5.18–20. For a fuller discussion of the cosmic model described here, with references to primary and secondary sources, see my *English Renaissance Tragedy*, 5–10, 236 n. 7, and *Shakespeare's Tragic Cosmos* (Cambridge: Cambridge University Press, 1991), 1–29, 229–32.

33 *The Two Noble Kinsmen*, ed. Wells and Taylor, 5.1.60–65. See also *Edward III*, 3.1.5–18; *2 Henry IV*, 4.1.63–6; Sir William Cornwallis, *Discourse upon Seneca the Tragedian* (1601) sig. Hiʳ ('Warre is the remedy for a State surfeited with peace, it is a medicine for Commonwealths sick of too much ease and tranquillitie'). Especially pertinent is Samuel Daniel's emphatic commentary on this theme at the start of his account of Henry V's reign in *The First Fowre Bookes of the Civile Wars Between the Two Houses of Lancaster and Yorke* (1595), bk 4, sts 18–21 (see also bk 3, st 108). The notion that peace corrupts and war is restorative is an unfortunate exaggeration of the fact that social divisions melt only when we are threatened by a common enemy. It lingered among the English upper classes until 1914 but could not survive the horrors of Gallipoli and the Western front.

34 Contemporary acounts of the nature of war, explains Nick de Somogyi, had constant recourse to the notion of contradiction. See his *Shakespeare's Theatre of War* (Aldershot and Burlington, Vt.: Ashgate, 1998), 46.

35 Ed. Wells and Taylor, *Complete Works*.

36 In the Quarto text of the play, the Dauphin's speeches in this scene are given to Bourbon. I am inclined to accept T.W. Craik's view (ed. *Henry V*, 18–19) that the Quarto text belongs with those 'surreptitious copies, maimed, and deformed by the fraudes and stealthes of inurious impostors' against whom Shakespeare's colleagues, John Heminges and Henry Condell, inveighed in their Preface to the First Folio.

37 For an especially forceful and witty example of this argument, see Bradshaw, *Misrepresentations*, 58–63.

38 Says J.L. Calderwood: 'Their burlesque of the main plot succeeds only in degrading themselves' – *Metadrama in Shakespeare's Henriad* (Berkeley, Calif.: University of California Press, 1979), 146.

39 The importance of the concept of *discordia concors* (or *concordia discors*) in this play has already been noted by Rose A. Zimbardo in 'The Formalism of *Henry V*', in *Shakespeare Encomium*, ed. Anne Paolucci (New York: City College, 1964), 16–24. In a comparable analysis, Gary Taylor emphasises the dialectical design of the play: 'a conflict of two peoples, two nations, each containing within itself variety and division. Out of diversity the play aspires to unity . . . It advances dialectically' (ed. *Henry V*, Introd., 71).

40 See Sir Thomas Elyot, *The Book of the Governor* (1531), bk 2, ch. 2 ('The exposition of majesty'), ch. 5 ('Of affability'); ed. S.E. Lehmberg (London: Dent, 1962), 99–102, 106–11. Concerning Henry V, Elyot says that he was 'in mine opinion . . . to be compared with any [king] that ever was written of in any region or country' (bk 2, ch. 6; ed. Lehmberg, 114). In his *Civile Wars*, Samuel Daniel refers to Henry's 'martiall cheere, / Seeming of dreadfull, and yet lovely sight. / Whose eye gives courage, & whose browe doth feare / Both representing terror and delight' (4.3).

41 Cf. Kent to the King in *Lear* (Folio text), ed. Wells and Taylor, 1.4.27–30: '[Y]ou have that in your countenance which I would fain call master . . . Authority'.

42 *King Edward III*, ed. Melchiori, 3.4.15–68.

43 In his edition of the play (37–8), Gary Taylor argues that the prisoners are killed on stage. But see Craik (ed.), *Henry V*, 309 (note on 4.7.35–8).

44 Cf. *Antony and Cleopatra*, ed. Wells and Taylor, 4.9.7–11, where Shakespeare intoduces the same paradox of divisive violence resolved into a loving oneness: 'You have shown all Hectors. / Enter the city, clip your wives, your friends, / Tell them your feats whilst they with joyful tears / Wash the congealment from your wounds, and kiss / The honoured gashes whole.' These lines are central to the imaginative vision of a tragedy in which the Mars-Venus-Harmonia myth is of great importance. See my *Shakespeare's Tragic Cosmos*, ch. 9.

45 Arguing that the play provokes extreme readings between which no compromise is possible, Norman Rabkin sharpens the extremes by alleging that the order to kill the prisoners is 'simply a response to the fair battlefield killing of some English nobles by the French' (*Shakespeare and the Problem of Meaning*, 55). This is clearly at odds with the text: [Henry] 'But hark, what new alarum is this same? / The French have reinforced their scattered men. / Then every soldier kill his prisoners! / Give the word through' (4.6.35–8). The *Alarum* [SD], which marks the despairing French decision to attack pell-mell, would have interrupted the dialogue at this point and required an anxious pause before Henry makes his momentous decision. Rabkin's mistaken interpretation is borrowed from H.C. Goddard's fiercely anti-Henry reading of the play: *The Meaning of Shakespeare* (Chicago: University of Chicago Press, 1951), 256. Although he argues for two mutually incompatible but equally valid interpretations, the bias of Rabkin's interpretation lies in its negative and sarcastic commentary on Henry's actions and motives.

46 About the order to take no prisoners we have heard enough in interviews with Second World War veterans who fought in the Pacific and on the Normandy beaches: humane objections to what they reported were often met with tears and the bitter and unanswerable, 'But you weren't there.'

47 Reinforcing his case against Henry, John Sutherland (*Henry V, War Criminal?*, 114) claims that he 'expressly ordered' that the other prisoners be killed. But not only are we presented here with a threat rather than an order, the threat itself is not delivered. Montjoy, the French herald, enters immediately to plead for mercy (which is granted), and the English herald remains on stage. See Craik (ed.), *Henry V*, note on 4.7.64.

48 Peter G. Phialas, 'Shakespeare's *Henry V* and the Second Tetralogy', *SP*, 72 (1965), 155–6.

49 Henry was also merciless in his treatment of some Frenchmen who continued to resist him after the treaty of Troyes.

50 With other forms of 'Romish' church plate, such as monstrances and censers, pyxes were melted down and minted as money in 1560. See David Starkey, *Elizabeth* (London: Chatto, 2000), 297.

51 Andrew Gurr (ed.), *King Henry V* (Cambridge: Cambridge University Press, 1992), Introd., 14.

52 Philippe Contamine, *War in the Middle Ages*, trans. Michael Jones (Oxford: Blackwell, 1984), 101–2.

53 According to the international lawyer Theodor Meron, Henry's emphasis on 'the King's exemption of responsibility for his soldiers' misdeeds such as pillage and murder is unremarkable for an era in which the concept of central authority over the army was still rudimentary' (*Henry's Wars and Shakespeare's Laws*, 65).

54 Froissart twice records that during Edward III's campaign in France the intervention of a knight saved a woman from rape by one or more of his own foot-soldiers (*The Chronicles*, 97, 99 [chs 124, 125]). And as we have seen (p. 46), even Tasso's romantic epic on the liberation of Jerusalem acknowledges the grim reality of rape.

55 In Holinshed, Henry sacks the city and expels its citizens; Shakespeare's Henry simply says, 'Use mercy to them all.'

56 Ed. Wells and Taylor, 3.4. 57, 1.2.141–3.

57 Edward abandons his 'folly's siege against a faithful lover' (the virtuous Countess of Richmond) and proceeds with his 'thrice valiant son' to France, where he will engage honourably in a different kind of siege (*Edward III*, 2.2.207–9).

58 This petty squabbling is a reflection of the divisiveness among the leading French nobles that the chroniclers and subsequent historians have cited as a major cause of Henry's success in France.

59   Froissart, *Chronicles*, 106: 'This night [after the battle of Crecy] they thanked God for their good adventure and made no boast thereof, for the king would that no man should be proud or make boast, but every man humbly to thank God' (cf. pp. 124, 175); *King Edward III*, 3.3.228, 3.4.18–22.

60   Ed. David Bevington (Oxford, 1987).

61   Edgar Wind, *Pagan Mysteries in the Renaissance* (London: Faber, 1958), 74.

62   As Holinshed points out, the allegation of French involvement in the assassination plot was false, being used by the conspirators to protect Mortimer and the heirs of Cambridge. There is no hint of this in the play, where Shakespeare makes use of the fiction to sharpen the English–French opposition (modified by the thought that the English conspirators have been infected by 'a malady of France'). Spanish involvement in the recent attempt to assassinate Elizabeth may be relevant too (note 19).

63   *The Discourses*, 3.40; ed. Bernard Crick (Harmondsworth: Penguin Books, 1970), 513.

64   Nick de Somogyi notes that *Henry V's* stress on solidarity echoes a commonplace in contemporary discussions of war and soldiership (*Shakespeare's Theatre of War*, 117–20).

65   This attitude in the French nobility might be ascribed to Shakespearean chauvinism; yet it is historically correct, the French aristocrat's class-conscious contempt for foot-soldiers being a major reason for the disastrous defeats at Crecy and Agincourt. See Charles Oman, *The History of the Art of War in the Middle Ages*, 2: 112.

66   In their cultural-materialist essay, 'History and Ideology: the Instance of *Henry V*', in *Alternative Shakespeares*, ed. John Drakakis (London and New York: Routledge, 1985), 206–27, Jonathan Dollimore and Alan Sinfield read the play as a manifestation of the Elizabethan regime's attempt to impose unity on the nation by means of ideological coercion and on Britain by imperialist domination of Ireland. The threats to unity which Shakespeare dramatises (unintentionally or accidentally, it seems) are interpreted by them as historical reality's challenge to the state's oppressive ideology of unity. My argument is that Shakespeare manipulates a notion of unity understood as intrinsically unstable; it's *raison d'etre* is *not* to 'occlude' conflict and contradiction (215) but to acknowledge them as always present and potentially dominant. Dollimore and Sinfield do in fact come near at one point to acknowledging that such a view of unity operates in the play: 'That the idea of a single source of power in the state was, if not a fantasy, a rare and precarious achievement is admitted in the Epilogue ... Many managers disperse power and unity falls apart' (220). But this 'admission' (by whom?) is seen by them as contradicting rather than extending the play's governing mode of thought (or 'ideology'). That Shakespeare's complex theory of unity serves in *Henry V* to legitimise a political order and a war which Dollimore and Sinfield do not approve of cannot, of course, be denied. The essence of my objection to their approach is that it disallows the play's artistic unity and the playwright's controlling intelligence.

67   'The fico for thee then!' (lines 55–64), says Pistol: that is, 'Fuck you!'

68   Anne Barton, 'The King Disguised: Shakespeare's *Henry V* and Comical History', in *The Triple Bond: Plays, Mainly Shakespearean, in Performance*, ed. Joseph Price (University Park: Pennsylvania State University Press, 1975), 92–114. In *Shakespeare and the Popular Voice*, Annabel Patterson refers to 'the disguised visit to the common soldiers' and treats it as 'crucial to Henry's characterization' (77). John Sutherland virtually equates Henry with the snooping Richard III at Bosworth: 'Henry ... is patrolling the lines incognito, pretending to be just another private soldier' (*Henry V, War Criminal?*, 115).

69   Cf. Gary Taylor (ed.), *Henry V*, Introd., 42–6.

70   Folio text; in the Quarto, it is Bates.
71   Puttenham, *The Arte of English Poesie*, 226.
72   Canterbury repeats Hal's imagery of death and renewal: 'his wildness, mortified in him, / Seemed to die too' (*H5*, 1.1.26–7). Nick de Somogyi (*Shakespeare's Theatre of War*, 200–21) argues that the death-life (or resurrection) motif is designed to reinforce the idea that the play brings the dead to life again on the stage. I doubt if Shakespeare would take such pains to signal a truism which is applicable to all his histories.
73   Ed. Wells and Taylor, *Complete Works*.
74   For an excellent analysis of Henry's wooing which complements my own, see Brian Vickers, *The Artistry of Shakespeare's Prose* (London: Methuen, 1968), 161–70. Vickers observes that this is Shakespeare's longest prose scene and that he 'has evidently taken considerable trouble with it . . . [T]he wit and brilliance of [Henry's] wooing language look forward to the high comedies which follow . . . [Henry] rises to the occasion, producing eloquence when it is needed, as he has done in the war.'
75   Compare Theseus, that great exponent of *discordia concors*, and lover of paradox and oxymoron: 'Out of this silence I have picked a welcome, / And in the modesty of fearful duty / I read as much as from the rattling tongue / Of saucy and audacious eloquence. / Love, therefore, and tongue-tied simplicity / In least speak most to my capacity' (*MND*, ed. Wells and Taylor, 5.1.100–106)
76   Both Michael Neill, in 'Broken English and Broken Irish: Nation, Language, and the Optic Power in Shakespeare's Histories', *SQ*, 45 (1994), 1–32, and Paola Pugliatti, in *Shakespeare the Historian* (Basingstoke: Macmillan, 1996), 138–40, note the importance of language in the play. They interpret it in the manner of Stephen Greenblatt as 'the perfect instrument of empire', a tool in the process of conquest and domination. My own argument posits language as a mediating and unifying factor and as symptomatic of affinities between the two peoples: we are not surprised that the Boy speaks French or Alice English and we respect Henry for acknowledging that his French could be much better than it is. Bilingualism is an implied ideal, and there is no trace of a suggestion that the French language should take second place to English in France. Language and language-learning is given a comparable significance in the indenture scene in *1 Henry IV*: see my *Shakespeare's Tudor History: a Study of 'Henry IV Parts 1 and 2'* (Aldershot and Burlington, Vt.: Ashgate, 2001), 110–11, 159. For a critique of the new-historicist mantra, 'Language is the perfect instrument of empire', and its use by Greenblatt, see Chapter 8.
77   See my *Shakespeare's Tragic Cosmos*, 62–5, 84, 203–4.
78   Ed. Wells and Taylor, *Complete Works*.
79   Discussing Donne's Ovidian elegy, 'Love's War', Rosalie Colie remarks: 'The analogy of love to war is too common in western poetry to require comment: not in poetry only, but in ordinary speech the relations of courtship and consummated love are described in terms of battle, siege, and conquest' (*Paradoxica Epidemica: the Renaissance Tradition of Paradox* [Princeton, NJ: Princeton University Press, 1966], 122).
80   The phrase occurs in each of the seven stanzas of the epithalamion which concludes Ben Jonson's marriage masque, *The Hue and Cry after Cupid*. The war is between 'the spouse and spoused' and is a continuation of the conquest worked on them by armed Cupid, who revels triumphantly at the start of the masque. The fruits of the bridegroom's 'invasion' are 'Games, Laughter, Sports, Delights'; while in the future, 'the jars, / And stings in wedlock; little strifes and wars' will become (or be) 'new wounds of love'. The metamorphic paradox of Strife and Love and of pain and joy (like Cleopatra's 'lover's pinch that hurts and is desired') could hardly be more emphatically expressed.

81   Holinshed, *Chronicles*, 3: 588; J.J. Scarisbicke, *Henry VIII* (London: Eyre & Spottiswoode, 1968), 37. Nashe alludes to the motto on the first page of *The Unfortunate Traveller* (1594): 'I followed the court or the camp . . . when Turwin lost her maidenhead, and opened her gates to more than Jane Trosse did.'

82   See J.H. and R. Pinches, *The Royal Heraldry of England* (London: Heraldry Today, 1974), 8, 24–5, 29, 47, 50–52, 154; also <www.hereditarytitles.com./page 31.html>. In *1 Henry VI*, Joan's sword, '[d]ecked with five flower-de-luces on each side' was heraldically out of date; she found it among 'a great deal of old iron' in a churchyard.

83   Ed. Wells and Taylor, *Complete Works*.

84   Elizabeth was given visibility and dramatic emphasis by John Barton and Peter Brook in *The Wars of the Roses*, their rewriting of *1–3 Henry VI* and *Richard III* as three plays. They thought this was necessary 'to bring out the historical and dramatic point'. See their *Wars of the Roses* (London: BBC, 1970), xxii.

85   Holinshed, *Chronicles*, 3: 190, following Edward Hall, *Chronicle* (1548); repr. 1809, 184–5.

86   *Misrepresentations*, 39.

87   *The Drama of Power: Studies in Shakespeare's History Plays* (Evanston, Ill.: Northwestern University Press, 1973), 331.

4   Perfect Answers: Religious Inquisition, Falstaffian Wit

1   For a thorough consideration of the evidence in favour of Shakespeare's satiric intention, see Gary Taylor, 'The Fortunes of Oldcastle', *ShS*, 38 (1985), 85–100. See also E.A.J. Honigmann, 'Sir John Oldcastle: Shakespeare's Martyr', in *'Fanned and Winnowed Opinions': Shakespearean Essays Presented to Harold Jenkins* (London and New York: Methuen, 1987), 118–32; Kristen Poole, 'Saints Alive! Falstaff, Martin Marprelate, and the Staging of Puritanism', *SQ*, 46 (1995), 47–95.

2   'Sir John Oldcastle: Shakespeare's Martyr', 126.

3   For James and Fuller, see David Bevington (ed.), *Henry IV, Part 1* (Oxford: Oxford University Press, 1987), 6–8; for Speed, see S. Schoenbaum, *William Shakespeare: a Compact Documentary Life* (Oxford: Clarendon Press, 1977), 193.

4   My references are to Bevington's edition of *Part 1* and to René Weis's edition of *Part 2* (Oxford and New York: Oxford University Press, 1997).

5   The New Variorum *Henry the Fourth Part I*, ed. Samuel Burdett Hemingway (Philadelphia and London: Lippincott, 1936), 403.

6   Variorum *Part I*, 421.

7   Variorum *Part I*, 431.

8   Variorum *Part I*, 441.

9   An undated reprint was issued in London a few years later. This is contained in Bale's *Select Works*, ed. Henry Christmas, Parker Society Publications (Cambridge: Cambridge University Press, 1849). My references are to this edition.

10   It is, however, *detectable* in Foxe; so it is just possible that Shakespeare acquired it indirectly from Foxe without having read Bale's original version.

11   *STC* 24045. It may have been edited by William Tyndale. No pagination.

12   Arundel's *Magnus Processus* is contained in the *Fasciculi Zizaniorum Magistri Johannis Wycliff cum tritico*, the only contemporaneous account of the rise of the Lollards. The *Fasciculi* is reprinted as vol. 5 of the Rolls Series, ed. W.W. Shirley (London, 1858). Bale and Foxe ascribe the authorship of this collection to Thomas Netter of Walden, a leading opponent of the Lollards.

13 There is no hint of any of this in *The examinacion*. But Bale was clearly inspired by the defiance with which in this account Cobham responds to his inquisitors, and owes to it some of the more impressive retorts which he imputes to his hero.

14 This legend in particular shows Bale's closeness to hagiographical tradition. Katherine is compared to the apostles armed with Christ's assurance that they should have no anxiety as to what they must say when brought before kings and princes; such indeed is the power of God's grace in her responses to the pagan philosophers who challenge her faith that they are filled with awe and completely overcome (*The Life of St Katherine . . . with its Latin Original*, ed. E. Einenkel, Early English Texts Society, No. 80 [London: Trubner, 1884], 31, 58, 61–2; Jacobus de Voragine, *The Golden Legende*, trans. William Caxton [1493], sigs Y3ᵛ–7). As Hippolyte Delehaye has shown, late-classical rhetoric played an important part in the growth of the martyr legend; he regards Katherine's debate with the pagan philosophers as an ingenious amplification of the standard interrogation of the martyr: see *Les Passions des martyrs et les genres littéraires* (Brussels: Bureaux de la Sociétè des Bollandistes, 1921), 169. Having been a Carmelite friar, Bale was steeped in hagiography and had in fact compiled his own collection of saints' lives for the benefit of his fellow Carmelites. See Leslie P. Fairfield, *John Bale: Mythmaker for the English Reformation* (West Lafayette, Ind.: Purdue University Press, 1976), 21–7.

15 In neither the *Examinacion* nor the *Magnus Processus* is there any warrant for Bale's repeated emphasis on the helpless confusion to which the inquisitors are reduced by Cobham's answers. This is a hagiographical motif which appealed to his dramatic instinct.

16 This answer is taken from the *Examinacion*. The 'most cheerful countenance' is Bale's characteristic addition, as is the following reference to the Archbishop's embarrassment. The original answer possibly marks the point at which Bale conceived the idea for his own version of Oldcastle's 'history'.

17 The confession is in the *Examinacion*, but the appeal to an audience is a typical example of Bale's theatrical heightening.

18 Cf. Baldassare Castiglione, *The Book of the Courtier* (1528), trans. Sir Thomas Hoby (1561) (London: Dent, 1966), 150: 'But among other merry sayings, they have a verie good grace, that arise when a man at nipping talke of his fellow, taketh the verie same words in the self same sense, and returneth them backe again, pricking him with his owne weapon.' Castiglione, it should be noted, likens perfect grace in speech and behaviour to divine grace: it is mysterious, not acquired by effort, 'the gift of nature and the heavens' (32, 44).

19 'Hit is unkyndly for a knight / That shuld a kynges castel kepe, / To bable the Bibel day and night' (Ballade). Cited in Wilhelm von Baeske, *Oldcastle-Falstaff in der englischen Literatur bis zu Shakespeare* (Palaestra, 1), 34.

20 Bale notes as a typical Romish slander Polydore Vergil's assertion in his *Anglica Historica* that Oldcastle 'cowardly fled' when he and other rebels were confronted by the King in person (*A Brief Chronicle*, 10).

5 Cultural Materialism and the Ethics of Reading

1 Brighton: Harvester, 1984; 2nd edn 1989. References here are to the second edition. For a measure of Dollimore's standing among ideologically oriented critics, see the reverential comments on his work ('to which so many of our contributors repair') in the introduction to *Ideological Approaches to Shakespeare: the Practice of Theory*, ed. Robert P. Merrix and Nicholas Ranson (Lewiston, NY, Queenston, Ont., and Lampeter: Edwin Mellen Press, 1992), vii.

2 *Radical Tragedy*, xliii; *Political Shakespeare*, ed. Dollimore and Alan Sinfield (Manchester: Manchester University Press, 1985), 9.

3 See Bertolt Brecht, *The Messingkauf Dialogues*, trans. J. Willett (London: Methuen, 1965), 59–63; *Brecht on Theatre*, trans. J. Willett (London: Eyre-Methuen, 1965), 37, 71, 190; M. Heinemann, 'How Brecht Read Shakespeare', in *Political Shakespeare*, 202–17; Raymond Williams, *Modern Tragedy* (London: Chatto, 1966), 35, 45–6, 48, 54, 67–73.

4 *Utopia and A Dialogue of Comfort*, trans. Ralph Robinson (London: Heron Books, n.d.), 130, 134.

5 *The Book of the Courtier*, trans. Sir Thomas Hoby (1561) (London: Dent, 1966), 110. See also 117–18, 128, 293.

6 *Essays* (London: Dent, 1906), 117, 118.

7 *The Discourses*, ed. Bernard Crick (Harmondsworth: Penguin, 1974), 207–8.

8 In the 1609 Dedication to his *Ciuile Wars* (1595), Samuel Daniel says: 'Ambition, Faction, and Affections, speake ever one language, weare like colours . . . feed and are fed with the same nutriments.' Sir John Hayward's *The Raigne of King Henrie IIII.* (1599) is premised throughout on the notion that history's repetitive patterns disclose the universal elements of human nature. See further, G.W. Trompf, *The Idea of Historical Recurrence in Western Thought: From Antiquity to the Reformation* (Berkeley and London: University of California Press, 1979), 3.

9 Thomas Hobbes, *Leviathan*, (London: Dent, 1928), 49–50, 63, 66.

10 *Essays*, trans. John Florio, 3 vols (London: Dent, 1910).

11 As in *Radical Tragedy*, and to avoid confusion, the text of *Lear* used here is that of the Arden, ed. Kenneth Muir (London: Methuen, 1966). For Shakespeare's other plays, the text is that of *The Complete Works*, ed. Wells and Taylor (Oxford: Clarendon Press, 1988).

12 Gloucester's situation at this point mirrors that of the good Germans to whom tribute is paid from time to time in the haunting diaries of the Jewish academic Victor Klemperer. See *To the Bitter End: the Diaries of Victor Klemperer 1942–45* (London: Weidenfeld and Nicolson, 1999).

13 *Sejanus*, ed. Jonas A. Barish (New Haven, Conn., and London: Yale University Press, 1965), 12–13.

14 'Macbeth: History, Ideology and Intellectuals', *CQ*, 28 (1986); reprinted in *Faultlines: Cultural Materialism and the Politics of Dissident Reading* (Oxford, Clarendon Press, 1992), and in '*Macbeth*': *Contemporary Critical Essays*, ed. Alan Sinfield (Basingstoke and London: Macmillan, 1992) (page references here are to the *Faultlines* version). Indicative of Sinfield's determination to disseminate cultural-materialist doctrine is his creation of an 'essay' entitled 'Tragedy and Literature' composed of extracts from no fewer than ten different places in *Radical Tragedy*, and placed immediately after his own essay on *Macbeth* in the *Critical Essays* casebook. Since this 'essay' contains not a single reference to *Macbeth*, its inclusion in the casebook departs strikingly from the standard format of the series.

15 Terence Hawkes, *Meaning by Shakespeare* (London: Routledge, 1992), 3.

16 Sara Suleri, 'Multiculturalism and Its Discontents', *Profession 93* (New York: Modern Language Association of America, 1993), 17.

17 See Richard Freadman and Seumus Miller, *Re-Thinking Theory: a Critique of Contemporary Literary Theory and an Alternative Account* (Cambridge: Cambridge University Press, 1993), 51–71. See also Eve Tabor Bannet, *Postcultural Theory: Critical Theory after the Marxist Paradigm*, 29–49.

18 Terry Eagleton, *Criticism and Ideology* (London: New Left Books, 1976), 176, 182.

6   Shakespearean Tragedy

1   Kenneth Muir, *Shakespeare's Tragic Sequence* (London: Methuen, 1972), 12, 16.
2   Dieter Mehl, *Shakespeare's Tragedies: an Introduction* (Cambridge: Cambridge University Press, 1986), 7.
3   Alistair Fowler, *Kinds of Literature: an Introduction to the Theory of Genres and Modes* (Oxford: Clarendon Press, 1982), 24. Cf. Raymond Williams, *Modern Tragedy* (London: Chatto, 1966), 15–46.
4   *Hegel on Tragedy*, ed. Anne and Henry Paolucci (New York: Harper and Row, 1975), 62, 67–71, 89, 237.
5   Friedrich Nietzsche, *The Birth of Tragedy and The Genealogy of Morals*, trans. Francis Golffing (New York: Doubleday, 1956), 19, 33–6, 42, 50, 64.
6   See my *Shakespeare's Tragic Cosmos* (Cambridge: Cambridge University Press, 1991), 11, 261–2.
7   *Oxford Lectures on Poetry* (1909; London: Macmillan, 1962), 83–4.
8   *Shakespearean Tragedy* (London: Macmillan, 1906), lecture 1.
9   Una Ellis-Fermor, *The Frontiers of Drama* (London: Methuen, 1948), 127–47. See also Bernard McElroy, *Shakespeare's Mature Tragedies* (Princeton, NJ: Princeton University Press, 1973), 1–28.
10 F.L. Lucas, *Tragedy in Relation to Aristotle's Poetics* (London: Hogarth, 1927), 55–6.
11 A.P. Rossiter, *Angel with Horns: Fifteen Lectures on Shakespeare* (London: Hutchinson, 1961), 265–72.
12 Catherine Belsey, 'Tragedy, Justice and the Subject', in *1642: Literature and Power in the Seventeenth Century*, ed. Francis Barker (Colchester: University of Essex, 1981), 166–86; Jonathan Dollimore, *Radical Tragedy: Religion, Ideology and Power in the Drama of Shakespeare and his Contemporaries* (Brighton: Harvester, 1984).
13 I.A. Richards, *Principles of Literary Criticism* (London: Routledge, 1926), 245–8; Northrop Frye, *Anatomy of Criticism* (London: Penguin, 1957), 37; T.R. Henn, *The Harvest of Tragedy* (London: Methuen, 1956), 14, 86–7.
14 On Seneca and the 'sympathetic universe', see Thomas G. Rosenmeyer, *Senecan Drama and Stoic Cosmology* (Berkeley, Los Angeles and London: University of California Press, 1989).
15 George Puttenham, *The Arte of English Poesie* (1589), ed. G.D. Willcock and A. Walker (Cambridge: Cambridge University Press, 1936), 26; Sir Philip Sidney, *An Apology for Poetry* (1595), ed. Geoffrey Shepherd (London: Nelson, 1965), 118.
16 Shakespearean references throughout this chapter are to the *The Complete Works*, ed. Wells and Taylor (Oxford: Clarendon Press, 1988).
17 Roland Mushat Frye, *Shakespeare: the Art of the Dramatist* (London: Allen and Unwin, 1982), 116.
18 See my *Shakespeare's Tragic Cosmos*, ch. 1.
19 On passion and suffering as marks of greatness in the hero, see especially Rossiter, *Angel with Horns*, p. 264, and Robert Kirsch, *The Passions of Shakespeare's Tragic Heroes* (Charlottesville and London: University of Virginia Press), 1990. See also my 'Tragedy, *King Lear*, and the Politics of the Heart', *ShS*, 44 (1992), 85–90.
20 *Hero and Saint: Shakespeare and the Graeco-Roman Heroic Tradition* (Oxford: Clarendon Press, 1971), 31.
21 Eugene M. Waith, *Ideas of Greatness: Heroic Drama in England* (London: Hutchinson, 1971), 106.
22 On this much discussed paradox, see especially A.D. Nuttall, *Why Does Tragedy Give Pleasure?* (Oxford: Clarendon Press, 1996).

23 *The Trojan Women*, lines 1179–80; in Seneca, *Four Tragedies and Octavia*, trans. E.F. Watling (London: Penguin, 1966), 203.
24 For a fuller account of the significance of time, see my *Shakespeare's Tragic Cosmos*, 13–18.
25 Donne, 'Holy Sonnets', no. xix. But see especially no. xviii.
26 Bertolt Brecht, *The Messingkauf Dialogues*, trans. John Willett (London: Methuen, 1965), 59.
27 *The Major Works*, ed. C.A. Patrides (Harmondsworth: Penguin, 1977), 144–5, 148.

7 *Coriolanus*: an Essentialist Tragedy

1 See Bertolt Brecht, *The Messingkauf Dialogues*, trans. J. Willett (London: Methuen, 1965), 59–63; *Brecht on Theatre*, trans. J. Willett (London: Methuen, 1965), 37, 71, 190; M. Heinemann, 'How Brecht Read Shakespeare', in *Political Shakespeare*, ed. Jonathan Dollimore and Alan Sinfield (Manchester: Manchester University Press, 1985), 202–17; Raymond Williams, *Modern Tragedy* (London: Chatto, 1966), 35, 45–6, 48, 54, 67–73.
2 'The New Historicism in Renaissance Studies', *ELR*, 16 (1986), 20, 23.
3 S. Kripke, 'Identity and Necessity', in S.P. Schwartz (ed.), *Naming, Necessity, and Natural Kinds* (Ithaca, NY and London: Cornell University Press, 1977), 66-101; id., *Naming and Necessity* (1972; Oxford: Oxford University Press 1980), esp. 39–53; H. Putnam, 'The Meaning of "Meaning"', in *Mind, Language and Reality* (Cambridge: Cambridge University Press, 1975), 215–71.
4 *Essentially Speaking: Feminism, Nature, and Difference* (New York and London: Routledge, 1989). In *Interpreting the Text: A Critical Introduction to the Theory and Practice of Literary Interpretation* (New York and London: Harvester Wheatsheaf, 1990), K.M. Newton points out that the anti-essentialism of cultural materialists is not anti-essentialist in the strict sense; these critics simply oppose liberal-humanist essentialism with a neo-Marxist (essentialist) alternative (124).
5 Paul Avis, *Foundations of Modern Historical Thought: From Machiavelli to Vico* (London: Croom Helm, 1986), 47–8, 74, 97–8; Machiavelli, *The Discourses*, ed. Bernard Crick (Harmondsworth: Penguin Books, 1970), 207 (1: 39) (cf. 266 [n. 1]).
6 *Shakespeare and the Popular Voice* (Oxford: Blackwell, 1989), 146–53.
7 *Radical Tragedy: Religion, Ideology and Power in the Drama of Shakespeare and his Contemporaries* (Brighton: Harvester, 1984), 204–5, 220–29. Terry Eagleton by contrast sees Coriolanus, not as a superannuated aristocrat, but as 'Shakespeare's most developed study of a bourgeois individualist' (*William Shakespeare* [Oxford: Blackwell, 1986], 73). The shared commitment to anti-individualism is unaffected by a fundamental difference in sociological analysis; either demonising category will do. Compare Dollimore's radical *King Lear* and Sinfield's reactionary *Macbeth*, both serving the same anti-liberal-humanist purpose.
8 P.N. Medvedev and M.M. Bakhtin, *The Formal Method in Literary Scholarship: a Critical Introduction to Sociological Poetics* (Baltimore and London: Johns Hopkins University Press, 1978), 129.
9 References to *Coriolanus* are to the New Arden text, ed. P. Brockbank (London: Methuen, 1976).
10 *A Treatie of Warres*, st. 25, in Fulke Greville, *The Poems and Plays*, ed. G. Bullough (Edinburgh: Oliver and Boyd, 1939).
11 Cf. R.F. Hill, '*Coriolanus*: Violentest Contrariety', *Essays and Studies*, 17 (1964), 12–23, who examines the play's 'pervasively antithetical and balanced' ordering of

'thought and verbal patterns'. Adrian Poole, *Coriolanus* (London and New York: Harvester Wheatsheaf, 1988), 104, notes 'violent contrarieties' in the animal imagery, and in the imagery of organic softness and inorganic hardness or 'constancy'.

12 On the Mars–Venus myth in *Tamburlaine, Othello*, and *Antony and Cleopatra*, see my *English Renaissance Tragedy* (London: Macmillan, 1986), 93–9; *Shakespeare's Tragic Cosmos* (Cambridge: Cambridge University Press, 1991), 7, 22, 131, 147, 230–32. In Shakespeare and Fletcher's *Two Noble Kinsmen* (*c.*1613), the Mars–Venus myth, with its theme of nature's concordant discord, is conspicuously associated with the chivalric ideal of love and valour: see *Shakespeare's Tragic Cosmos*, 43–4.

13 *Coriolanus*, ed. Brockbank, 21, 23, 93.

14 The description of Young Martius 'in one on's father's moods' emphasises a compulsive disregard for limit: 'when he caught it, he let it go again, and after it again, and over and over he comes, and up again, catch'd it again' (1.3.61–3).

15 Coppelia Kahn, *Man's Estate: Masculine Identity in Shakespeare* (Berkeley and Los Angeles: University of California Press, 1981), 167–8.

16 *Critical Practice* (London: Methuen, 1980), 96.

17 Thomas Sorge, 'The Failure of Orthodoxy in *Coriolanus*', in *Shakespeare Reproduced: The Text in History and Ideology*, ed. J.E. Howard and M.F. O'Connor (New York and London: Routledge, 1987), 227–30.

18 Cf. A.C. Bradley, '*Coriolanus*'; reprinted in B.A. Brockman (ed.), *Coriolanus: a Selection of Critical Essays* (London; Macmillan, 1977), 70–71; K. Stockholder, 'The Other Coriolanus', *PMLA*, 85 (1970), 230.

19 Cf. Una Ellis-Fermor, '*Coriolanus*'; reprinted in Brockman (ed.), *Coriolanus*, 139: 'For despite his confusion, Coriolanus appears to be striving rather to be the man he is, a man, it may be, that neither he nor she [Volumnia] knows; the very fact of the strife is perhaps an index of his frustration.'

20 In 'The Other Coriolanus', Katherine Stockholder presents 'the other Coriolanus' as the human Martius – subject to pain and death – whom Virgilia sees (230). But she goes on to argue that he is so enslaved to the hard, militaristic self-image created for him by his mother that he never acknowledges this other self in any way. Thus he ends almost as a comic figure – a boasting *miles gloriosus*. With this, it will be apparent, I do not agree.

21 *Coriolanus*, ed. Brockbank, 326 (Appendix).

22 In Renaissance iconography, 'Venus Victorious' (*Venus victrix*) or 'Venus Armed' (*Venus armata*) is dressed in armour, and represents the strength that comes from love.

23 E.A. Colman, 'The End of Coriolanus', *ELH*, 34 (1967), 19; Poole, *Coriolanus*, 118.

24 Pierre de la Primaudaye, *The French Academie*, trans. T. Bowes *et al.* (London, 1618), 180. (He is discussing the contrarious order of nature.)

25 McAlindon, *Shakespeare's Tragic Cosmos*, 174–83.

26 On the identification of heroic nobility with 'magnanimity', greatness of heart or soul, see Curtis W. Brown, *Shakespeare and the Renaissance Concept of Honor* (Princeton, NJ: Princeton University Press, 1960), 106–7, 468. For most Renaissance moralists, however, 'greatness of heart' or magnanimity signified highmindedness, courage, and constancy (106–7). Shakespeare's emphasis on feeling seems to be idiosyncratic. Elizabeth Storey Donno, '*Coriolanus* and a Shakespearean Motif', in *Shakespeare and the Dramatic Tradition: Essays in Honor of S.F. Johnson*, ed. W.R. Elton and W.B. Long (Newark, London, and Toronto: University of Delaware Press, 1989), 47–68, considers the heart image in *Coriolanus* from a perspective

different from my own: 'The disjunction between what the heart thinks and the tongue speaks, which . . . became for Shakespeare a kind of motif in projecting character, also represents a topical issue in its reflection of the antirhetorical attitude that developed in the course of a rhetorically attuned period. In his final tragedy he employs it as a means of particularizing his hero's integrity in his persistent, if overinsistent, belief that speech should mirror the speaker's true response to the occasion' (59).

27   'He knows not himself. For this strength of hating in a noble heart is the same as the force of loving' (H.A. Taine, *A History of English Literature* [1883], cited in *Coriolanus*, ed. Brockman, 46). On intensity of feeling or greatness of heart as the primary attribute of Shakespeare's tragic heroes, see A.P. Rossiter, *Angel with Horns* (London: Hutchinson, 1961), 263–4; Marilyn French, *Shakespeare's Division of Experience* (London: Cape, 1982), 254; Arthur Kirsch, *The Passions of Shakespeare's Tragic Heroes* [*Hamlet, Othello, Lear, Macbeth*] (Charlottesville and London: University of Virginia Press, 1990). It must be acknowledged, however, that Martius' change of heart is unreflecting and apparently untouched by remorse or regret; and that partly for that reason he is a lesser tragic figure than his great Shakespearean predecessors.

8   The Discourse of Prayer in *The Tempest*

1   All citations of Shakespeare in this chapter are from *The Complete Works*, ed. Stanley Wells and Gary Taylor (Oxford: Clarendon Press, 1988).

2   Quoted in Stephen Greenblatt, *Learning to Curse: Essays in Early Modern Culture* (New York and London: Routledge, 1990), 16–17 (first printed in *First Images of America: the Impact of the New World on the Old*, ed. Fredi Chiapelli [Berkeley: University of California Press, 1976]). Greenblatt's source for the Bishop's punchy maxim (by now a new-historicist mantra) is Lewis Hanke, *Aristotle and the American Indians: a Study in Race Prejudice in the Modern World* (Bloomington and London: Indiana University Press, 1970), 8. Hanke's source is J.B. Trend, *The Civilisation of Spain* (London: Oxford University Press, 1944), 88. Trend's maxim is a very free version of six lines in Antonio Lebrija (or Nebrija), *Grammatica Castellana 1492*, (facsimile repr., Menston, Yorks: Scolar Press, 1969, sig. Aiiii–v). Neither the word 'perfect' nor the idea of perfection occurs in these lines. What the Bishop indicated is that linguistic skill is *necessary* if one is to give laws to conquered peoples who speak 'peregrinas lenguas'. This banal observation implies a less restrictive (politically specific) view of language than Trend's maxim suggests. Other colonialist interpretations of *The Tempest* may be found in Francis Barker and Peter Hulme, '"Nymphs and reapers heavily vanish": the Discursive Con-texts of *The Tempest*', in *Alternative Shakespeares*, ed. John Drakakis (London and New York: Routledge, 1985), 191–205; Peter Hulme, *Colonial Encounters: Europe and the Native Carribean, 1492–1797* (New York and London: Methuen, 1986), 1; Howard Felperin, 'Political Criticism at the Crossroads: the Utopian Historicism of *The Tempest*', in *The Tempest*, Theory in Practice Series, ed. Nigel Wood (Buckingham and Philadelphia, Pa.: Open University Press, 1995), 29–66, 44–51. Sceptical approaches to colonialist readings of *The Tempest* are currently unfashionable, but not impossible to find. See especially Meredith Ann Skura, 'Discourse and the Individual: the Case of Colonialism in *The Tempest*', SQ, 40 (Spring 1989), 42–69; Debora Willis, 'Shakespeare's *The Tempest* and the Discourse of Colonialism', SEL, 29 (1989), 277–89; Alden T. Vaughan and Virginia Mason Vaughan, *Shakespeare's*

Caliban: A Cultural History (Cambridge: Cambridge University Press, 1991), passim; Jeffrey Knapp, *An Empire Nowhere: England, America, and Literature from 'Utopia' to 'The Tempest'* (Berkeley, Los Angeles, Oxford: University of California Press, 1992), 220–42; Brian Vickers, *Appropriating Shakespeare: Contemporary Quarrels* (New Haven, Conn. and London: Yale University Press, 1993), 242–8; Ben Ross Schneider, '"Are We Being Historical Yet?": Colonialist Interpretations of Shakespeare's *The Tempest*', *ShakS*, 23 (1995), 120–45.

3 For a very different approach to the language of prayer in *King Lear* and the romances, see Elena Glazov-Corrigan's 'Speech Acts, Generic Differences, and the Curious Case of *Cymbeline*', *SEL*, 34 (1994), 379–99, which applies speech act theory to the use of language in *Cymbeline* and, more generally, to all the genres. The coherence of this ambitious scheme of generic distinctions depends to a considerable extent on bypassing the abundant curses and prayers in *King Lear* and the fact that prayer occurs not just in the Epilogue of *The Tempest* but throughout.

4 Henry Peacham, *The Garden of Eloquence* (1593), ed. William G. Crane (Gainsville, Fla.: Scholars' Facsimile Reprints, 1954), 4, 64–5, 71.

5 Shakespeare's audience was familiar with the biblical notion of the lawful curse. The last item in the Elizabethan Prayer Book was 'A Commination Against Sinners', a sequence of curses against the ungodly (based on Deuteronomy 27), followed by a prayer that 'Christ wil deliuer us from the curse of the law, and from the extreme malediction which light upon theym, that shal be set on the left hand . . . and geue us the blessed benediction of hys father.' See *The Prayer-Book of Queen Elizabeth, 1559*, ed. William Benham (Edinburgh: John Grant, 1911), 142–6.

6 Peacham, *The Garden of Eloquence*, 81–2.

7 See C.T. Onions, *A Shakespeare Glossary*, rev. Robert D. Eagleson (Oxford: Clarendon Press, 1986), 119. In the Quarto and the Folio, 'God be wi' you' is usually 'God buy you'. Modern editors, however, emend to 'God be wi' you'. (There are two instances in the Folio *Hamlet* of 'God buy you' meaning 'goodbye'.)

8 *A Werke for Householders or for them that haue the guydyng or gouernance of any company* (London, 1530), sig. D4v.

9 *The Lives of the Right Hon. and Rev. Dr. John North together with an Autobiography of the Author*, ed. Augustus Jessop (London: Bell, 1890), 8. Compare also R. W[illis], *Mount Tabor or Private Exercises of a Penitent Sinner Serving for Daily Practice of the Life of Faith* (London, 1639), 211. (I am indebted to Keith Thomas, *Religion and the Decline of Magic: Studies in Popular Beliefs in Sixteenth and Seventeenth Century England* [London: Weidenfeld and Nicolson, 1971], 505–6, for directing my attention to these texts.) See also Lawrence Stone, *The Family, Sex and Marriage in England, 1500–1800* (New York: Harper and Row, 1977), 171.

10 Gerald Brenan, *A History of the House of Percy*, 2 vols (London: Freemantle, 1902), 2: 194.

11 *The Tempest*, New Variorum Edition, ed. Henry Howard Furness (Philadelphia, Pa. and London: Lippincott, 1892), 17, note on 1.1.44, citing B. Nicholson (who notes that 'there are no less than five omissions so marked in Middleton's *A Chaste Maid in Cheapside*'). Frank Kermode (ed.), *The Tempest* (London: Methuen, 1962), 6, accepts this conjecture. Stephen Orgel demurs, observing that 'blasphemous' could mean simply abusive, slanderous (ed. *The Tempest* [Oxford: Oxford University Press, 1987], 98). But this overlooks the fact that in the last scene Gonzalo specifically associates the boatswain's blasphemies with oaths.

12 Francis Bacon, *Essays* (London: Dent, 1906), 15. Compare Geffrey Whitney, *A Choice of Emblems* (1586), ed. Henry Green (New York: Blom, 1967), 137: 'whilst that man dothe saile these worldlie seas'. Of obvious relevance, too, is the

iconographic motif of the ship riding in safety through the storms, symbolic of Christians and the Church protected by God in a world of abounding wickedness (F. Edward Hulme, *The History, Principles and Practice of Symbolism in Christian Art* [New York: Macmillan, 1909], 211–12). Chaucer integrated this theme to his hagiographical romance *The Man of Law's Tale*, a version of the well-known medieval story of Constance. This saintly queen is twice consigned to 'the wilde se' in 'a ship al steerelees' (once, like Prospero, with her infant child). She is protected throughout voyages of astonishing length (between Rome, Syria, England, and Rome again) by the divine 'comandour' of the tempest, 'hym . . . That is to me my seyl and eek my steere' (Chaucer, *The Complete Works*, ed. F.N. Robinson, 2nd edn [London: Oxford University Press, 1974] lines 338, 506, 833). Since the tale of Constance (recounted also in Gower's *Confessio Amantis*, Shakespeare's source for *Pericles*) belongs to the same narrative genre as Shakespeare's romances (the tale of injustice, separation, marvellous journeys and adventures, reunion, reconciliation, and providential governance), its impact on *The Tempest* is arguably greater than any of the other voyages alluded to in the play – those of Aeneas from Troy via Carthage to Rome (2.1.71–7), of St Paul from Palestine to Rome via Malta (see p. 141 and n. 13), and of European colonists to Virginia and the land of 'Setebos' via 'the still vexed Bermudas'. The point to be emphasised, however, is that these voyages are historically and ontologically remote from one another. The play blends the universal and the historically specific – like *The Winter's Tale*, where an actual sixteenth-century painter, Julio Romano, inhabits a fictional, antique world where Renaissance courtiers worship the god Apollo. Strongly politicised interpretations of *The Tempest* tend to emphasise its Virgilian analogue (Aeneas being a colonist) at the expense of its palpable indebtedness to the popular tradition of separation romance (which stresses family reunion, reconciliation, and homecoming). On the structure and dissemination of the separation romance, see my article, 'The Medieval Assimilation of Greek Romance: a Chapter in the History of a Narrative Type', in *REAL. Yearbook of Research in English and American History*, 3 (1985), 23–56.

13   Virgil, *Aeneid*, ed. H. Ruston Fairclough (London: Heinemann, 1935), 264.

14   For Greek and medieval precedents, see McAlindon, 'The Medieval Assimilation of Greek Romance', 44–6; and for Renaissance precedents, Kermode (ed.), *The Tempest*, 37, note on 1.2.427.

15   Since it is clear that both Perdita and Ferdinand are the uncorrupted creatures they seem to be, unlike some who have come to the island, Caliban's parody of worship is hardly meant to ironise their mutual wonder and reverence. As noted above, too, divinising is typical of the quasi-Platonic characterisation of the noblest individuals in the romances.

16   In response to the sneers of Antonio and Sebastian, Gonzalo points out that his ideal-commonwealth speech is tongue-in-cheek, 'merry fooling' to distract the King (line 182). Yet critics habitually side with the sneering conspirators and describe the speech as naive and ridiculous.

17   The act of speaking is emphasised at the start of the conspiratorial dialogue. *Antonio*: 'th' occasion speaks thee . . . Do you not hear me speak?' *Sebastian*: 'I do, and surely / It is a sleepy language and thou speakst / Out of thy sleep' (lines 212–17).

18   As well as the adventures of New World voyagers, the shipwreck of St Paul may well have been in Shakespeare's mind here. Scarcely had he landed on the island of Melita (Malta) than he was attacked by a viper, but 'shaking off the beast into the fire [he] suffered no harm'. The natives had expected him to die, but 'seeing that there came no harm to him, changing their minds, they said he was a god' (Acts 28: 3–6 [Rheims]).

19 Further examples are: 'The church's prayers made him so prosperous' (*1H6*, 1.1.32); 'Henry the Fifth, thy ghost I invoke: / Prosper this realm' (*1H6*, 1.1.52–3); 'you [Oberon] come / To give their bed joy and prosperity?' (*MND*, 2.1.72–3); 'God prosper our sport!' (*MWW*, 5.2.12); 'God in thy good cause make thee prosperous' (*R2*, 1.3.78); 'So I leave you / To the protection of the prosperous gods' (*Tim.*, 5.2.67–8); 'You have . . . petitioned all the gods for my prosperity!' (*Cor.*, 2.1.167–8); 'The glorious gods sit in hourly synod about thy particular prosperity, and love thee no worse than thy old father . . . does!' (*Cor.*, 5.2.69–71).

20 Bacon, *Essays*, 15 ('Of Adversity').

21 *Shakespeare's Caliban: A Cultural History*, 33–4.

22 Caliban's alcoholic jingle curiously exemplifies cacemphaton or cacophaton, one of the classified vices of style in rhetorical tradition: 'many sillables of one sound together . . . like a continuall iarring upon one string' (Peacham, *The Garden of Eloquence*, sig. G3v). Cf. Joannes Susenbrotus, *Epitome Troporum ac Schematum et Grammaticorum et Rhetoricorum* (London, 1621), 212 and Index s.v. 'cacemphaton'. With etymological exactness, George Puttenham terms it 'the figure of foule speech' (*The Arte of English Poesie*, ed. G.D. Willcock and A. Walker [Cambridge: Cambridge University Press, 1936], 212).

23 Orgel (ed.), *The Tempest*, 55. No textual evidence is adduced in support of this interpretation; it would seem to be offered as correct on the grounds that contemporary royal marriages were 'arranged primarily to please their fathers' (52). In contrast to Orgel, James Black (much like myself) reads the plot as incorporating a benign 'process of marital negotiations'. See 'The Latter End of Prospero's Commonwealth', *ShS*, 43 (1991), 29–41.

24 Felperin, 'Political Criticism at the Crossroads', 53, 55. This ignores not only Prospero's explanation for the storm ('in care of thee') but also the speech in 3.3 where Ariel, watched by Prospero and following his 'instruction' (line 85), explains to the distracted 'men of sin' that only 'heart-sorrow / And a clear life ensuing' will save them from 'ling'ring perdition' (lines 70–85). It is imperative to recall this scene when considering Prospero's reaction in 5.1 to Ariel's mention of pity. Prospero acknowledges being furious and 'struck to th' quick' by the 'high wrongs' of his enemies but adds: 'They being penitent, / The sole drift of my purpose doth extend / Not a frown further' (lines 24–30). Clearly, his purpose has not changed, though he may well have been tempted to change it. Nevertheless, Stephen Orgel's assumption that Prospero's marriage plan is a mere bid for power leads him to conclude that the alleged fifth-act renunciation of 'vindictiveness and vengeance', with its suggestion that 'he becomes at last fully human', is 'in fact' inauthentic (ed. *The Tempest*, 52).

25 *The Prayer-Book of Queen Elizabeth, 1559*, ed. Benham, 124–6.

26 The theme of blessing is even more conspicuous in the popular pre-Reformation version of the wedding ceremony given in the Sarum manual: see M. Searle and K.W. Stevenson, *Documents of the Marriage Liturgy* (Collegeville, Mass.: Liturgical Press, 1992), 163–77.

27 The same paradox figures in the richly paradoxical design of *King Lear*. The Fool tells Lear that he 'did the third [daughter] a blessing against his will' (1.4.102), meaning that 'by cursing and banishing her he had made her Queen of France and saved her from marrying Burgundy' (Kenneth Muir, ed. *King Lear* [London: Methuen, 1966], 41).

28 See Heather Dubrow, *A Happier Eden: the Politics of Marriage in the Stuart Epithalamium* (Ithaca and London: Cornell University Press, 1990), 78.

29 The true colonist of the story is surely Caliban's mother Sycorax, a criminal reject of the Old World who consigned the island's original inhabitant to eternal misery because he refused to obey 'her earthy and abhorred commands' (1.2.274).

30   See Vickers, *Appropriating Shakespeare*, ch. 7 ('Christians and Marxists: Allegory, Ideology').

9   Marlowe Plus and Minus 'Theory'

1   *Renaissance Self-Fashioning: From More to Shakespeare* (Chicago and London: University of Chicago Press, 214–21).
2   Jacques Derrida, *Writing and Difference*, trans. Alan Bass (London and Henley: Routledge, 1978), 292 (Derrida's italics).
3   Simon Shepherd, *Marlowe and the Politics of Elizabethan Theatre* (Brighton: Harvester, 1986), 95.
4   Roger Sales, *Christopher Marlowe* (Basingstoke: Macmillan, 1991), chs 1, 2, and 7.
5   'Ludam scilicet illudar' ['I would play in order, of course, to be deceived/mocked'], warns St Bernard of Clairvaux, referring to sin and temptation (*Epistola* 87.12, in *Patrologia Latina*, ed. J.P. Migne, vol. 182, p. 217). See also Migne, 49: 516, 529, 749, 777; 76: 670–71; 83: 664, 668. Compare the *Ancrene Riwle*, an early Middle English treatise on the ascetical life: 'The fiend beholds all this game: laughs till he bursts' (ed. Mabel Day, EETS.OS, 225 [1952]), 93–5.
6   Russell Fraser, *The War against Poetry* (Princeton, NJ: Princeton University Press, 1970), 93–5; Jonas Barish, *The Antitheatrical Prejudice* (Berkeley, Los Angeles, and London: University of California Press, 1981), 91–2.
7   The entertainments presented by Hieronimo in Acts 1 and 4 of *The Spanish Tragedy* vividly embody this distinction; so too do the contrasted disguisings and plottings of Edgar and Edmund in *King Lear*.
8   I use Roma Gill's New Mermaid edition (2nd edn, London: Black; New York: Norton, 1989). This edition is based on the shorter A text but has an appendix containing those scenes from the B text that are 'either straightforwad additions to the play presented in the A text' or 'have been substantially reworked' (69). The B-text material in Gill's appendix has no lineation; my quotations from this material, therefore, are followed only by a page reference (thus, B.85). Citations from the B-text material not given in Gill's appendix are from W.W. Greg's parallel edition of the two texts (Oxford: Clarendon Press, 1959) and are followed by line reference (thus: Greg, 280). Citations of Gill's A text are followed by scene and line reference (thus, '2.109' is scene 2, line 109) or chorus and line reference ('chor. 4.6' is chorus 4, line 6).
9   Faustus quotes Romans 6: 23 ('The reward of sin is death') and 1 John 1: 8 ('if we say we have no sin, we deceive ourselves'), but ignores the immediately following verse, which in each case emphasises God's forgiveness.
10 David Ormerod and Christopher Wortham (eds), *Dr. Faustus: the A Text* (Nedlands: Western Australia University Press, 1985), 52, trace '*Homo fuge*' to 1 Timothy 6: 11–12 ('But thou, o man of God, flee from these things, and follow after righteousness, godlines, faith, love, pacience, & meeknes. Fight the good fight of faith: laye hold of eternal life'). They suggest that 'Whither should I fly?' is an echo of Psalm 139: 7–8.
11 For a fuller account of this play, and in particular for its specifically tragic dimension, see my '*Doctor Faustus': Divine in Show* (New York: Twayne, 1994).

Appendix

Critiques of 'Theory': a Select Bibliography

Abrams, M.H. *Doing Things with Texts*. New York and London: Norton, 1989.

Alter, Robert. *The Pleasures of Reading in an Ideological Age*. New York: Simon and Schuster, 1989.

Anderson, Perry. *In the Tracks of Historical Materialism*. London: Verso, 1983.

Bannet, Eve Tavor. *Postcultural Theory: Critical Theory after the Marxist Paradigm*. Macmillan: Basingstoke, 1993.

Burke, Seán. *The Death and Return of the Author: Criticism and Subjectivity in Barthes, Foucault and Derrida*. Edinburgh: Edinburgh University Press, 1992.

Butler, Christopher. *Interpretation, Deconstruction, and Ideology: an Introduction to Some Current Issues in Literary Theory*. Oxford: Clarendon Press, 1984.

Clarke, Simon. *The Foundations of Structuralism: a Critique of Lévi-Strauss and the Structuralist Movement*. Brighton: Harvester, 1981.

Dews, Peter. *Logics of Disintegration: Poststructuralist Thought and the Claims of Critical Theory*. London: Verso, 1987.

Donoghue, Denis. *Ferocious Alphabets*. London and Boston: Little, Brown, 1981.

Edmundson, Mark. *Literature against Philosophy, Plato to Derrida: a Defence of Poetry*. Cambridge: Cambridge University Press, 1995.

Ellis, John M. *Against Deconstruction*. Princeton, NJ: Princeton University Press, 1989.

————. *Literature Lost: Social Agendas and the Corruption of the Humanities*. New Haven, Conn.: Yale University Press, 1997.

Freadman, Richard, and Miller, Seumus. *Re-Thinking Theory: a Critique of Contemporary Literary Theory and an Alternative Account*. Cambridge: Cambridge University Press, 1992.

Good, Graham. 'The Carceral Vision: Theory, Vision, Ideology, Cultural Studies'. *The Critical Review*, 38 (1998), 88–102.

————. *Humanism Betrayed*. Montreal: McGill-Queens University Press, 2001.

Graff, Gerald. *Literature Against Itself: Literary Ideas in Modern Society*. Chicago and London: University of Chicago Press, 1979.

Harris, Wendell V. *Interpretive Acts: in Search of Meaning*. Oxford: Clarendon Press, 1988.

————. *Literary Meaning: Reclaiming the Study of Literature*. Basingstoke: Macmillan, 1996.

Hilfer, Tony. *The New Hegemony in Literary Studies: Contradictions in Theory*. Evanston, Ill.: Northwestern University Press, 2003.

Himmelfarb, Gertrude. *The New History and the Old*. Cambridge, Mass.: Harvard University Press, 1987.

Hirsch, E.D. *Validity in Interpretation*. New Haven, Conn.: Yale University Press, 1967.

————. *The Aims of Interpretation*. Chicago: University of Chicago Press, 1976.

————. 'Meaning and Significance Reinterpreted'. *Critical Inquiry*, 11 (1984–5), 202–25.

Jackson, Leonard. *The Poverty of Structuralism*. Harlow and New York: Longman, 1991.

————. *The Dematerialisation of Karl Marx*, Harlow and New York: Longman, 1994.

Lamarque, Peter, and Olsen, Stein Haugom. *Truth, Fiction, and Literature*. Oxford: Clarendon Press, 1994.

Levin, Richard. 'Feminist Thematics and Shakespearean Tragedy'. *PMLA*, 103 (1988), 125–38.

————. 'The Cultural Materialist Attack on Artistic Unity, and the Problem of Ideological Criticism', in *Ideological Approaches to Shakespeare*, ed. Robert P. Merrix and Nicholas Ranson. Lewiston/Queenston/Lampeter: Edwin Mellen Press, 1992, 39–56.

————. 'The New Interdisciplinarity in Literary Criticism', in *After Poststructuralism: Interdisciplinarity and Literary Theory*, ed. Nancy Easterlin and Barbara Riebling. Evanston, Ill.: Northwestern University Press, 1993.

————. 'The Historical and Political Turn in Literary Studies', *REAL. Yearbook of Research in English and American Literature*, 11 (1995), 425–48.

Merquior, J.G. *Foucault*. London: Fontana, 1985; 2nd edn 1991.

————. *From Prague to Paris: a Critique of Structuralist and Poststructuralist Thought*. London: Verso, 1986.

Nuttall, A.D. *A New Mimesis: Shakespeare and the Representation of Reality*. London: Methuen, 1983.

Olsen, S.H. *The End of Literary Theory*. Cambridge: Cambridge University Press, 1987.

Simpson, David. 'Literary Criticism and the Return to "History"'. *Critical Inquiry*, 14 (1988), 721–47.

Sokal, Alan, and Bricmont, Jean. *Intellectual Impostures*. London: Profile Books, 1998.

Stewart, Stanley. *'Renaissance' Talk: Ordinary Language and the Mystique of Critical Problems*. Pittsburgh, Pa.: Duquesne University Press, 1997.

Tallis, Raymond. *Not Saussure: a Critique of Post-Saussurean Literary Theory*. Basingstoke: Macmillan, 1988; 2nd edn 1999.

————. *In Defence of Realism*. London: Arnold, 1988.

————. *Enemies of Hope: a Critique of Contemporary Pessimism*. Basingstoke: Macmillan, 1997.

————. *Theorrhoea and After*. Basingstoke: Macmillan, 1999.

Thompson, E.P. *The Poverty of Theory and Other Essays*. New York and London: Merlin, 1978.

Vickers, Brian. *Appropriating Shakespeare: Contemporary Critical Quarrels.* New Haven, Conn. and London: Yale University Press, 1993.

Washington, Peter. *Fraud: Literary Theory and the End of English.* London: Fontana, 1989.

Webster, Richard. *Why Freud Was Wrong: Sin. Science, and Psychoanalysis.* London: Harper Collins, 1995

Wellek, René. *The Attack on Literature and Other Essays.* Brighton: Harvester, 1982.

Index

198 *Index*

Index